the cinema of AGNÈS VARDA

DIRECTORS' CUTS

Other selected titles in the Directors' Cuts series:

the cinema of ALEXANDER SOKUROV: *figures of paradox*
JEREMI SZANIAWSKI

the cinema of MICHAEL WINTERBOTTOM: *borders, intimacy, terror*
BRUCE BENNETT

the cinema of RAÚL RUIZ: *impossible cartographies*
MICHAEL GODDARD

the cinema of MICHAEL MANN: *vice and vindication*
JONATHAN RAYNER

the cinema of AKI KAURISMÄKI: *contrarian stories*
ANDREW NESTINGEN

the cinema of RICHARD LINKLATER: *walk, don't run*
ROB STONE

the cinema of BÉLA TARR: *the circle closes*
ANDRÁS BÁLINT KOVÁCS

the cinema of STEVEN SODERBERGH: *indie sex, corporate lies, and digital videotape*
ANDREW DE WAARD & R. COLIN TATE

the cinema of TERRY GILLIAM: *it's a mad world*
edited by JEFF BIRKENSTEIN, ANNA FROULA & KAREN RANDELL

the cinema of TAKESHI KITANO: *flowering blood*
SEAN REDMOND

the cinema of THE DARDENNE BROTHERS: *responsible realism*
PHILIP MOSLEY

the cinema of MICHAEL HANEKE: *europe utopia*
edited by BEN McCANN & DAVID SORFA

the cinema of SALLY POTTER: *a politics of love*
SOPHIE MAYER

the cinema of JOHN SAYLES: *a lone star*
MARK BOULD

the cinema of DAVID CRONENBERG: *from baron of blood to cultural hero*
ERNEST MATHIJS

the cinema of JAN SVANKMAJER: *dark alchemy*
edited by PETER HAMES

the cinema of NEIL JORDAN: *dark carnival*
CAROLE ZUCKER

the cinema of LARS VON TRIER: *authenticity and artifice*
CAROLINE BAINBRIDGE

the cinema of WERNER HERZOG: *aesthetic ecstasy and truth*
BRAD PRAGER

the cinema of TERRENCE MALICK: *poetic visions of america (second edition)*
edited by HANNAH PATTERSON

the cinema of ANG LEE: *the other side of the screen*
WHITNEY CROTHERS DILLEY

the cinema of STEVEN SPIELBERG: *empire of light*
NIGEL MORRIS

the cinema of TODD HAYNES: *all that heaven allows*
edited by JAMES MORRISON

the cinema of ROMAN POLANSKI: *dark spaces of the world*
edited by JOHN ORR & ELZBIETA OSTROWSKA

the cinema of JOHN CARPENTER: *the technique of terror*
edited by IAN CONRICH & DAVID WOODS

the cinema of MIKE LEIGH: *a sense of the real*
GARRY WATSON

the cinema of NANNI MORETTI: *dreams and diaries*
EWA MAZIERSKA & LAURA RASCAROLI

the cinema of DAVID LYNCH: *american dreams, nightmare visions*
edited by ERICA SHEEN & ANNETTE DAVISON

the cinema of KRZYSZTOF KIESLOWSKI: *variations on destiny and chance*
MAREK HALTOF

the cinema of GEORGE A. ROMERO: *knight of the living dead*
TONY WILLIAMS

the cinema of KATHRYN BIGELOW: *hollywood transgressor*
edited by DEBORAH JERMYN & SEAN REDMOND

the cinema of
AGNÈS VARDA

resistance and eclecticism

Delphine Bénézet

WALLFLOWER PRESS LONDON & NEW YORK

A Wallflower Press Book
Published by
Columbia University Press
Publishers Since 1893
New York • Chichester, West Sussex
cup.columbia.edu

Copyright © Delphine Benezet 2014
All rights reserved
Wallflower Press® is a registered trademark of Columbia University Press

A complete CIP record is available from the Library of Congress

ISBN 978-0-231-16974-5 (cloth)
ISBN 978-0-231-16975-2 (pbk.)
ISBN 978-0-231-85061-2 (e-book)

Series design by Rob Bowden Design

Cover image of Agnès Varda courtesy of the Kobal Collection

CONTENTS

Acknowledgements vii

Introduction: Beginnings   1

1   Agnès Varda: A Woman Within History   9
2   Aesthetics and Technique   41
3   Varda's Ethics of Filming   71
4   Poetics of Space   89
5   Cinécriture and Originality   111

Conclusion   139

Filmography   145
Bibliography   150
Index   159

ACKNOWLEDGEMENTS

I would never have been able to write this book without the support of many friends and colleagues in London, Montreal, France and elsewhere.

I am grateful to Yoram Allon, Commissioning Editor at Wallflower Press, for his interest in the project at the very beginning, and his ongoing support as the manuscript gradually took shape over the months and years. Several colleagues read early drafts of chapters and provided invaluable feedback, including Vincent Bouchard, Jenny Chamarette, Sébastien Côté, Libby Saxton and Frank Runcie. Naomi Segal and Gill Rye offered advice and opportunities to present some of this project as a work in progress while I was a visiting fellow at the Institute of Germanic and Romance Studies at the University of London.

Friends inside and outside academia have helped by providing distraction and encouragement when needed, and here I wish to thank Abi Brown, Donna Barry, Tess Marais, Izabella Potapowicz, Aino Rinhaug, Caroline de St Quentin and May Telmissany.

Last, but certainly not least, my family have been there for me throughout. My husband, Chris Minns, offered both unwavering patience and a ruthless critical eye, and Colin and Lucy have provided a daily reminder of the importance of life beyond the 'life of the mind'. This book is for them.

INTRODUCTION

Beginnings

'Working from the cinema or on the cinema means starting from the film, and going back to it.' (Lagny 1994: 41)

'Les femmes soit disant on est toutes les mêmes! Emmerdeuses, futiles, bavardes, connasses, salopes, etc!' ('Because we women are supposedly all the same! Nuisances, frivolous, gossips, bitches, sluts, etc!')
                                  Quote from *Réponses de Femmes* (Agnès Varda, 1975)

Je suis comme je suis
Je suis faite comme ça
Quand j'ai envie de rire
Oui je ris aux éclats
                                               Jacques Prévert, *Paroles*

Agnès Varda: A Director 'au féminin singulier'

The year is 1962 and Paris is full of young people ready to enthuse about the political and social changes afoot in Cuba. Among these young people are filmmakers Chris Marker and Agnès Varda and writers Michel Leiris, Jean-Paul Sartre, Simone de Beauvoir and Marguerite Duras. Many of these intellectuals collaborate with Cuban institutions such as the Cuban Institute of Cinematographic Art and Industry (ICAIC). Today some might frown at a film praising Castro's dictatorship, but at the time, Cuba is a fresh new cause. *Salut les Cubains!* (1964) is a distinctive political documentary, mostly made of animated photographs that Agnès Varda took on a trip to Cuba in December 1962 and January 1963. But while grounded in the 'here and now' of the 1960s in France and Cuba, it also features many of the traits found in Varda's other artistic projects. It is informed by its political and historical context and shaped by the conditions in which it was made. With a simple camera (a Leica) and light portable technology (the Nagra tape recorder and cameras seen in the film's opening), Varda was able to experiment with still images, sound and music to make an elaborate film accompanied by a double off-screen commentary, a sort of dialogue between herself and Michel Piccoli.[1]

The opening scenes of *Salut les Cubains!* offer a vibrant introduction to Varda's practice. A rooster crows over the Pathé Cinéma logo on a black screen and after a cut, we discover a crowd of people watching a display of photos portraying soldiers, Fidel Castro and beautiful women in Cuba as Piccoli's voice-over situates the action for us: 'Paris, St Germain des Prés, Juin 1963'. Suddenly the lively rhythm of congas, the voice of a singer and heady music take over the narrative and bring us from the gallery where the band plays to an impromptu performance on the streets of Paris where filmmakers and photographers (including Varda and Alain Resnais) are seen capturing the band's song and their audience *in situ*. The noise of the buses driving past, dancing feet and smiling customers in the cafés add to the joyous cacophony, and to the sense that then and there two worlds are meeting and responding to the same musical rhythm.

Varda's film is the retelling of the story of the Cuban Revolution and she could have limited her account to the carefully planned coup organised by the Castro brothers and Che Guevara, or presented Cuba as a charming, exotic place where progress rules. Even though she underlines changes in terms of education (notably increased literacy levels) and cultural politics brought by Castro's government, she also shows a population in need of many things, like agricultural technology. Interestingly when Varda tells the story of the coup, as Piccoli's voice describes the preparation and efforts of the resistance with concrete information (80ft-long boat, 82 men, eight-day sea trip, and so on), Varda's voice interjects with amusing details connected to his description of the group: 'Salut les révolutionnaires au mal de mer!' ('Here's to the seasick revolutionaries!'), 'Salut aux révolutionnaires romantiques!' ('Here's to romantic revolutionaries!'). This slightly irreverent and comical treatment of Cuba's male revolutionaries is further enhanced by the emphasis the film lays on women. Varda goes well beyond references to national machismo, by portraying Cuban women as essential contributors, whether they are militia, students, artists, mothers or elders who keep precious artistic traditions alive. Admired for their beauty, their determination and their strength, Cuban women are presented as equal revolutionaries and political partners.

From the beginning, Varda ignores the interminable speeches of the leaders and privileges women and music as engaging features of the island in the shape of a cigar. Repeatedly, women and music are filmed together, in harmony, as they dance to celebrate the simple fact of being together, thus giving the audience a musically- and physically-driven respite from the two-person commentary. Far from hindering the pace of the film, these series of animated photographs of dance provide a lively rhythmical pulse to the film's narrative. The long final section focusing on the *cha cha cha* of Sara (Sarita) Gómez, the first female and black Cuban filmmaker, like an earlier scene where the late Benny Moré was singing and dancing, oblivious to his surroundings, gives an impression of boundless energy that is hard to resist. The sequences invite the spectators to join in this hopeful celebration of a better life that remains to be forged, as well as testifying to Varda's commitment to an experimental and collaborative *cinécriture* which relies on elaborate combinations of images, voices and sound.

Salut les Cubains! is an excellent illustration of what can be gained from looking at Varda's production beyond the well-beaten track that follows *Cléo de 5 à 7/Cleo from 5 to 7* (1961) and *Sans Toit ni Loi/Vagabond* (1985), as well as beyond the exclusively feminist lens often used in the scholarly literature considering her work. Agnès Varda is well-known for her notable commitment to feminist causes, and perhaps because of this, her work is rarely considered outside of a feminist perspective. She signed the 1971 manifesto of 343 French women who declared that they had had illegal abortions. This text, which generated outrage at the time, initiated debates about women's reproductive rights, and eventually led to the legalisation of abortion in January 1975. But *Salut les Cubains!* shows us that there is much more to Varda's work, as she engages with Cuba's cultural history and the people she met as much as with historical events in order to re-tell their particular story. Forging original portraits is something she had already done at the time, notably in shorts like *L'Opéra Mouffe* (1958) and feature films like *Cléo de 5 à 7*. Today, her influence on French cinema and female filmmakers is broadly acknowledged by scholars, but surprisingly few have ventured beyond the almost canonical *Cléo de 5 à 7* and *Sans Toit ni Loi*.

In her profession and in her life, Varda has always been an outsider. She trained as a photographer and made her first film, *La Pointe Courte* (1954), with little money and few other resources, and without awareness that she was going against the grain of the practices in the industry. Her background is strikingly different to the contemporary new wave group associated with the magazine *Les Cahiers du cinéma*. These well-known directors, such as Jean-Luc Godard, Eric Rohmer, Claude Chabrol, Jacques Rivette and François Truffaut, were discerning critics and devoted film-buffs. She is often associated with the Left Bank group comprising of Chris Marker and Alain Resnais, but as the chapters that follow will show, her first feature in 1954 was already ahead of the technical and aesthetic changes associated with the new wave years later.[2] Her different background and her alternative approach to filmmaking make her a special case, or '*cas d'espèce*', that needs to be fully understood and re-evaluated.

This project emerged from the realisation that in spite of Varda's long and productive career which includes successful political documentaries like *Les Glaneurs et la glaneuse/The Gleaners & I* (2000), more obscure short and feature films like *Documenteur* (1981) and *Plaisir d'Amour en Iran* (1976), art installations as well television series like *Agnès de ci de là Varda* (2011), there was an obvious gap in the critical literature. Scholars who wrote about Varda frequently used selective clusters of her work to suit their purposes, and in focusing on a restricted corpus, they were missing important aspects of her cinema, such as her witty use of the polemical potential of the corporeal. Since the only comprehensive attempt to cover all her films (Smith 1998) Varda has made a series of art installations, and film theory has seen significant critical extensions *via* phenomenology, philosophy and ethics, offering potentially enriching 'critical openings' (Cooper 2007: i). This book reviews Varda's career as a whole with a focus on her neglected films, and offers an original perspective on her career. It is informed by a close critical engagement with her less well-known and well-received works, like her installations and TV series, and it looks at cinema as both an aesthetic and ethically-driven collaborative practice, and as a synaesthetic art form.

Ten years ago, surprisingly little had been written about Agnès Varda compared to other new wave filmmakers. Susan Hayward's surprise at finding Varda's *cinécriture* 'passed over in silence in anthologies on women's film' (1990: 285) prompted her analysis of *Sans Toit ni Loi* as a political and feminist film. In *To Desire Differently: Feminism and the French Cinema*, Sandy Flitterman-Lewis discusses Varda in terms of female authorship and analyses the various constructions of femininity in her films like *Cléo de 5 à 7* (1996: 264).[3] Alison Smith offers a comprehensive view of Varda's cinema through the 1990s, but her approach does not engage at length with film theory, in particular recent developments since 2000, such as the work of Laura U. Marks (2000), Vivian Sobchack (2004) and Martine Beugnet (2007).[4] Finally, Carrie Tarr and Brigitte Rollet's ambitious survey (2001) is limited to a small number of examples, which only provides a partial view of Varda's work.[5]

As Varda began re-issuing some of her older films on DVD with extra material (the precious *boni*, as she calls them) and as her work as a visual artist became more prominent, other scholars started writing about her films (see Valerie Orpen (2007), Rebecca J. DeRoo (2008), Shirley Jordan (2009), Kelley Conway (2009, 2010) and Kate Ince (2012)). A new strand of critical conversations had been started because these scholars embraced recent theoretical changes, like the phenomenological and ethical turn (see Cooper 2006, Ince 2012); because they grounded their interpretations in substantial archival research (see Orpen 2007, DeRoo 2008 and Conway 2009, 2010), and because they considered installations for the first time (see Jordan 2009, Barnet 2011, Chamarette 2011, 2012). All these publications testified to groundbreaking changes in terms of the options at hand to discuss Varda's visual meditations and *rêveries*, and this study contributes to the emerging view of Varda as a female auteur, an ethical and experimental filmmaker and a technological innovator. Varda's willingness to embrace technological changes, her consistent principles, and her interest in issues as diverse as waste and poverty in the Western world and the representation of old age and feminism in the twenty-first century no doubt contribute to her importance. In the flesh, Varda is also an engaging, obstinate and witty figure, not the quiet and passive 'grandmother' that critics have sometimes portrayed. Now that she is in her eighties, she often comments that she is offered prestigious trophies for life-long achievements,[6] but the truth is she remains an influential figure and a director '*au féminin singulier*' whose full oeuvre merits a careful reappraisal.[7]

The Cinema of Agnès Varda: Resistance and Eclecticism is more than an *auteurist* interpretation of this prominent director's work. It is a thorough re-evaluation of Varda's contribution to cinema in the last fifty years and one that takes into account recent changes in the discipline of film studies. A critical appraisal of the dialogue between Varda's films and the social and cultural context of production highlights the critical self-reflexive nature of her cinematographic practice. Rather than using examples drawn from her films to illustrate a specific definition of counter cinema, this book analyses some of Varda's neglected films to shed new light on her personal repertoire of images, characters and settings. It recognises the diversity of Varda's work and builds bridges between her various pieces and those of other artists of the time. The first aim of this book, then, is to redress gaps and absences in the scholarship, to revisit neglected portions of Varda's production and to re-situate these within their cultural and political context. The second aim is to analyse Varda's eclectic yet consistent conception of cinema, in which feminism is not 'a relic from the past' (Vincendeau 1987: 4), and spectators are not only bodies and minds to be solicited, but also 'subjects of (potential) agency and actors in history' (Rabinowitz 1994: 8).

There is no easy way to deal with the variety of films, photos and installations that constitute the sum of Varda's work. Categorising her body of work according to different modes as some have done (notably Timothy Corrigan with a different corpus in *The Essay Film: From Montaigne, After Marker* (2011)) is difficult due to the overlap between many of the works at hand. Adopting a specific terminology to interpret Varda's oeuvre as a whole is problematic given the frequent slippages of her work between fiction and non-fiction, film and other media. It thus became obvious that the best analyses were those whose authors admitted that one could not master all the 'magic moments' (Powrie 2011: 80) and 'insistent apparitions' (Chamarette 2011: 33) that Varda's work contains. I therefore embrace the variety of her production by writing a consistent ensemble of detailed, informed and hopefully insightful analyses which offer a new outlook on Varda's contribution to cinema through careful consideration of her eclectic and unorthodox installations, documentary and fiction work.

Whatever the role she plays in her films, and her involvement notably varies from fictional character to off-screen narrator, Varda is a striking case of the '*cinéaste passeur*' (Baqué 2004: 186). This concept, which was developed by Dominique Baqué in reference to Raymond Depardon and Jacqueline Salmon, provides new insight into Varda's work. My interpretation of the *cinéaste passeur* views the filmmaker as a mediator not only between the filmed subjects and the spectators, but also between a specific space and time and the moment of the screening. Varda's work will therefore be considered in its historical, social and cultural context of production as well as in relation to its audience, then and now. *Salut les Cubains!* is a good example of a film whose reception is bound to have changed since its initial release, if only because of our knowledge of the repression and crimes committed in the name of the Cuban Revolution.[8] By looking at Varda as an inventive mediator, who weaves a patchwork of images concerned with the body, memory, politics and art, I also aim to establish her work as a 'cinema of the senses' (Beugnet 2007: 13). By using the concept of the *cinéaste passeur*, this book extends the analysis of the spatial dialectic in Varda's films (discussed by Smith (1998), Wagstaff (2005) and Orpen (2007), but only in terms of *flânerie*) and explores other shared fundamental traits of her work. It is my contention that Varda's cinema and artwork is distinctive because of its particular mix of eclecticism and resistance, and that a thorough exploration of these notions can contribute to a better understanding of her place in film history.

A Cinema of Resistance

The strategies that Varda deploys in her films testify to her lasting commitment to represent women within history. This concern not only with women on screen but with the act of '*filmer en femme*', as she calls it, makes her an important figure in the fields of film, gender and cultural studies. Susan Hayward and Sandy Flitterman-Lewis have shown that Varda's films are often both feminist and political in their conception and message. Their analyses demonstrate how Varda mediates the experiences of embodied subjects and problematises gendered representations. I want to extend their reading by showing that Varda articulates an original 'haptic cinema' (Marks 2000: 170), which invites us to engage with and question our own experience. This analysis aims to explore how by filming bodies and telling stories, Varda creates a cinema of the senses that takes the audience on an intellectual and sensory journey of discovery.

More than sixty years have elapsed since she directed *La Pointe Courte* in 1954, yet this film still generates debate among critics and historians. Claire Johnston, for instance, who was a fervent supporter of the idea that new images of women needed to be made by women, attacked *Le Bonheur/Happiness* (1965) by describing Varda's colourful and unconventional love triangle as retrograde. So should she be labelled a feminist, a member of the Rive gauche group, a precursor of the new realism of the 1990s, or more simply an *auteur* (see Hayward 2000: 21)? How has her activism and her representation of political issues evolved? How should one consider her most provocative creations like *Le Bonheur* and *Réponses de Femmes* (1975)? Throughout her career, Varda has used a variety of formats in her work. What has made her a voice of resistance is her commitment to resist norms of representation and diktats of production.

The first part of this volume examines several aspects of her films that demonstrate her alternative position within cinema. In chapter one, 'Agnès Varda: A Woman Within History', I make a phenomenological re-appraisal of Varda's work by looking at *L'Opéra Mouffe*, *Daguerréotypes* and *Les Veuves de Noirmoutier* (2004–5). No critical consensus has been reached on the place of Varda's work within film history and feminist cinema, but it is clear that her position is one of exception, if only for the fact that in the 1950s she is, apart from Jacqueline Audry, one of the very few female directors in France.[9] Because her cinematographic practice has always engaged with the corporeal, this chapter argues that Varda's production constitutes a decisive contribution to feminism. Analysing images of women, reassessing the role of bodies in these three films (and installation), and discussing the experimental and essayistic nature of Varda's work establishes how the subjective and personal intersect with collective experiences and memory. In other words, this chapter shows how 'her' story and history (or rather women's history) are intimately interlaced.

The following chapter, entitled 'Aesthetics and Technique', continues to look at the specificity of Varda's production within its historical context, but it also adopts a revisionist perspective *vis à vis* hardcore *auteurism*. By focusing on the collaborative nature of filmmaking, by reassessing the role of other contributors like the editor and the composer, and by looking at Varda's own performances of authorship, this chapter revisits the idea of the filmmaker as the all-mighty single *auteur* of her films. Taking *La Pointe Courte* and *Agnès de ci de là Varda* as two very different examples, this chapter aims to reconsider some of the filmmaker's preoccupations across time and to evaluate what sort of contribution other artists and collaborators have made to Varda's cinema. This in-depth analysis shows how each of these projects is the result of a complex amalgam of efforts, encounters and influences.

A comprehensive analysis of Varda's work is an exciting yet daunting task due to the profusion of works she has made. It would be hard (but probably not impossible) to find commonalities between her documentary on the vibrant art scene, history and culture of Los Angeles in the 1980s (*Mur, Murs*, 1980) and the story of an improbable romance between an apprentice clairvoyant and a guide in the catacombs of Paris (*Le Lion volatil*, 2003). Varda's own reflection on her practice provides invaluable tools to understand the connections between contrasting fragments of her work. The three chapters of the major section entitled 'The Attraction of Eclecticism' focus on different films and installations but each attempts to make these work together to discuss different issues relating to Varda's practice. In chapter three, entitled 'Varda's Ethics of Filming', I focus on the figure of the *cinéaste passeur*, and discuss two basic elements that I identify as foundational for Varda's ethics of filming. Her approach is, I would argue, based on the encounter with the other, and marked by a consistent concern for the capture and preservation of images and this is most visible in the four films discussed in this section *Mur, Murs, Documenteur* (1980–81), *Sans Toit ni Loi* and *Les Glaneurs et la glaneuse*. In chapter four, 'Poetics of Space', I look at how Varda articulates a model of cinema that subverts classical theory through the following questions: how does Varda approach space when she films or sets up installations, are there notable common elements that she focuses on in her otherwise disparate filmography, and is her approach to space unique at all? These questions are raised in relation again to a set of very different works including the films *Cléo de 5 à 7*, *Du Côté de la Côte* (1958), *Plaisir d'Amour en Iran*, and the installations: *Ping Pong Tong et Camping* (2005–6), *La Cabane de l'Échec* (2006) and *Dépôt de la cabane de pêcheur* (2010). Finally, chapter five, 'Cinécriture and Originality', is concerned with Varda's *cinécriture*, that is to say her unique approach to conceiving cinema as an elaborate and potentially powerful combination of moving images, sound and music. Varda's reluctance to follow pre-set production standards and her desire to experiment contribute to her singular approach in all the works under scrutiny in this chapter: *Elsa la Rose* (1966), *Uncle Yanco* (1967), *Les Glaneurs et la glaneuse, Deux Ans Après, Ydessa, les ours et etc., 7p., cuis., s. de b., ... à saisir* (1984) and *Réponses de Femmes*. This chapter relies on analyses to establish Varda's visual work as one that solicits the spectator's body as much as his/her intellect. As in the previous chapters, the aim is to plunge the reader into Varda's multifaceted *rêveries*, revealing how her eclectic and unorthodox *cinécriture* is the key to her influential and groundbreaking contribution to cinema.

Notes

1   This is Piccoli's first experience with Varda, but they will collaborate on several other occasions. Piccoli is a household name in France and has had a long and successful career working with well-known French and foreign directors including Claude Chabrol, Louis Malle, Claude Sautet, Alfred Hitchcock, Marco Ferreri and Manoel de Oliveira. By 1960, his career on screen was already well-established, since he played with Simone Signoret in Luis Buñuel's *La mort en ce jardin/ Evil Eden* (1956) and had been directed by Jean Renoir, René Clair and Alex-

andre Astruc. The 1960s were marked by two of his most famous roles, alongside Brigitte Bardot in Jean-Luc Godard's *Le Mépris* (1963) and Catherine Deneuve in Buñuel's *Belle de jour* (1967).

2 Periodisation is, as expected, a debated issue. Richard Neupert in his *History of the French New Wave Cinema*, writes that the new wave is 'a complex network of historical forces, including all films made by young directors exploiting new modes of production as well as unusual story and style options. The new wave *per se* lasts from 1958 through 1964' (2007: xviii).

3 When referring to passages of Flitterman-Lewis's book, I am using the second, expanded edition published in 1996 but it first came out in 1990.

4 As the publication dates suggest, this is probably because her monograph precedes by a few years the wave of new 'theory of the senses'.

5 The panoramic nature of Tarr and Rollet's project does not enable an in-depth discussion of Varda's production. More importantly, they view Varda's documentaries of the 1980s as depoliticised (see Tarr and Rollet 2000: 148), a claim that I would dispute, especially in the case of her Californian diptych *Mur, Murs* and *Documenteur* and *Daguérreotypes*.

6 The opening of *Deux Ans Après* (2002), a film that Varda made following the astounding response she got for *Les Glaneurs et la glaneuse*, shows her self-deprecating humour, when she quickly shows all the trophies the film earned, and moves on to more interesting matters.

7 The phrase '*au féminin singulier*' (Bastide 2009) is a subversion of the title of Geneviève Sellier's seminal book on the new wave (*Masculine Singular: French New Wave Cinema*). Varda's nomination as the head of the *Caméra d'Or* at the Cannes film festival in 2013 proves that her insight is both valued and recognised.

8 *Salut les Cubains!* was re-released on screen in 2004 as part of *CineVardaPhoto*, a triptych composed of *Ulysse* (1982) and *Ydessa, the Bears and etc./Ydessa, les ours et etc* (2004).

9 Rollet and Tarr note in the opening of their book *Cinema and the Second Sex* that 'in 1949 Jacqueline Audry was the only woman director making feature films (a handful others were making documentaries and shorts)' (2001: 1).

CHAPTER ONE

Agnès Varda: A Woman Within History

Varda's Place Within Film History

After almost sixty years behind the camera, Agnès Varda's filmography may not include any box office blockbuster (although *Sans Toit ni Loi* received a Golden Lion in Venice in 1985), but it has earned her a *succès d'estime*. After many years interacting with the audiences for her films and exhibitions, Varda is a well-known and established filmmaker at home (be it France or Belgium) and abroad. She has been fascinated by images for a long time, at least since she studied art history at the prestigious École du Louvre. Her interest turned into a profession when she started working as the official photographer for the Théâtre National Populaire (TNP), a famous French theatre company directed by Jean Vilar from 1951 to 1963. Her cinematographic career began by chance in 1954 when she decided to use a small sum recently inherited to make a film with Alain Resnais in Sète, a fishing village in the south of France. Featuring only two professional actors, Philippe Noiret and Silvia Monfort, and local participants found *ad hoc*, Varda and Resnais filmed and edited *La Pointe Courte*, an unconventional love story shot in black and white. After this first feature, she alternated between commissioned shorts like *Les Dites Cariatides* (1984), personal shorts such as *l'Opéra Mouffe* and *7p., cuis., s. de b., ... à saisir* and features like *Cléo de 5 à 7* and *Les Glaneurs et la glaneuse*.

Studies by Sandy Flitterman-Lewis, Susan Hayward and Ginette Vincendeau have contributed to the recognition of Varda's work, but their seminal analyses do not mean that Varda's place in the history of French cinema is set in stone. In Henri-Paul Chevrier's *Le Cinéma de répertoire et ses mises en scène*, for instance, Varda is swiftly assimilated with the Rive gauche group, then associated with feminist cinema in the 1970s, and finally described as a filmmaker practicing minimalist cinema (2004: 14,

90, 168). In her article 'Who Killed Brigitte Bardot?: Perspectives on the New Wave at Fifty', Vanessa Schwartz argues for a long overdue reconsideration of Varda's work. She demonstrates how *La Pointe Courte* has been 'sent to the morgue' in most books written about the new wave (2010: 148) even if many characteristics of Varda's first film clearly point to it as the inaugural new wave film. Schwartz's analysis of this important exclusion is incisive and to the point: 'To remember it [*La Pointe Courte*] would give too much credit, too early, to someone other than Truffaut' (ibid.). Varda's films are indeed often quickly pigeon-holed and interpretations like Chevrier's are frequently based on incomplete and limited readings of her work, something that this book aims to remedy.

Because of her double status as a woman and as a filmmaker who did not belong to the *Cahiers du cinéma* group formed of Godard, Rivette, Truffaut and Chabrol who were 'lumped together under the banner of the New Wave' (Hayward 2004: 233), Varda has always been perceived as a bit of an outsider, a *persona* that the filmmaker has even cultivated for various reasons, including her desire to assert her individuality.[1] Another reason for her debated place in French cinema and in its historiography is the number of films which were classified as either minor productions or of limited critical interest. These include *Le Bonheur*, *L'une chante, l'autre pas/One Sings, the Other Doesn't* (1976), and her Californian diptych *Mur, Murs* and *Documenteur*. Recent scholarship, however, has re-evalued Varda's eclectic body of work. Her 'minor' or forgotten films have recently been reconsidered and analysed as significant if often misunderstood feminist pieces (see Hottell 1999, DeRoo 2008, 2009 and Bénézet 2009 for more detailed analyses). The many re-edited and augmented DVDs that Varda has released in the last decade, and her recent foray into the world of contemporary art, has also attracted the attention of a growing number of scholars and *cinephiles* (see, for example, McNeill 2010 Chamarette 2011 and McMahon 2012).

My intention in this chapter is to reappraise a sample of selected films to argue that Varda's cinematographic practice has always engaged with the corporeal, and that as a consequence it constitutes a decisive contribution to feminism. The three pieces chosen – *L'Opéra Mouffe*, *Daguérréotypes* and *Les Veuves de Noirmoutier* – were shot years apart and span Varda's career. The first two films can be considered as part of the 'cinéma de quartier' ('local cinema shooting') that Varda frequently practices. Both were shot in Paris and focus on a well-defined space and its residents. The conditions of exhibition of *Les Veuves de Noirmoutier* were different from those of the two earlier films selected, but this installation piece makes for a more comprehensive and wide-ranging corpus.[2] In spite of these differences, I will argue that all these films exemplify the central character of the body in Varda's production and that Varda's focus on bodies is politically significant.

1: L'Opéra Mouffe
An essay between ethnographic and surrealist experiment

The scholarly reception of *L'Opéra Mouffe* is both interesting and revealing. Parallels have been made between this and later films, like *Les Glaneurs et la glaneuse*, on the basis of their shared concern for 'the disenfranchised and the have-nots' (Rosello 2001: 29). The autobiographical nature of *L'Opéra Mouffe* has been identified by Valerie Orpen, who describes the film as 'a semi-autobiographical documentary, recording the altered and subjective viewpoint of a pregnant woman in the then-seedy neighbourhood of the rue Mouffetard' (2007: 5). Despite these references, feminist critics and film scholars alike have largely avoided *L'Opéra Mouffe*, maybe because they found the film pretentious (see Tyler 1959) or essentialist (see Orpen 2007: 88).

Following Laura Rascaroli's (2011) analysis, *L'Opéra Mouffe* is best described as an experimental and 'essayistic' work. It is shot in black and white with a 16mm camera. There is no synchronised sound because Varda had deliberately chosen to film alone. When she evokes the circumstances of this film, Varda emphasises the repetitiveness and independence necessary to carry out her project: 'J'allais tous les matins avec ma petite chaise m'installer rue Mouffetard et je filmais' ('Every morning, I would take my little chair to the rue Mouffetard where I would get settled and start shooting'; Varda's interview in the *DVD Tous Courts* edition). Each section of the film begins with a very short song followed by Georges Delerue's music. The film is divided into ten vignettes, all introduced by intertitles (except the first one) in the manner of silent films. At the same time, *L'Opéra Mouffe* is resolutely modern as the film uses a musical soundtrack throughout, rather than a musical performance or a *bonimenteur*.[3] In terms of narrative, there is a sense of continuity between some of the vignettes, but no direct causality between the film's various sections. One of them focuses on a couple named 'Les amoureux', another titled 'Des angoisses' illustrates a pregnant woman's anxieties. The juxtaposition of sequences like 'Quelques uns' and 'L'ivresse', showing people sleeping rough, with the more idyllic love scenes in 'Les amoureux' illustrates the contradictory feelings and anxieties experienced by the pregnant woman mentioned in the film's subtitle: *Carnets de notes filmées rue Mouffetard à Paris par une femme enceinte en 1958*, commonly translated in English as *Diary of a Pregnant Woman*. Without veering too much in the direction of an interpretation solely informed by biographical information, it is important to underline that, in many interviews, Varda mentions that the film was in part a reaction to her subjective experience of pregnancy: '*L'Opéra Mouffe* was a short film about the contradictions of pregnancy. I was pregnant at the time, told I should feel good, like a bird. But I looked around on the street where I filmed, and I saw people expecting babies who were poor, sick and full of despair' (Varda and Peary 1977). The alternation between the *rêverie*-filled diary of a pregnant woman and the more Griersonian-inclined vignettes showing La Mouffe allows *L'Opéra Mouffe* to develop into an essayistic film focusing on the corporeal.

The fact that the spectator does not really know if the film has a plot line, or if it is based on free associations, makes it all the more enigmatic. The opening of *L'Opéra Mouffe* is a case in point. The names of the handful of people involved in the project roll over the image of a naked woman, sitting on a bench, her back to the spectator. The credit scene is immediately followed by a series of close-ups on the chest and belly of a pregnant woman. After a minute or so, a cut takes the spectator to the market where a pumpkin is cut open and emptied of its seeds to be displayed on a market stall. In refusing to show us the face of the woman,[4] Varda makes clear that the film is

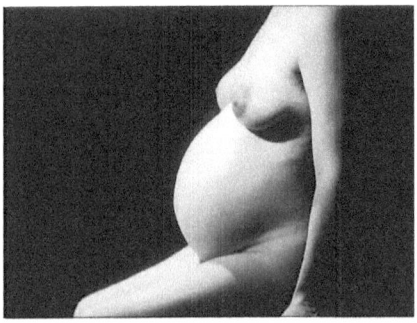 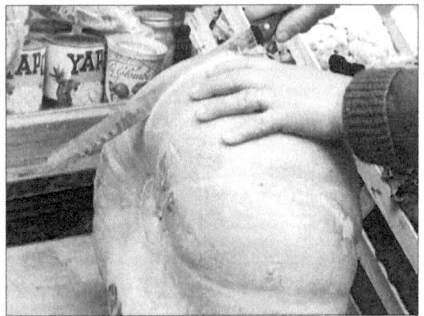

The mysterious pregnant woman the spectator is presented in the opening, in profile (left); an example of Varda's striking juxtapositions: a pumpkin being cut open at a market stall which evokes the woman's pregnant belly (right)

going to present a collection of willingly enigmatic and ambiguous images rather than a set of straightforward representations. The captions may help but they are not doing all the work and neither are the images. The spectator immediately understands that he will need to be active to make sense of this particular film. Varda's frequent use of close-ups satisfies our curiosity and desire to look closer to understand what we see. Her editing also helps, since it provides clues to interpret some of the film's vignettes. But the spectator needs to get involved and to rely on their senses to make sense of the film. In the opening sequence, the analogy established between the pumpkin and the belly is obvious, if unusual. The juxtaposition of the nude close-ups and the violent removal of the pumpkin's seeds makes the pregnant woman's fears manifest and palpable. The contrast between the peaceful rhythm of her breathing lying down and the firm grasp of the hands slicing the pumpkin open could not be more telling. The physical reaction of the audience one often observes is the result of this sudden and surprising juxtaposition.[5] Orpen's reading of Varda's nudes as 'beautiful […] but never titillating [and] either staged, posed, […] abstract, or very playful' (2007: 71) confirms my interpretation because the naked body here is meant to trigger a reaction but not one of visual pleasure. Varda shows the spectator how overwhelmed the pregnant woman of the subtitle feels when she considers the precarious nature of her unborn child. By compelling spectators to be active in their reception of the film, Varda increases their sensitivity to the minute details on screen; she forces them to tune in and to open up to evocative associations. Her close-ups of the belly of a pregnant woman are not meant to be titillating but to make the audience ponder and wonder at its perfectly round shape and at its slow movement as the woman inhales and exhales.

Another point that needs to be examined besides the combination of the evocative images with the film's soundscape is the multiplicity of bodies in *L'Opéra Mouffe*. The opening of the film is a clear homage to surrealism and the artistic practice of collage. Unashamedly, the film also reminds the audience of its theatrical construction. The superposition of hand-drawn theatre curtains synchronised with the typical opening tap of a conductor's stick at the very beginning is a playful nod to the spectators. This clever suturing of sound and images feels like the director is telling the audience: 'Show time!'

The film's opening is not only theatrical but also inventive and self-reflexive with its hand-drawn curtains and evocative soundscape

One of the most striking features of *L'Opéra Mouffe* (besides its meticulous editing and evocative soundscape) is the oscillation that takes the spectator from the crowds of La Mouffe to the sections devoted to the other two discernible female subjectivities: the radiant lover (played by Dorothée Blank) and the pregnant woman. But how are all these bodies orchestrated in the film? Are they simply edited to create an aesthetically pleasing portrayal of Paris in the late 1950s, or do they tell us something about that period in France? How significant is the treatment of these bodies on screen? Are the two women a sort of alter ego of the filmmaker, or do they have a different function? All these questions need to be addressed to establish the significance of the corporeal in *L'Opéra Mouffe* and the importance of the two women who are visually singled out in the film: the lover and the mother-to-be also need to be assessed.

The evocation of pregnancy in *L'Opéra Mouffe* is from the very start mysterious because we cannot clearly associate the nude shots in the opening with the pregnant woman present in the sections 'Des angoisses' and 'Des envies', or with Varda herself. In a double movement that conceals and reveals, this woman is turning her back to us and showing her bump. One could consider the vignettes associated with the mother-to-be as a subjective evocation of pregnancy, but if it is then it is clearly an evocation that Varda wants to experiment with. The fact that Varda does not play the role of the pregnant woman herself and that she keeps this film in the third person is important too. It underlines her determination to maintain a distance between her personal experience and the representation of pregnancy that she creates.[6] Varda is neither composing a

The dove, a recurring image in the film, is shown here struggling to escape from a fish bowl (left), while a young woman, running in slow-motion through ruins, evokes freedom and insouciance (right)

pamphlet on pregnancy nor simply presenting her subjective experience of pregnancy. Rather she invites the spectator to experience the vignettes associated with the mother to be as 'little sensory haikus' inflected by the music and songs as much as by her editing.[7] In these, the association of certain images is telling as is the soundscape, which 'when linked to the image [...] provides and writes the narrative, directing, constructing, and emoting these words perceptually' (Sinclair 2003: 27).

Four vignettes in total are related to pregnancy, namely the opening, 'De la grossesse', 'Des angoisses' and 'Des envies', but they do not necessarily follow each other. A sense of continuity is created between the opening and 'De la grossesse' through the image of the dove. In the opening, the cutting of the pumpkin occurs against the backdrop of tins, on which we can clearly read the word 'La Colombe' ('the dove'). In 'De la grossesse', the singer's four-line song includes the word 'dove' twice and we get to see a dove desperately trying to escape from a fishbowl. The close-ups of the bird's physical struggle contrast with the apparent happiness of the young woman who is shown running in slow-motion in the long take that follows. She runs in a minimalist space, scattered with ruins and naked trees, her summer dress floating as she approaches the camera, as if she was embodying youth and freedom. Yet her insouciance is quickly tempered by the images that immediately follow. A sprout growing out of a cabbage cut in two and the image of a small doll in its cradle accompanied by the rhythmic percussion of a metronome-like sound evokes the impending deadline of a due date or of time flying fast. So she may look free, happy and as innocent as a dove, but this woman's growing 'bud under her skin' ('le bourgeon dans la peau' of the introductory song) is what awaits her eventually.

The other two occurrences where we see the mother-to-be are different because she is heavily pregnant. In the section 'Des angoisses', a tracking shot follows her as she struggles to walk and carry heavy groceries. This scene is preceded by images of a hammer violently smashing light bulbs, followed by a hatchling struggling to get out of its shell. Again the image of the bird, here a baby bird, establishes continuity with the two sections discussed earlier. The soundtrack throughout 'Des angoisses' is a high-pitched, piercing whine. This incites the spectator to consider the sequence as a continuum, in which the violent hammering, the silenced chips of the fragile hatchling and the struggling woman are connected. This editing and clever use of sound makes the woman's slow progress look all the more difficult and it certainly makes the spectator empathise with her. The woman's slow physical progress is miles away from the picture of velocity and youth projected by the young woman running earlier.

In the other scene related to pregnancy called 'Des envies', the tone changes drastically when Varda manipulates the woman's contrasting food cravings. The vignette starts at the market with several close-ups of the market's offal and meat carcasses before it cuts and takes us to a florist's shop. In a way, we have come full circle, back to the market, with its *nature mortes* even if, this time, the focus is on animals rather than on plants and vegetables. The pregnant woman walks out of the florist, carrying a bunch of flowers that she smells before munching on them. This scene illustrating her unexpected cravings is funny and light and its final position needs to be taken into account when analysing these two consecutive vignettes representing pregnancy. This scene's humorous tone and the subsequent closing of a nearby shop's iron curtain, followed by the intertitle 'Rideau', prevents the spectator from interpreting the film as a solemn and categorical project. *L'Opéra Mouffe* should be considered, on the contrary, as an irreverent and playful piece.

Varda presents us with various facets of the life of a young woman who is sometimes gay and happy, sometimes tired and gloomy. It is as if we were turning the pages of her *rêverie*-filled diary, which creates a perfect opportunity for the director to explore this woman's sensual experiences and the potential of visual associations. In 'Des envies', for instance, she subverts the belief that associates pregnancy with food cravings by juxta-

The pregnant woman munching on roses, an unusual case of cravings in the section called 'Des Envies'

posing a series of unappetising *nature mortes* with the unusual consumption of flowers by the pregnant woman. At other times, Varda paints a grimmer picture of pregnancy as if the mother-to-be was overwhelmed by the transformation of her former self. The '*Travail, famille, patrie*' motto of the Vichy government was not *de rigueur* anymore, but the late 1950s remained a pronatalist era. In 'Des angoisses', the physical weariness of the mother-to-be combined with people's visible indifference (like the nun who does not offer to help and walks right past her) foreground the daily difficulties and unpleasantness associated with her pregnancy. Her changing shape provokes changes in the way she is looked at in the public sphere as well as in her sense of self. Her walk through nearly empty streets mimics the long process of adjustment that she has to go through. The unidentified high-pitched, piercing whine that accompanies the tracking shot where she is seen tottering and finally leaning against the wall out of exhaustion highlights her corporeal fatigue.

Varda's decision to represent the challenges of this woman as she changes physically and the surreal associations that she establishes go against the traditional representation of pregnancy as an idyllic period. Rather than making a film that fits into the norms of an idealised and mythical version of motherhood, she highlights the difficulties that come with some of the changes that the mother-to-be undergoes when pregnant. Her realistic rather than idealised representation of pregnancy subverts many of the classical images of maternity. During the interwar period and well into the 1950s, female identity was associated with three competing images as Sandra Reineke explains in *Beauvoir and her Sisters*. These three competing images were: 'the 'modern woman', who represented change from earlier gender ideals; the 'mother', who represented continuity and tradition and who served the state through sacrificing her body in birth; and the 'single woman', who oscillated between the other two, but more generally reflected postwar demographic concerns over France's birthrate 'in the absence of marriageable men' (Reineke 2011: 12). These archetypes are interesting when looked at in connection with the two women in *L'Opéra Mouffe* since it could be argued that the film questions these stereotypes.

Varda's vision is not political in the sense that her film does not advocate for the control of women's fertility, but it does not support a pronatalist agenda either. Rather, it suggests that there is a plurality of ways to represent women and to evoke their experience on screen whether they are single, pregnant, married or not. Varda's rejection of a fixed version of female subjectivity is in itself proof of her feminist stance. *L'Opéra Mouffe* is a playful and carefully crafted invitation to review the preconceptions held in the 1950s and engage in new perceptions of women. The images of Dorothée Blank, the radiant lover, are another symptomatic instance of Varda's refusal to create a static and stereotyped version of the modern woman. Varda's unconventional take on female subjectivity underlines 'how ideologies of feminity are produced and re-produced in media representations' (Thornham 2007: 7) and demonstrates that one can also create thought-provoking alternatives.

In *L'Opéra Mouffe*, Dorothée Blank's character is associated with the idea of the modern woman in many ways. For example, a scene where she is passionately kissing one of her lovers is followed by a significant close-up on the word 'la Moderne' written on her Singer sewing machine. In the absence of dialogue and of a realistic soundtrack, all visual clues are crucial. The juxtaposition of these two shots is an example of how Varda's editing establishes meaningful connections between specific images and ideas, here the naked lover and the modern woman. The sewing machine's label is associating the lover with modernity and progressiveness. Surprisingly Dorothée Blank's character is not as unambiguous as one may expect. Until the end, she remains an evanescent character whose story is left voluntarily undeveloped. We know nothing of her occupation, for example. For all we know she could be anything, an actress, a singer, or perhaps even a seamstress? We know, however, that she has three different lovers and that she lives by herself. The main difficulty for the spectator is that it is impossible to say whether the sections devoted to her are her subjective experience, *rêveries*, or even one of her lovers' nostalgic recollections.

The most notable difference between her and the mother-to-be is that she is almost always associated with a man whether it is in her bedroom, in her courtyard, or at the market. So why is that the case? Is this emphasis on her couple(s) telling the film's audience that she defies conventions and enjoys sexual freedom? Or is it asking us to question the meaning of the term 'modern' when associated with women? The only moment when she is by herself occurs in the courtyard where she is seen lying sideways on her bed and naked. Like the woman on the bench in the opening, she is turning her back to us, but here she looks absorbed and happy to be looking at her own reflection in a mirror. So is she performing what a modern woman is supposed to look like? Or is she simply enjoying her time alone in the absence of a male companion? And who is imagining this

Is this tableau an actress performing femininity, a mirror held to the spectator, or what a modern woman looks like according to Varda?

scene, her or someone else such as her frustrated ex-lover? In the two vignettes where she appears, 'Des Amoureux' and 'Joyeuses Fêtes', things are far from clear-cut.

One way to interpret her character is to consider her as a free-spirited counterpart to the more contemplative mother-to-be. But overall her evanescent nature is meant to trigger our curiosity and to force us to fill in the blanks. Are her nudity and the way she interacts with her lovers ideal representations of love and heterosexuality, or a series of masks which reveals the director's desire to question the performative nature of our own selves both in private and public? 'Joyeuses Fêtes' begins with a long scene showing children wearing masks and chasing each other. On a daily basis, our performances are certainly more subdued and less provocative than the childrens' here, but they are part of almost anyone's day to day life. Another way to look at this woman and her performance is through the perspective of the film. Dorothée Blank is indeed filmed in an almost self-reflexive way when her first lover plays with the lamp over her bed, when he puts her in the limelight and admires her face, so perfect and smooth before he turns the lamp off and they embrace again. Could this be a game of hide and seek not only between the woman and her lover(s) but also between the uncertain spectator and the definitely elusive young woman? Dorothée Blank, like Cléo, another of Varda's beautiful heroines, has very little privacy and is constantly defined and circumscribed by the gaze of others. Her nudity is very much staged as are her appearances on screen. At the market, she stands out from the crowds of La Mouffe because of her beauty and because of her passionate displays of affection. On screen, she stands out because Varda juxtaposes her exceptional beauty and free sexuality with the nitty-gritty of the locals' less glamourous daily life. In one of the bedroom scenes Varda, in a manifest homage to Man Ray's famous *Violon d'Ingres* (1924), frames Dorothée's back against the dark volutes of her iron bed. Visually she is all performance and plasticity, but ideologically she is a single woman whose 'modernity' I would argue is not yet acquired.

In a pronatalist society where women cannot freely control their own fertility, the choices available to this character remain limited. Varda's representation of Dorothée Blank as an icon of modernity is in that respect only tentative. The label may tell us 'la Moderne' but it is on a tool, the sewing machine, associated with domesticity. Many external accounts testify to Varda's political commitment and demonstrate that she strongly believed in women's right to reproductive freedom. So looking at the way Dorothée Blank's supposed modernity rubs against the representation of pregnancy and examining the alternative versions of female subjectivity offered in the film is essential. The creation in 1956 of the Mouvement français pour le planning familial (MFPF) alongside the women's liberation movement and the radical doctors of the Groupe Information Santé (GIS) led to a push in the 1960s and early 1970s for free access to contraception and abortion, but none of these changes had occurred when Varda was filming *L'Opéra Mouffe*. So is Dorothée Blank's character as free as she looks, or is she restricted by her legal rights? She may be the subject of gossip and admiration at the market, but the reality is that the more permissive image she projects should be carefully evaluated in the light of the period she lived in. Like the mother-to-be who has to live through a pregnancy that cannot be reversed, Dorothée

Blank's character is limited because she is a woman who does not have the same rights as men in France in the late 1950s. Like many women at the time, Varda was aware of the work of intellectuals like Jean Paul Sartre and Simone de Beauvoir. De Beauvoir's much criticised *The Second Sex* published in 1949 also presents the body in ambiguous terms 'oscillating between reductive biological stereotyping and critical elaboration of controlling cultural practices' (Reineke 2011: 26). In De Beauvoir's book, like in *L'Opéra Mouffe*, the corporeal may be at times 'a burden' as in the section 'Des Angoisses' and at other times 'a marvellous double' to be contemplated 'in a mirror with amazement, [...] a work of art, a living statue' (2009: 672) as in 'Des Amoureux'. Varda's determination to question the corporeal and her desire not to limit herself to stereotyped versions of female subjectivity shows that *L'Opéra Mouffe* is as feminist as De Beauvoir's writing.

But what of the other women (and men) presented in *L'Opéra Mouffe*? Now that Varda's feminist position is established, why linger on the locals of La Mouffe? The locals do not simply provide an air of authenticity that counterbalances the more artistic and surrealist vignettes devoted to the pregnant woman and the radiant lover. They are doing more than adding *couleur locale* to the film. Rather, they further reinforce some of the issues discussed earlier in that they illustrate how varied female subjectivity can be. The fact that Varda's montage compels the spectator to question his participation in interpreting film will also be looked at in this analysis of the residents and their role.

In the sections focusing on the locals of La Mouffe, there is a strong focus on women; women who are buying things, women who are trading goods and women who are talking to one another. Many of these women, especially in the opening vignettes are animated, talkative, as well as clearly curious. The market is shown as a place where they meet acquaintances, where they exchange news and gossip, and where they parade all dressed up in their furs and hats. It is both an economically important place and a public theatre where people perform and interact. Focusing on these daily exchanges and documenting these lives, even if Varda's editing transforms them, is reminiscent of the theoretical move towards a more inclusive and less elitist historiography, which pays attention to the everyday as practiced by Michel De Certeau. By choosing this location, the filmmaker also confirms her ideological position: she wants us to focus on a path less travelled and more specifically on a neighbourhood less explored. Her interest in capturing the life of the rue Mouffetard is inscribed in the title itself: *L'Opéra Mouffe*. As the public space of the street stands at the core of Varda's project, her film could be analysed as an ethnographic documentary on Paris in the late 1950s and on the role women played at the time. Her vision may be very personal, structured, and operatic, but the film undeniably contains 'fragments' of daily life in La Mouffe. The time of her shooting should not be undervalued either since the film documents life on this street in the winter of 1957, three years after the well-known winter of 1954. Reacting to a particularly alarming number of deaths on the streets, Abbé Pierre called for help on the radio and in the press in order to set up aid centres to help homeless people to survive the cold.[8] So the bare branches of the trees seen in the lover's courtyard, as well as near the buildings of La Mouffe should be regarded not only as a symbol of dormant life, but also as a reminder of the hardships experienced by many in Paris.

L'Opéra Mouffe may not be a *film à message* per se, but it is politically inclined, and it should be analysed both as a historical document and a more personal testimony. Despite the strict geographical focus and the short format of the film, Varda offers the audience a kaleidoscopic view of the neighbourhood at the time. We get to see the street market, the back alleys, the local houses as well as some of the shops of La Mouffe. The film's oscillation between the subjective evocation of the pregnant woman's experience and the documentary sections on the locals echoes Renov's analysis of the new autobiography in the 1980s, when he remarks that this type of work: 'straddles the received boundaries of documentary and the avant garde, [and] regards history and subjectivity as mutually defining categories' (2004: 109). Varda's complex editing and the lingering sense of mystery (even after several screenings) suggest that the woman's experience (regardless of whether we take her to be Varda's alter ego, or any French woman at the time) and the historical and social context are fundamentally intertwined and mutually defining. In the long tracking shot where the pregnant woman staggers under the weight of her groceries, several including Orpen have noted the importance of the graffiti on the wall which reminds us of the distant but no less menacing war in Algeria (see Orpen 2007: 17). In *L'Opéra Mouffe*, one cannot literally dissociate the private, the public and the historical as they are clearly intertwined. What Varda undertakes in this film is a poetic evocation of this neighbourhood's history through the private and associational (of the diary). The *avant garde* character of the film may have prevented critics and scholars to consider it alongside other films of the period, but this would not be Varda's first atypical piece.[9] It is indeed as we have seen by now hard to categorise and tentative on many occasions. But it offers a provocative perspective through its particular soundscape and through its questioning of the fragile boundaries between documentary and fiction.

The fast-paced editing of some of the sequences devoted to the locals may give the impression that the director is solely interested in looking at repetitive behaviour, at people limping, tidying up their hair, or wiping their nose. But when examined carefully these vignettes are significant because of the variety of people that Varda includes in the final montage. The charismatic *'causeuses'* who open the film at the market are as important as the slower and more contemplative shots of the other locals: the drinkers and rough-sleepers. In the vignette called 'De l'ivresse' where almost all the participants look back at the camera, the music and pace of editing suggest that we are dealing with a more meditative section, one on which we are supposed to pause. In 'De l'ivresse', regular drinkers do not seem to be considered by the market-goers as abnormal or out of character. They are simply part of the social fabric of the neighbourhood. But for all its apparent normality, there is one remarkable fact in the vignette 'De l'ivresse' and this is the inclusion of women. When showing women who drink alongside men, Varda chooses a transgressive image, one that is far from the romantic notion of *ivresse* often associated with love.[10]

This transgressive image is meant to provoke the audience and to trigger their reaction. Female alcoholism tends to be a secret and lonely practice (see Charpen-

Men and women drinking together in a Parisian bistrot, a documentary and subversive vignette

tier 1981) and medical discourse has often associated female alcoholism with underlying psychological problems, while male alcoholism is often seen as a ritual of male bonding and a sign of virility. So showing male and female locals together, as drinking equals and companions, is a levelling of gender, as well as a visual violation of the patriarchal construction of femininity.[11] Varda's vision is that women who defy society's conventions should not be relegated to the periphery but included in a representative picture of Paris in the late 1950s. The song's final two lines emphasise this idea of an inclusive examination of society, since it mimics the saying 'Qui dort dîne' (those who sleep will have dinner) with a humorous made up maxim 'Qui boit dort' (those who drink will sleep). At the same time, Varda creates a sense of continuity between all the Griersonian-inclined sections focusing on La Mouffe through visual echoes. Visually, the close-ups on the drinkers' faces are reminiscent of the fixed gaze of some of the '*gueules cassées*' (war veterans with severe facial injuries) encountered at the market in the earlier section 'Quelques Uns'. Their gaze testifies to their awareness of the film-making process, and is similar to the shots showing the inquisitive nature of the women at the market. The locals may not perform like the actress Dorothée Blank, lying naked in front of a mirror or embracing her lover, but the fact that they are returning the gaze, if only momentarily, creates a disjunction in the narrative flow that compels the spectator to pause and think about his own participation and role. In her analysis of essay films, Rascaroli notes that this 'constant interpellation' whereby 'each spectator, as an individual and not as a member of an anonymous, collective audience, is called upon to engage in a dialogical relationship with the enunciator, [...] to become active, intellectually and emotionally, and interact with the text' (2009: 35) is a defining feature of the film essay. This interpellation occurs in *L'Opéra Mouffe* time and again, and when it does not the absence of a realistic soundtrack titillates the spectator's curiosity and compels her to compensate and engage with the images and music composed by Delerue.

In the opening sequence at the market where Varda focuses on conversations, the intensity of these women's facial expressions incites the spectator to try to imagine the subject of their spirited exchanges. We may not hear the women's voices, but Varda's close-ups on their faces and the mimicking of these women's voices by brisk musical phrases alternating between woodwind and brass instrument provide a sense of immediacy and liveliness to the scene. The film's changing soundscape enables us to examine how the music and songs suture images together and create the emotional world of diegetic involvement. Varda's decision to do away with a realistic and synchronised soundtrack is what I would call inviting because the spectator can fill in this absence with whatever she wishes. Michel Chion, who writes extensively about sound, music and cinema, regards breaks, interruptions, and sudden changes of tempo (all practiced in *L'Opéra Mouffe*) as typical of an external logic of sound which 'brings out effects of discontinuity and rupture as interventions external to the represented content' (1994: 47). This is consistent with the form of the film essay in general as well as with its intention which is to make the spectator an intellectually and emotionally active participant. One can make sense of the different vignettes by comparing and contrasting them, by examining their order and tempo. But they could also be looked at as self-sufficient units, which are meant to trigger in the audience various impressions. Like in the opening where juxtaposed images create significant analogies, the music and songs' rhythms and poetic contents defy expectations and produce strong reactions. At the end of *L'Opéra Mouffe*, the spectator is left to decide whether this film is about the cinematographic re-creation of a pregnant woman's subjective impressions, the different ages a woman goes through (childhood, youth, pregnancy and old age), the inequalities and difficulties that afflict women in France in the fifties, or the daily life of the locals of La Mouffe. The spectator's conclusion may very well vary from one screening to the next, but whatever it is, it will depend on her understanding of what the corporeal stands for in the film, on her conscious efforts to make sense of the images and on her (usually) unconscious interpretation of sound.

2: Daguerréotypes
Manipulating stereotypes and enchanting daguerréotypes

(A) *Daguerréotypes' Working Bodies*

Daguerréotypes was originally produced for television and later screened in various film festivals. Like *L'Opéra Mouffe*, *Daguerréotypes* focuses on a specific geographical location rue Daguerre, the street where Varda lives in Paris. The circumstances that surround the shooting are worth mentioning since they determine the format of the film. In 1975, Varda had recently become a mother for the second time and decided that her next project, a '*carte blanche*' for the ZDF, a German television channel, would be filmed locally. The idea was that she would not go further than the eighty metre cable between the camera and her home allowed and that this would make it easier for her to look after her son Mathieu Demy. 'I started with the idea that women are attached to the home. So I attached myself to my home, literally, by imagining a new kind of umbilical cord. I attached an electric cable to the electric meter in my house which, when fully uncoiled, turned out to be 80 metres long. I decided to shoot *Daguerréotypes* within that distance' ('Je suis donc partie de cette idée, de ce fait, que les femmes sont attachées à la maison. Et je me suis moi-même attachée à la maison. J'ai imaginé un nouveau cordon ombilical. J'ai fait tirer une ligne électrique du compteur de ma maison, et le fil mesurait 80 mètres. J'ai décidé de tourner *Daguerréotypes* à cette-distance là') (Varda 1975: 39–40). When presented this way, the film is almost like an *exercise de style*, that is to say a formal experiment as much as a test.

Daguerréotypes has not attracted much critical attention from scholars. In a recent exception Kate Ince evokes the film but not at length to discuss important aspects of Varda's work including her use of haptic imagery and feminist strategies (2012). My ambition is therefore to open the discussion by analysing the way Varda presents the body throughout the film and to show the political potential of this particular project.

Daguerréotypes is a film that is definitely part of Varda's *cinéma de quartier* if only because of the technical limits that Varda imposed on her team and herself. It is anchored in rue Daguerre, in the vicinity of the filmmaker's home, and intends from the start to offer the spectator a very subjective snapshot of the neighbourhood. *Daguerréotypes* is a film set in Paris as shown by the image of the Eiffel Tower in the opening shot, but it is also an original take on this street where magicians, musicians, hairdressers and tailors will be filmed as they work and live together. In the very beginning, Varda's off-screen commentary reveals that she had always been mesmerised by the old-fashioned paraphernalia of the Chardon Bleu shop, but she also explains what her ambition is for this film. In *Daguerréotypes* she intends to trade her customer's clothes to spend time on the other side of the counter. She wants to be inside the local shops with the shopkeepers as they spend their day working, waiting and dealing with customers. The shops that she has chosen to focus on are the ones most people went to on a daily basis in the 1970s: the bakery shop, the butcher's, the grocery, and the *quincaillerie* (a kind of DIY-hardware store). To this selection of shops she adds a few more quaint places including a tailor's workshop, a hairdresser, a clock-maker, an accordion store and a driving school. The local cafe is also filmed but not like any of the other shops. We do not know who the owner is and we are never taken in the cafe during its daytime opening hours. Scenes from the magician Mystag's show held at the cafe are nonetheless crucial to the film since they are interweaved with the locals' daily activities in the second half of *Daguerréotypes*. So the cafe is used as a centre of convergence and coherence, almost like a symbolic theatre where Varda can tie together the various strands of the story that she is trying to tell.

If we consider that *Daguerréotypes* is a picturesque portrayal of the neighbourhood articulated around the shops of the street, it is essential to consider those who own these shops as well as those who use them everyday. Varda makes no secret that her portrayal is going to be highly stylised and personal from the very start. Mystag's definition of a 'daguerréotype' in the first scene of the film and the filmmaker's confession that *Daguerréotypes* originates from her fascination and curiosity are blatant proof of this. So what sort of representation does Varda offer of her neighbourhood in this film? Are the local shopkeepers filmed all day and at work only? Or does she give them the opportunity to speak and participate in the project? And also, how is the corporeal of interest again in this specific film?

After explaining what she intends to do in the introduction of *Daguerréotypes*, the filmmaker makes herself more discreet during a series of longer sequences representative of the shopkeepers's routines. This section is characterised by its stylistic sobriety and constructed as a 'day in the life' type of documentary. It starts like *L'Opéra Mouffe* with a theatrical lift of the curtains but the stars of the show are of a different nature, as Varda explains: 'Au théâtre du quotidien les stars sont: le pain, le lait, la quincaille, la viande, le linge blanc, l'heure juste, le cheveu court et toujours l'accordéon'.[12] The filmmaker takes the audience from one shop to another and shows us a series of uninterrupted exchanges between the shopkeepers and their customers. These exchanges illustrate both their expertise and their familiarity with most customers. The latter are varied and include an old lady who wants to buy condensed milk, two young men getting bread, and a mother and her child who want some laundry detergent and a toy. Whoever they are dealing with, the shopkeepers remain attentive and considerate even when they face unclear demands or long queues of people. The banality of these verbal exchanges may make them sound inconsequential but the camera's long takes on the choreography of the bodies on screen is remarkable.

First, the camera lingers on the hands of the baker's wife when she touches the bread to pick one with just the right crust, then it remains on them while she rummages through her drawer to find the exact change. Maria's knowledge is literally hands on and filmed as such. Instinctively she knows when to ask about someone's health and when to be more politely detached. The coming ins and going outs are punctuated by the door's bell which creates an almost lulling sense of repetition. The position of her body slightly leaning towards the counter tells us that her routine is made of many moments of relative calm interrupted by short and to the point exchanges of goods for money. The slow ballet of bodies continues as the camera shifts its attention to another local couple who are opening their DIY store. Here, there are gas bottles to be taken out, panels and doors to be opened, items to be displayed on the pavement. In a dialogue-free long take that slowly pans from one partner to the other, the couple moves in and out of the shop, synchronised and in harmony. Their mutual understanding and effortless dexterity (probably achieved through daily repetition) highlights the couple's dependence on each other. In all these places but the grocery shop which is operated by four Maghrebi men, the wives work alongside their husbands and play a fundamental role.[13] The baker, who we have not seen at this point, utterly depends on his wife to tend to the shop. Similarly, the butcher needs his wife to settle financial transactions and to keep waiting customers happy. At the hairdresser's store the space may be more clearly divided since female and male customers have a separate dedicated space, but the sound of magazines being flicked through and the ambient chit-chat illustrates the central role played by women in this business too. What the camera shows us is that these businesses rely on the harmonious choreography of both the partners' bodies to strive and flourish. This equilibrium may not always be easy to maintain but the looping structure of this series of sequences which ends with the closing of the DIY shop and the same accordion melody shows the audience that women are as significant as their male counterparts in the life of rue Daguerre. *Daguerréotypes* makes them visible as much as their partners and points to their knowledge, dexterity and dependability. If one considers that this film constitutes a historical document which shows what the capital was like in the 1970s, then this sequence demonstrates that women play a critical role in the local economy and in society overall. They may be associated in the media with their home and children and in the world of advertisement with seduction, but in Varda's film their bodies are as active as the men's and firmly anchored in the world of labour.[14]

This first series of scenes focusing on a day in the life of a shop is not the only section of the film where the filmmaker adopts what I would describe as an affirmative and corrective viewpoint. In the first series of direct interviews, Varda asks the participants to tell her where they come from. She then draws the conclusion that, in this working class neighbourhood, many of the tradesmen are economic migrants who came from outside the capital, a practice which to this day is still called in French 'monter à Paris' (to go up to Paris). In doing so, Varda makes it clear to non-native speakers[15] that these individuals who may have fitted their stereotype of the Parisian have in fact not been living in the capital for generations. This is a significant moment since it is the first time that Varda's off-screen commentary rectifies a common misconception about Parisians.

In the second series of interviews, which interestingly does not focus on work, Varda asks each partner another apparently innocent question: how they met their significant other. Here two characteristics are of particular importance. First, even if the sequence is thematically linked by the specifics of the couple's first romantic encounter, it is edited so that out of the six couples interviewed, only two men get to speak first: the owner of the Chardon bleu shop (whose wife is arguably not the most voluble) and the hairdresser. The women are therefore given pre-eminence in the sense that they are given the opportunity to articulate first how they met their husbands. The second notable characteristic of this series of interviews is that the men are the only ones who talk of not only love at first sight (in French '*coup de foudre*') but also their children, while the women tend to be more factual and sometimes even sound *blasé* (the seamstress and Janine the hairdresser in particular). This subversive montage favours a representation of men that goes against the grain of traditional masculinity since they are shown as sensitive and more romantically inclined individuals (in particular Yves the hairdresser and the baker). This sequence is also worth mentioning because it is the first time that they share aspects of their private rather than professional lives. By focusing on the women's key role in the day to day running of the shops and by letting them speak first when focusing on romantic encounters, Varda demonstrates that there are alternative and affirmative ways to portray the women of her street. She also shows that women need not be confined to traditional roles on screen and that they should be seen as sensible and articulate economical agents.

(B) *Daguerréotypes' Conflicting Images of Women*

In this chapter, I have chosen to concentrate on three of Varda's works which are not chronologically close partly because each of these films sheds light on some of the major social and political changes that occurred in France during the second half of the twentieth century. Varda's career spans over fifty years and her conception of cinema and its role was most certainly affected by some of the social and political changes she experienced. Scholars have recently started analysing the intersections between personal and collective experience in Varda's work. DeRoo's article on *Le Bonheur* is for example a case in point, which demonstrates the importance of analysing films in relation to their cultural and social context. In exploring the film's social and historical context, DeRoo demonstrates that *Le Bonheur* should be regarded as a subversive response to the dominant iconography representing women in the 1960s. Her essay, which uses archival excavation of imagery from magazines like *Elle* and *Marie Claire*, demonstrates Varda's irony when she applies these representations to the 'subjects, characters and poses of *Le Bonheur*' (DeRoo 2008: 191).

The 1970s were a period of intense political debate and many historians describe the period as the culmination of the long sexual revolution (see Briggs 2012: 542). As a result, one may wonder if *Daguerréotypes* through its concern with the local is not also a politically inclined work. A short sequence claims that people from this end of the street refrain from discussing politics because 'it's not good for trade', contrary to what takes place at the other end of the street where political manifestos and heated discussions are plenty. This disclaimer meant to justify the absence of political discussions on screen only illuminates the polarisation of the rue Daguerre. Besides, if one takes a step back to consider the range of women represented in the film, it is clear that *Daguerréotypes* not only surveys but also interrogates the different images of women that circulate at the time.

On several occasions in the film, Varda includes commercial images of women that appear on the covers of magazines. In the first ten minutes of the film, when a woman and her child walk past a newspaper stand whose prominent display includes *Le Nouveau Détective* front page, we clearly see a black and white full size photograph of a naked blonde, just as tall as the little girl who turns towards the camera. This juxtaposition is witty because of the contrast between the naked yet passive woman on paper and the inquisitive gaze of the child whose mother has wrapped up in many warm layers. It is also cleverly inserted less than a minute after a longer sequence devoted to two '*causeuses*' whose conversation focuses on a local victim of domestic violence. So even if Varda is not making a direct connection between conjugal violence and the objectification of women's bodies, she definitely suggests here that the proliferation and impact of these images should be questioned. And through this 'cascade of free associations' (Gorbman 2012: 55) she makes her subjective voice heard.

In the hairdresser's shop, where women gather and talk, a variety of commercial images are on display. The glossy pictures of fashionable hairstyles epitomise an unattainable ideal of beauty and youth dictated by magazines. These women are embodying an ideal of conformism through beauty. Other images, notably those of a magazine like *Jour de France* flaunting *La Bardot* on its cover refer to a different type of aspirational icon that at the time symbolises sexual liberation. To a contemporary spectator, Brigitte Bardot may look all dolled up and as affected as the commercial pictures of hairstyles we see in the salon, but what she evokes is very different. The *clichés* attached to Bardot's film persona are 'her youth, modernity, confidence, and freedom. [...] she was no pinup who acted but rather a moving picture star who could also be stopped long enough to be photographed' (Schwartz 2010: 149). In *Daguerréotypes*, none of these images of women are innocuous. I believe that in this scene Bardot's photo shows the kind of new attitudes towards women that are gradually emerging at the time, even if they occur in a traditional looking hair salon of the rue Daguerre full of chatty middle-aged women. Some of the images promoted by popular culture (including film and music) clashed with the more traditional and conformist view of feminine beauty held by some. The cultural popularity of sexualised icons like Bardot may not always have coincided with social acceptance in the 1960s, but this sequence suggests that in 1975 many things are changing, even if these changes are part of a slow and gradual evolution. Scholars like Dagmar Herzog have argued that the idea of a 'long sexual revolution' is a more accurate description of what was happening in France.[16] Herzog also claims that the legalisation of the pill in France in 1967 was only part of a larger development of new attitudes concerning sex.[17] So Varda's attention to Bardot as a symbol of a new sexualised youth culture when inserted in the context of the local hair salon could suggest that, in the mid-1970s, people have put the clash of ideals behind them, and that they are ready to accept new political and social changes.

France Soir's headline, or how French politics and the future of women irrupt in Mystag's magic show

The most significant front page of *Daguerréotypes* is the one that the young figure skater holds for all to see during the magician's show situated at the end of the film. On the cover of *France Soir*, the title is impossible to ignore: 'Avortement, c'est l'heure de vérité' ('Abortion: now is crunch time'). The film may focus on the magician's tricks, but this is a significant close-up, especially coming from someone who signed Simone de Beauvoir's polemical manifesto four years before this film. In 1971, Varda signed 'le manifeste des 343' published in *Le Point* which called for the legalisation of abortion. Signed by three hundred and forty two other women including Marguerite Duras, Bernadette Lafont and Françoise Sagan, it read as follows: '*One million women get an abortion in France every year. They're doing it in dangerous conditions because they're condemned to clandestineness, although medically controlled abortion is a simple thing. Everyone keeps silent about those million women. I declare I am one of them. I had an abortion. As well as demanding free access to contraceptive means, we are demanding free abortion*'.[18] At the time, Varda was involved in the feminist movement called MLF (mouvement pour la libération des femmes). With her friend, the actress Delphine Seyrig, she went to demonstrations and held meetings in her kitchen which are vividly remembered by her daughter Rosalie.[19] So even if *Daguerréotypes* does not include any discussion of abortion *per se*, it certainly acknowledges the turning point that French politics has reached by 1975. This paper is much more than a part of Mystag's magical trick, it is a window on the political changes which will affect the life of many young women like the figure skater and the butcher's daughter. It is also a reminder of the commitment and struggle of militants who are pushing for this bill to be passed.

Daguerréotypes draws our attention to the variety of women's images in the media, and the film itself captures a remarkable range of images of women. As explained earlier, the working body is central to Varda's affirmative take on the role of women in society. In many other sections of the film, Varda also includes many other women such as the young figure skater who is both full of aspirations and determined, the enigmatic older Léonce (alias Mme Chardon Bleu), and the 'causeuses' and 'concierge' with their assertive opinions. These many participants contribute to the film's narrative and show that women cannot be confined to a single reductive image. As the interviews clearly demonstrate, they come from different places and have had different experiences. Some are old and others are young. The only thing that ties them together is the fact that they live on the same street and that maybe some of the political aspirations of the older generation will become realities for the younger ones.

(C) *A Non-Definitive and Self-Reflexive Take on Portraits*

Varda takes a clear position in giving visibility to working women in *Daguerréotypes*. But her way of capturing the lives of the people of the rue Daguerre on film is far from being presented as a definitive take. Rather, she is asking the audience to look again, even if it is to look at something that they think they already know. She is also, I would argue, questioning the notion of the portrait and its claims to authenticity. When Varda decides not to edit out moments when the non-professionals of *Daguerréotypes* perform or when their body language acknowledges the camera, she invites the spectator to reassess what it is that they are watching. In most of the scenes focusing on the locals' working day, the participants seem oblivious of the camera. They are seen chatting away with their customers and serving them as if nothing was out of the ordinary. Sometimes, however, it is clear that the camera is not as unobstrusive as it seems, like at the end of the first sequence in the clockmaker's shop. In this sequence, the customer's natural attitude and spontaneous banter have made the situation sound perfectly authentic. But after the clockmaker walks out of the frame to attend to something in the shop off screen, his wife is awkwardly standing behind the counter, visibly hesitant and furtively looking towards the camera, as if looking for a signal. Her posture reveals how the filmmaking process disrupts the reality of the world it is documenting. In this case, her body cannot lie, nor can it act seamlessly.

The other occurrences that remind the spectator of the documentary process generally coincide with sections focusing on the driving instructor. On these occasions, he sounds like he is performing for the camera and looks rather uncomfortable. His diction and tone of delivery in particular sound artificial. This is all the more surprising considering that a fairly long sequence is devoted to his classroom teaching, which one would expect should have prepared him to be more at ease than other participants in front of an audience. Could it be that these individuals who are visibly confortable in their shops when busy and working feel that they have an obligation towards the filmmaker and the camera? Did something happen that made them uncomfortable just before these takes? Varda's decision to keep these moments of awkward stillness and indecision remind us that one of the film's main subjects is the idea of the portrait.

The Daguerréotype was a photographic process invented by Louis Daguerre in 1837 which enabled people to make portraits or photos of landscapes. It required ten minute exposure and remained popular until the 1850s. Posing for the camera or acting in front of the camera is not necessarily an easy task, something that all will be doing naturally. In *Daguerréotypes*, Varda is experimenting with the idea of the cinematographic portrait and the end sequence which gathers several shots like 'family photos' illustrates this. Throughout the film, she is manipulating the codes associated with the portrait, and reappropriating them. She encourages the audience to pause and contemplate some of the following issues: how do the traditions and codes of portraits (whether pictural or photographic) affect her cinematographic project? How do you draw someone's portrait on film at a time when television has become an established mode of representation? Do you need genuine shots of a person who is unaware of the process, or can you show their personality through interviews? And how does a long term relationship between the filmmaker and participants impact on the end result, if it does at all? When Varda establishes a contrast between the natural-looking activities of the shopkeepers and the corporeal hiccups, she points to something that I associate with Sartre's description of the barmaid and other workers and his discussion of the ceremony that society expects from him. I will quote Sartre's text at length here:

> There is the dance of the grocer, of the tailor, of the auctioneer, by which they endeavor to persuade their clientele that they are nothing but a grocer, an

auctioneer, a tailor. A grocer who dreams is offensive to the buyer, because such a grocer is not wholly a grocer. Society demands that he limit himself to his function as a grocer… There are indeed many precautions to imprison a man in what he is, as if we lived in perpetual fear that he might escape from it, that he might break away and suddenly elude his condition. (2003: 82–3)

In this passage Sartre eloquently demonstrates that in the collective imaginary specific roles are set for tradesmen. These roles and ceremonies are performed by the tradesmen's bodies, through the way they walk, lean, talk. All impersonate the type of tradesmen that they are supposed to be. Could it be that in the scenes mentioned earlier the driving instructor finds it difficult to perform his role in front of the camera? When Varda begins her film, the audience probably expects a cinematographic snapshot of the street that will include such performances and ceremonies, and maybe even some stereotypes. Soon enough, however, the filmmaker requires her audience to reconsider their preconceptions by showing three important things. First, by focusing on the body of women at work, she incites the spectator to think about professional and social hierarchies in France in the 1970s. She makes the audience not only look at the repetitive nature of their routine but also at their reliability and intelligence. Secondly, by reframing the way these individuals and their bodies are represented on screen, she questions the idea of the portrait and links this back to earlier traditions and codes. Finally, by drawing attention to the effect of the cinematographic process, she makes a polemical statement and demonstrates that a documentary film can never be true to reality, and that in truth it is 'a multi-layered, performative exchange between subjects, filmmakers/apparatus and spectators' (Bruzzi 2006: 10).

Our perception and understanding of the corporeal in *Daguerréotypes* will depend on our experience and on our willingness to engage with the images and sounds that Varda mixes up. While sections of the film are voluntarily kept slow and 'empty' of dramatic actions (for instance the 'day in the life' opening), others force us to process an incredible amount of information. Mystag's show for example requires that we reconsider the 'professional' sections, since we get to see all the tradesmen out of their shops. Drinking and smoking, chatting and laughing, they are in fact free of the 'social ceremony' their bodies are contrived to during the day, and they indeed look very different without their work clothes on. That evening in the café is exceptional; it is a turning point when they are asked to observe the magician's rules. When Mystag asks Yves, the hairdresser, to relax before he hypnotises him into stillness, the roles are suddenly reversed. Yves is no longer the one asking his customer to lean back while he is busy trimming his hair. The filmmaker's witty editing takes us unexpectedly from the butcher's hands cutting meat to Mystag's spectacular self-stabbing, and from the driving instructor's lesson discussing the dangers of traffic to the trick where Mystag makes his assistant's head disappear. These 'professional close-ups' that the spectator has sometimes already seen are reframed and given a new meaning when they are inserted throughout the show. What is performance and what authenticity? Is Mystag's show the ultimate performance or a revelatory opening enabling the audience to see the participants' true selves? Is this a show of attractions or a documentary?

The film's final section focuses on the participants' private lives, showing their homes for the first time. When Varda asks them about their dreams, she is definitely trying to get them to talk about something other than work. Many maintain that they cannot escape from work even in their dreams which are haunted by customers, students and mistakes. The butcher's wife is categorical: 'Rêver? On n'a pas le temps, le dimanche c'est télé et on dort!' ('Time to dream? We have none, on Sundays we watch TV and we sleep, that's it!'). Others are more sentimental, nostalgic, and even original. The baker's wife admits, for instance, that she makes funny dreams where she travels to different places even if she always wakes up in the same place, her bed, and needs to get herself ready to work. By enchanting their daily gestures, choreographing their bodies and giving them the chance to talk about their dreams, Varda lays emphasis on alternative aspects of the participants' lives and personalities. She requires that we review our stereotypical expectations and engage with her film which she refuses to categorise but describes as a reportage and homage to her neighbours, the mysterious and outspoken locals of the rue Daguerre.

While the first section of *Daguerréotypes* is more observational, concentrating on the shared space of the street's shops, the second half is more unconventional and ambiguous both in its content and style. The mysterious habits and mannerisms of Mme Chardon Bleu may have been exposed but they remain unexplained, the mundane activities of the tradesmen and their daily routine are known to us but all in all we know very little about their lives. *Daguerréotypes* is a tentative and self-reflexive film based on the enchanted and enchanting encounters that Varda creates in front of the camera. Its most valuable lesson is certainly in its reassessment of the polemical potential of the corporeal on screen.

3: Les Veuves de Noirmoutier

(A) *Un auto-allo portrait polémique et corporel*

Scholars and critics alike have often described Varda's cinema as autobiographical. There is no denying that some of the subjects she reflects on as well as her use of the voice-over suggest such a tendency, although a more detailed analysis of this particular device reveals that Varda often undermines and subverts the spectator's expectations. Films like *Jacquot de Nantes* (1990) and *Les Plages d'Agnès* are undeniably linked with Varda's personal experience. Yet, by interpreting these films as merely autobiographical, one misses the director's interest in gleaning elements of a specific history and place as well as her personal impressions. In her analysis of Varda's exhibition *L'Île et Elle*, Barnet rightly reminds us of this tendency: 'The individual is linked to the collective, and vice versa, in a way that is always socio-political and highly charged with feminist influences. As Varda stated in 1975, and as is echoed in *Les Veuves de Noirmoutier*, 'Je suis une femme mais je suis aussi toutes les femmes' (Barnet 2011: 106).

The installation *Les Veuves de Noirmoutier* was created at the Galerie Martine Aboucaya in early 2005 and displayed at the Fondation Cartier in Paris from June to October 2006 as part of Varda's exhibition *L'Île et Elle*. A week after the exhibition ended, Arte France broadcast a documentary film entitled *Les Veuves de Noirmoutier* based on some of the footage that Varda shot in preparation for the installation. The film, however, includes three additional widows and Varda's intention in making it is clear: she wants to make these women not only visible but also heard outside of the restrictive 'white cube of the gallery'.[20] Since 2006, Varda's installation has been included in many of her exhibitions such as *Y'a pas que la mer!* in Sètes (to which I will refer extensively since this is where I last saw this work in 2012).[21] I will therefore be as specific as possible to support my analysis of Varda's work in its particular context. In order to differentiate between the formats of this project I will use the following abbreviations: *Les Veuves de Noirmoutier* (I) for the installation, *Les Veuves de Noirmoutier* (F) for the film, and finally *Les Veuves de Noirmoutier* (C) for the catalogue published as an accompaniment to the 2012 exhibition in Sètes.

In her book *Selfless Cinema? Ethics and French Documentary* (2006), Sarah Cooper describes *Les Glaneurs et la glaneuse* as an example of 'auto-/allo-portraits'. My objective in the first part of this section on *Les Veuves de Noirmoutier* will be to expand on this term to demonstrate that this work can be analysed as a corporeal auto-/allo-portrait. In the second part of this section, I will turn to the invisible to show how this work tries to make the intangible palpable.

> Much has been written about the early and middle stages of women's lives, up to and including menopause, but sustained feminist analyses of experiences such as widowhood, grand-mothering or sexuality in old age have been few and far between, and while the physical and emotional experiences of younger women are dwelt upon, there has been little attentiveness to those of the old. (Jordàn 2011: 139).

Varda is therefore an exception since her work has for over a decade exhibited a sustained interest and engagement with the experiences of ageing, widowhood and mourning. Shortly after the release of *Les Glaneurs et la glaneuse* in 2000, Rosello expertly analysed Varda's film as a 'Portrait of the Artist as an old Lady' (2001: 29–36). Shirley Jordan commenting on the same film wrote that it 'calls us to witness the socially and existentially unpalatable textures of aging' (2009: 581). So even if the experiences of the old have not received much critical attention, Varda's concern certainly did not go unnoticed.

In *Les Veuves de Noirmoutier* (I+F), Varda continues her exploration of aging but takes it one step further, even if as often she refrains from offering a set definition of old age or widowhood.[22] The *dispositif* of *Les Veuves de Noirmoutier* (I) (i.e. the audio-visual setting of the gallery space) confronts head-on some of the common assumptions made about widows such as their age. Just looking at the fourteen monitors around the central big screen, it is obvious that some of these women are still part of Noirmoutier's 'population active' (or working force) like Inès Allorant, and certainly not retired. The multiplicity of the faces displayed on these screens illustrates the diversity that characterises this category. Varda does not confine her representation of widows to the stereotype of a lonely, wrinkled, white haired woman. Neither does she restrict her project to a series of interviews with alter-egos or look-alikes meant to reflect her own experience. On the contrary, *Les Veuves de Noirmoutier* (I) which touches on the personal and raw subject matter of bereavement for Varda is characterised by a meticulously planned audio-visual environment heaving with eclectic characters.[23] Varda's *dispositif* is elaborate and emphasises from the get-go the fact that widowhood can be perceived in a number of ways. In the room where the lights are dimmed, thus inviting the visitor to slow down and maybe sit for a while as in a theatre, fourteen chairs face fourteen small monitors arranged around a much bigger screen. While the central panel shows a nine-minute looped video of all the widows (but Varda) walking on the beach, each small monitor is reserved for one single female participant. To engage with each widow's experience, the visitor needs to sit down and pick one pair of headphones to listen to a specific testimony. The oblong shape formed by the chairs corresponds to the configuration of the screens and a short description encourages people to move from chair to chair to listen to each widow. The space is large enough to allow other visitors to move around the chairs and circulate freely as they please.[24]

The big screen in the centre is different from the others since it is accompanied by a specific soundscape and more pictorial in its composition as noted by Chamarette (2011: 40). The fourteen widows, all dressed in black, gradually congregate and silently walk around a large wooden table incongruously placed on the beach *à la Magritte*. The sound of the waves on the sand is overlapping with the melancholy melody of Ami Flammer's violin, but no words are ever pronounced during the 9-minute looped film. To Jordan, the central monitor represents and invites 'the ritual exercise of grief, while also questioning the reductive construction of an entire social category' (2009: 585). While I agree that *Les Veuves de Noirmoutier* (I) challenges the restrictive confines of widowhood, I would interpret this central screen slightly differently.

I see this video as an attempt to shed light on the difficulty of communicating grief and on the impossibility of portraying loss. The widows' grief, which is explicitly referred to in many interviews as taboo, is given central stage here. The widows' bodies take possession of the beach, a space more often associated with joyful holidays and romantic encounters. Their slow procession and resolute silence makes the scene both mysterious and poignant. The game of '*chaises musicales*' and the circling that the visitor is meant to do in the space of the gallery echoes the slow-paced choreography of the central screen. To relate to these women's experiences and to unveil the mystery of this central scene, the visitor needs to physically engage with the installation and to let the testimonies permeate him. The various positions that the visitor can adopt *vis à vis* Varda's *dispositif* encourage her to question how included or excluded she feels from the scene that she is watching and listening. While the smaller monitors encourage the visitor to engage with the idiosyncrasies of each individual life and to meet the singularity of what Comolli calls a '*corps parlant*',[25] the big screen reminds us that no words can really approximate the widows' difficulties and woes. Through its slow rhythm and morose music, this choreography of bodies summons a poignant evocation of the women's pain. It also tells the visitor that these women should be given a space of their own in order not only to grieve, but also to remember and celebrate their lost ones.

The visitor who devotes a fair amount of time to watching the individual portraits will inevitably start to draw parallels. She will see echoes as well as differences between the widows' *'corps parlants'* and their narrated experience. Some women tell Varda that because their husband's profession took them at sea for extended periods, they were already used to long absences and the feeling of an empty house. Others, like Inès, who have not gotten used to the absence of their partners or husbands, find this experience excruciating. Many of the women show incredible resilience and stamina. Several of them talk of the daily reminders of their husband's presence; they show old photographs and tell of happy memories. When the flow of anecdotes carries the conversation towards other subjects, the camera's attention often turns to the widows' hands absently playing with their wedding rings, a visual reminder of their loss. These widows may not be sociologically representative because Varda's sample is limited geographically, but many of the difficulties they talk about correspond to the concerns of people who want to improve the life of individuals and/or old people who find themselves in the same situation.

One of the project's immediate and undeniable achievements is the fact that *Les Veuves de Noirmoutier* (I+F) drew these women out of their husbands' shadows and into the public eye. Varda gives these women the opportunity to have a say and to tell others what living as a widow is and feels like. This is one of the reasons why *Les Veuves de Noirmoutier* (I+F) should not only be interpreted as an autobiographical piece; it is an 'allo-portrait' as much as an 'auto-portrait'. The project is both a poetical re-appropriation of a specific territory and an opportunity to make these voices heard which can potentially make the visitor realise how we are all implicated in defining and shaping the image of widows. Varda's enterprise can be looked at as a reflection on the implication of various subjectivities in social and historical discourses. In her work on ethnography, Catherine Russel explains how an autobiographical project can be concerned with more than a single subject: 'Autobiography becomes ethnographic at the point where the film- or video-maker understands his or her personal history to be implicated in larger social formations and historical processes. Identity is no longer a transcendental or essential self that is revealed, but a "staging of subjectivity" – a representation of the self as performance' (1999: 276). This turning of the mirror towards oneself is something that Varda does in her installation since one of the smaller monitors includes her own take on bereavement. Because of its distinctive character, it needs to be discussed and assessed separately.

Varda's video is located at the bottom right of the set of monitors. Because of Varda's silence, this auto-portrait is probably the most difficult to watch of all. Unlike the other women, Varda is not filmed in her home in Paris or Noirmoutier,[26] but sitting on the beach in a chair very much like the ones in the room. Next to her is an empty chair which foregrounds 'the spectral presence of an intangible other' (Chamarette 2011: 43), Jacques Demy, the absent 'Il' in the exhibition *L'Île et Elle*. For anyone accustomed either to her assertive public persona or to her playful voice-over on film, this is an aural shock. In this video, Varda makes no compromise and exposes herself as she is filmed weeping and isolated. At one point, in a quiet voice-over, she is heard singing Jacques Prévert's *Des Monts et des Merveilles*, a poem which features at the end of the film *Jacquot de Nantes*. This video is a bold statement and an intimate display of grief. Varda's video may differ formally from that of the other widows in that it is 'physically staged and painterly' (Jordan 2009: 586) but it is not given pre-eminence at all in the *dispositif*. Unlike the other women, in her video, Varda shows the visitor rather than tells her, maybe because as the instigator of the project she is aware that her voice could drown or undermine that of the other widows. The empty chair captured in the present of the video is a reminder of the past, of the lost one. It is an unsettling but also touching reminder of the past relationship that Varda is still firmly attached to. Varda confronts the visitor as she sits on the beach 'at once widow and artist, the organizing subject and the object of study' (Jordan 2009: 587). Her testimony (or lack thereof) is in close proximity to the ones of the other widows and does not dominate the installation. Her video may, like the video on the central screen, resist interpretation but the fact that she is including herself testifies of her desire to commit to this bold, self-expository piece of work.

(B) *Bereavement and Art: Making the Intangible Palpable*

Scholars who write about Varda's recent works often make connections between her cinematographic work and her installations. This is critical especially since in the last ten years, Varda has used her footage and films as a source of inspiration and as an easily accessible audio-visual database.[27] In this section, I want to move away from the particularities of the auto-allo portraits to consider the invisible and intagible that they gesture towards. Many visible traces accumulated through the *dispositif* explain to the visitors that these women experience difficulties, that several dislike being only defined by their status as widows and that misconceptions and taboos often hinder their self-development. *Les Veuves de Noirmoutier* (I) relies on the specific experiences of the interviewees to foster the visitor's engagement, but the project as a whole also suggests something else, something bigger. *Les Veuves de Noirmoutier* (I) shows that art can summon the intangible and shed light on the relational ties that both define us and make us a community.

Les Veuves de Noirmoutier (I+F) offers a collection of examples of how women deal with loss. Their testimonies reveal what they miss most and how they deal with the everyday: 'J'allume la cheminée [...] ça fait une chaleur' ('I light up the chimney and it warms up the room') says Alice. 'Le manque, c'est le manque de toucher [...] la maison est encore pleine de la présence de Thierry, de son odeur' ('I miss, I miss being able to touch him. I can still feel Thierry's presence in the house everywhere, I can smell him') says Inès. The *dispositif* makes us stop and sit to share even for a little while these women's experiences. The headphones intensify this feeling since for a moment we cut ourselves from the room's noise to listen to an individual confession. The repeated allusions to loss underscore the widows' sufferings but their testimonies do not simply act as an act of exposure. They also open up a space for reflection and meditation.

These women's words invite us to recognise ourselves as vulnerable and to think about our own losses too. As spectators or visitors, we are invited to be with them.[28]

Judith Butler emphasises the importance of this notion of loss: 'Despite our differences in location and history, my guess is that it is possible to appeal to a "we", for all of us have some notion of what it is to have lost somebody. Loss has made a tenuous "we" of us all. And if we have lost, then it follows that we have had, that we have desired and loved, that we have struggled to find the conditions for our desire' (2003: 10). The trivial anecdotes and picturesque evocations of the lost one may trigger in the viewer a feeling of kinship and recognition. Thinking about our own loss(es) makes us realise how bound we are to others and how our relationships define us. In the 'Notes d'intention' that Varda wrote when *Les Veuves de Noirmoutier* (F) was broadcast, she highlights the significance of our connections to others and writes that the exchanges she had with these women while shooting for the film taught her as much about them as it did about herself.[29]

Varda's impulse may have been cathartic but the fact that she represents herself as lost for words in her video is telling. She will neither provide an explanation, nor make *Les Veuves de Noirmoutier* (I+F) a subjective exploration only. She wants the visitor to engage with *Les Veuves de Noirmoutier* (I) and to think about her personal experiences. Losing one's significant other means losing one's bearings, whether this person is a husband, a wife, a partner, or another relative. *Les Veuves de Noirmoutier* (I+F) could be interpreted as a project meant to shed light on the grieving selves most communities are made of. Butler again describes the overwhelming feeling of being lost very well: 'It is not as if an "I" exists independently over here and then simply loses a "you" over there, especially if the attachment to "you" is part of what composes who "I" am. If I lose you, under these conditions, then I not only mourn the loss, but I become inscrutable to myself. Who "am" I, without you? When we lose some of these ties by which we are constituted, we do not know who we are or what to do' (2003: 12). This undoing of our identities is a central thread in the many testimonies and what is left to do and how to fill time is a recurring question in *Les Veuves de Noirmoutier* (F+I). When she assembles *Les Veuves de Noirmoutier* (I), Varda is simultaneously looking for herself and redefining her own self.

By documenting these women's experiences, by bringing them into the white cube and the home of many television viewers, Varda is asserting the validity of their experiences. They may form an eclectic group but their testimonies should not be ignored. Naming these women and giving them an opportunity to be heard establishes them as a community of grieving selves as vulnerable as ours. Butler argues that the feeling of loss as incapacitating as it may be, holds an important political potential. This sense of human vulnerability can remind us that we have a collective responsibility for the physical lives of others (2003: 19). By exposing us not to finitude *per se* but to its consequences, Varda reminds us of the ones we have lost, of our own sense of self, and of the ones we can still be with. By making the intangible palpable, she underscores the political potential of art. *Les Veuves de Noirmoutier* (F+I) re-affirms the importance of considering the many experiences of the margins, whether these are defined by gender, class or any other restrictive category, and it also re-asserts our capacity of 'being with' responsibly (see McMahon 2012: 15–20).

Notes

1. For an illuminating account of Varda's clever self-positioning, see DeRoo 2009: 258.
2. *Les Veuves de Noirmoutier* was exhibited in the Fondation pour l'art Jacques Cartier in Paris in 2006. The installation later travelled to various locations including Nantes and Sète.
3. *L'Opéra Mouffe* was not a commissioned film and was promoted by Varda herself to people like Amos Vogel in the 1960s (see Vogel 1997). If Varda had wanted to produce a real silent film look-alike (or rather sound-alike), this alternative context of distribution would probably have enabled her to show the film with a live *bonimenteur* or pianist.
4. Because of their posture and of Varda's framing, the spectator cannot tell for sure if he is watching one or two women. This undecipherable opening is consistent with Varda's playful and self-reflexive attitude throughout the film.
5. I would like to thank the people who attended my presentation on *L'Opéra Mouffe* at the Institute of German and Romance Studies in March 2009. Their physical reaction confirmed my interpretation of the scene as one appealing to the senses as much as to the intellect.
6. This choice is significant, especially since Varda appears to play with her persona in later films like *Les Plages d'Agnès* (2008) which has been described as a facetious autobiography in the first person.
7. When Michel Chion, who has written extensively on sound, music and cinema, talks about one of Wim Wenders' contemplative films, he uses the expression 'little sensory haikus', which I find compelling when analysing the ten sequences of *L'Opéra Mouffe* (1994: 47).
8. Despite the sixty years or so that separate us from this particular winter, 1954 remains a memorable date in French history. For years, Abbé Pierre was the most appreciated public figure in France. An example of his actions' resonance in cultural spheres is *Hiver 54, L'abbé Pierre* directed by Denis Amar in 1989.
9. *La Pointe Courte* is another example of an atypical work. Even if it has received more critical attention than *L'Opéra Mouffe*, it often remains on the margins of historiographies of the new wave.
10. This section may focus on drunkenness but the couple tottering down the steps of the local café could be looked at as a much less attractive version of the couple 'Des Amoureux'. The expression *ivre de bonheur* which means 'blissfully happy' comes to mind in French, especially since Dorothée Blank and her lovers are always captured as they kiss or embrace passionately.
11. For an insightful analysis of the perception of a public figure associated with female alcoholism, see Renate Günther's article on Marguerite Duras (2004).
12. 'At the theatre of everyday life, the stars are the bread, the milk, DIY items, the meat, the white laundry, the exact time, short hairs, and always the accordion.'
13. In a later interview the audience will learn that their wives have not moved to the capital and still live in Morocco.

14 For a wide ranging analysis of women in the media, see Maggie Allison's article 'Women and the Media' (2000).
15 It is worth remembering that the film was originally produced for a foreign audience. To native speakers, the provincial accent of several of the participants is a clear give away well before this sequence which sheds light on their exile to Paris.
16 For more details see Dagmar Herzog's article 'Between Coitus and Commodification' (2006).
17 In Dagmar Herzog's *Sex After Fascism: Memory and Morality in Twentieth-Century Germany* (2005), chapter 4; and Hera Cook's *The Long Sexual Revolution: English Women, Sex, and Contraception, 1800–1975* (2004).
18 In the manifesto of the 343, Le Nouvel Observateur, #334, April 5, 1971, available at http://tempsreel.nouvelobs.com/actualites/societe/20071127.OBS7018/le_manifeste_des_343_salopes_paru_dans_le_nouvel_obs_en.html. Accessed November 2012.
19 For more details, see Rosalie Varda's informative interview, available at http://madame.lefigaro.fr/societe/enquetes/266-etre-feministe-en-2008–3–5-rencontre-avec-rosalie-varda/2 Accessed November 2012.
20 For details on the idea of the white cube see O'Doherty's *Inside the White Cube: The Ideology of the Gallery Space* (2000) and for a confirmation of Varda's intentions, see the *'Notes d'intention'* made available by Arte France http://medias.unifrance.org/medias/196/62/81604/presse/quelques-veuves-de-noirmoutier-2005-presskit-francais-1.pdf Accessed November 2012.
21 I realise that many difficulties pave the way for such a section since installations are by nature ephemeral and always experienced *in situ*. For a perceptive discussion of the subjective experience of installations, see MacNeill (2010: 51–3 and 70–6).
22 Any definition is bound to be culturally specific since each society determines who is 'considered' old based on its own set of varying criteria.
23 Varda is a widow herself since 1990 when Jacques Demy, who had been her partner for years as well as the father of her second child Mathieu, died from AIDS.
24 On the side of the installation a visual map indicates the names of the participants and a caption explains: 'Face aux quatorze écrans, quatorze chaises munies d'un casque. À chaque chaise correspond un écran. Passer de chaise en chaise pour écouter le témoignage de chaque veuve.' ('Fourteen screens face to face with fourteen chairs and headphone-sets. Each chair matches a screen. Go from chair to chair to listen to the testimony of each widow.')
25 Comolli, a well-known French critic and filmmaker, promotes the use of sound and live recording to listen intently to participants in documentary cinema: 'C'est bien le corps parlant qu'il s'agit de filmer aujourd'hui – le sujet tout entier, non mutilé, pris dans sa parole et ses silences, pris en lui-même […] butant contre lui-même comme ce qui résiste encore au règne du calcul.' ('Filming a talking body is what is at stake today, filming a whole subject, un-cut, caught up in his speech and silences, caught up in himself […] fighting himself as if he was trying to resist reflection and calculation') (2004: 690–1).

26 Varda's production company CinéTamaris and her main home are located at rue Daguerre in Paris but she also owns a family house in Noirmoutier. Jacques Demy was the one who took her there for the first time years ago. He was particularly fond of this place since he had spent some of his holidays there as a child. It is therefore a particularly significant place for Varda who will always associate it with meaningful events and people in her life.
27 For an analysis of Varda's aesthetic vision and use of her cinema as a database see Conway 2010: 125–39.
28 Laura MacMahon makes an illuminating reading of a scene of *Les Plages d'Agnès* where Varda's camera in its extreme proximity to Demy is 'a mode of accompaniment, a mode of [...] *being with* him as he dies' (2012: 19).
29 The last paragraph of her seven-page notes is explicit: 'Les veuves de Noirmoutier ne m'ont pas déçue. Je suis l'une d'elle, mais j'avais beaucoup à apprendre sur elles (et sur moi!)' ('The widows of Noirmoutier surely did not disappoint. I may be one of them, but I had so much to learn about them as well as about me!')

CHAPTER TWO

Aesthetics and Technique

'Une certaine tendance du cinéma français', Truffaut's famous text published in *Les cahiers du cinéma* in 1954, made the case for a new type of *auteur* cinema, breaking away from the 'tradition of quality' (also called 'cinéma de qualité' and 'cinéma de papa') and its reverence to the screenwriter. This emphasis on the *auteur* rather than on the *metteur en scène* prompted much debate. Andrew Sarris's use of the term 'auteur theory' to discuss films produced by American studios also generated much criticism. 'Predicated upon the recognition of the film director as the personality responsible for the aesthetic and artistic coherence of a film, the French concept of auteur bespeaks an idealistic and essentialist view of cinema…' (Maule 2008: 20). This model encourages an analysis of the recurrent themes and motifs within an *auteur*'s corpus but it often downplays the commercial context of the film production, as well as its context of distribution.[1] In Europe, re-readings of important groups of directors like those of the new wave by Geneviève Sellier, have made it obvious that auteurism really is in fact a fantasy, and a 'partenogenesis' (2008: 26) to be questioned rather than accepted as a given.[2] Scholars such as Hayward and Flitterman-Lewis have demonstrated that Varda's cinema can be interpreted as a coherent corpus characterised by specific patterns and common preoccupations (for more details, see Hayward 1992 and Flitterman-Lewis 1996). But does Varda's work perfectly fit the profile of an auteur's cinema, and is this concept a panacea? Mary P. Wood has a point when she writes that 'contemporary Europe still produces directors with *auteur* status, but the majority no longer fit the "great white male" template of directors' (2007: 24).

Because Varda is not a great white male to start with, and because the labels most often associated with her *persona* such as 'the grandmother of the new wave' are either erroneous or reductive, I want this chapter to challenge more traditionally *auteurist* interpretations of her work. By re-centring the focus on the collaborative nature of filmmaking, by re-assessing the role of other contributors like the editor and the composer and by looking at Varda's own performances of authorship, I want to revisit the idea of the filmmaker as the all-mighty and sole *auteur* of his films.

1. Collaborative Filmmaking

One could argue that from the moment of its first public screening a film becomes a collaboration between the filmmaker and the viewer, not because the viewer modifies the film *per se*, but rather because his/her idiosyncratic reaction will impact his/her understanding and interpretation of the film. This section does not intend to discuss how audiences responded to a specific film or a group of films by Varda. It will not be concerned either with the collaborative documentary *Loin du Vietnam/Far from Vietnam* (1967), a project instigated and edited by Chris Marker, which involved footage from Joris Ivens, William Klein, Jean-Luc Godard, Alain Resnais, Claude Lelouch and Varda.[3] What I intend to do instead is to take up some of Berys Gaut's remarks on the limitations of auteurism to establish that other participants should also be credited as artistic contributors.[4] Therefore in this section, Varda will not be looked at as the only sovereign maker of her films, but rather as an individual who controls many but not all the elements giving shape to her films. By looking at specific examples within Varda's filmography, I want to demonstrate that the idea of a creative collaboration can illuminate an *auteurist* reading, which traditionally privileges the director over a set of other less often credited actors.

(A) *La Pointe Courte: A Radical Collective Enterprise*

The film I will start with is Varda's first feature film *La Pointe Courte*, which has become a reference despite its rather uncertain beginnings. Varda shot it in the South of France in 1954 with the help of a limited team and the locals in Sète. She managed to raise enough money thanks to a small inheritance and the participants' agreement that they would not get paid unless the film made profit. Michel Noiret and Sylvia Montfort, the only two professional actors, gave their time and experience. Many locals contributed by telling Varda family anecdotes that she weaved into her script and by letting the crew use items from their household and/or workplace. The script's structure was inspired by William Faulkner's *The Wild Palms* (1939) in that it alternates between contrasting sections which focus on the couple played by Noiret and Montfort and scenes inspired by the fishermen and their families. Varda only shot images on location and as a result had to record and synchronise dialogue once she was back in Paris. Alain Resnais kindly agreed to edit the film for free after she had finished the shooting in Sète. According to Varda, he was keen to be as faithful as possible to her original script. The film was shown at the Cannes Film Festival in 1955 and André Bazin, the famous critic at *Cahiers du cinéma*, wrote a rave review of it. Distributing it was, however, impossible because it had not been shot with the CNC's authorisation (Centre national du cinéma/National Centre of Cinematography). Its first public screening occurred in 1956 at the Studio Parnasse and was coupled with Jean Vigo's *À propos de Nice* (1930), a fittingly unconventional yet accomplished piece. *La Pointe Courte* certainly did not go unnoticed at the time, and remains a subject of interest to scholars working on French cinema in the 1950s and 1960s. In his *History of the French New Wave*, Richard Neupert sums up many of the points that make the film a decidedly radical work: 'An elegantly restless camera, deliberate character gesture and motion, crisp use of shadow, long shot durations [...], and evocative depth of field make Varda's film one of the most unusual and beautiful motion pictures of 1950s France and a wonderful example of what could be produced by this new era's calls for personal cinema' (2007: 62).

My analysis of *La Pointe Courte* will be organised around three main points: first the film's detailed script and its various sources; second the film's soundtrack; and finally Resnais' editing. Varda's script had from the very start two objectives: the first, to document and show the life of a small community of fishermen in Sète; the second, to tell the story of two people, one born in the village, the other in Paris, who are married but trying to decide whether they should stay together or split up. The couple's situation is, however, not the only event involving emotional turmoil in the film and both narrative strands include several points of tension. The opening sets the scene as it shows how the fishermen of la Pointe Courte are threatened by the local authorities. Two inspectors are sent to try to collect evidence showing that the locals fish where they are not supposed to and that in doing so they risk contaminating people with shellfish unfit for consumption. Raphaël, the young and dashing man enamoured with Anna, a sixteen-year-old local girl, is sent to jail in Montpellier after being caught by the coastguards soon after the inspector's first visit. At the same time, Daniel, a child whose mother can barely cope with her seven other children, falls ill and dies. Finally, Raphaël, after being successful at the local '*joutes*' is finally accepted as a suitable suitor for Anna after many family arguments.

Varda's family lived for a few years in Sète after they had left Belgium during the war. Varda remained a regular visitor after her family moved to Paris and she often says in interviews that the village holds a special place in her heart and work. Her script shows a definite ear for the local dialect ('*le parlé local*') while her camera is fascinated by the intricate patterns drawn by the fishing nets, the laundry lines and the rugged contours of the low houses of la Pointe Courte. The events that shake the tranquil life of la Pointe Courte were inspired by the stories that she collected from the locals. The fact that Varda credits the inhabitants of la Pointe Courte alongside herself in the opening as writers and directors testifies to their role in making the film what it is. The man playing Raphaël, for instance, is re-enacting the story of his parents, who originally had a hard time convincing their own parents that they should be allowed to see each other ('*fréquenter*' being here an understatement in French of course). This story and others are weaved into Varda's script and into the life of this tight knit community on screen. One could say that the film is a patchwork of fictionalised anecdotes interrupted by sequences devoted to the couple.

The film underlines the precariousness of the fishermen's lives and the fact that they are at the mercy of officials and regulations. Even if the local families form a cohesive front against the authorities, they cannot protect themselves from everything.

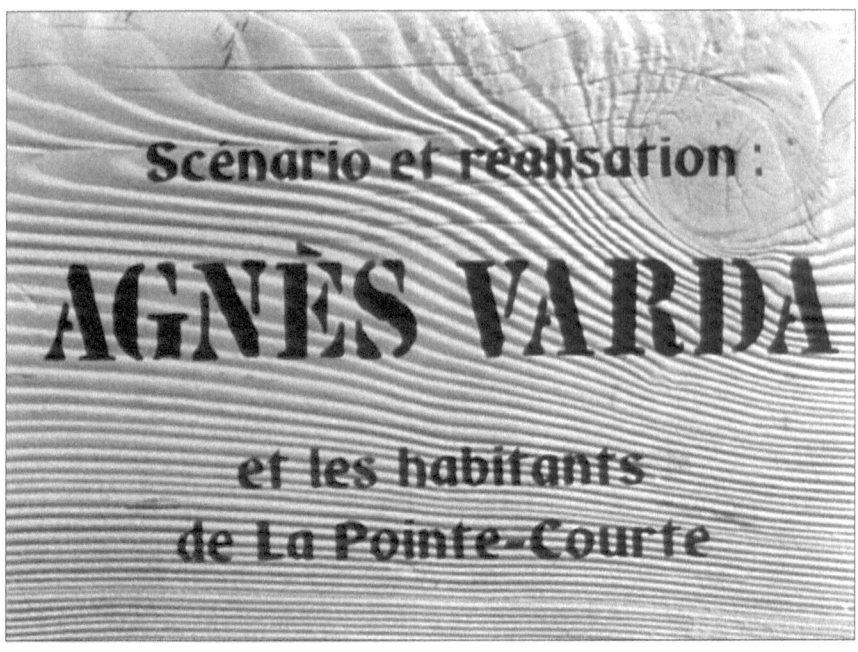

La Pointe Courte's credits are explicit; this film is a truly collective enterprise

They may assist one another through adversity but they are also presented as vulnerable. The death of Daniel, for instance, is not explained (even if based on the doctor's description, we can assume that he suffered from meningitis), but the fact that the house he lives in looks overcrowded and bare adds to our impression that many in this community can barely make ends meet. In one particular scene, several men are seen discussing the fact that fishing is becoming unsustainable since they are simultaneously cheated by the people who buy from them (the '*mareyeurs*' or merchants) and limited by the regulators. Even after the more joyful episode of the '*joutes*', two of the locals evoke their future and their repeated failure at making others realise that they are entitled to certain rights. One of them is adamant they should carry on putting pressure on the authorities ('on va continuer à les bassiner') while the other thinks that they should probably resign themselves to the idea of moving or of being expelled from la Pointe Courte. The editing of the sequence at this point is telling, since not much can be made of these men's expressions as they stand in profile, but their voices remain clear while the camera focuses on the tottering feet of kids and grown ups who try to get to a flag by walking on a slippery pole over the water. This may just be a game, but its principle evokes the fishermen's attempts. However, optimistic and tenacious, their future remains uncertain and nobody knows what will happen in the long term to their community. This threat and uncertainty was certainly not imagined but real. During the summer of 1954, when Varda shot the film, people in the nearby village of Mèze were trying to get the locals expelled from la Pointe Courte since they had turned their cabins into homes without official permission.[5] This idea of a clash between official and accepted practices and their unauthorised and spontaneous counterparts runs deep into the film's script. Many of the questions asked in the film actually relate to whether it is acceptable to do certain things, like to catch fish and establish your home where you want to, or to say certain things such as 'I want to marry you', or 'I don't think our love is what it used to be'. The only difference is that some of these questions manifest themselves in the domestic arena while others do so in the public sphere.

The family stories and real life struggles incorporated into the script contribute to the authenticity of the resulting film. Two other elements that the film exploits are la Pointe Courte's natural environment and the bodies of the locals. The contrast between the fishermen's side of the harbour, dark and geometric with its fishnets and wooden structures, and the light and windy side where the women chat and laugh while washing their laundry is a photographer's heaven. The narrow streets provide a perfect place for long meandering tracking shots which allow snapshots into the various families' lives. In the first ten minutes of the film, the spectator sees Daniel's overcrowded house with his mother and siblings gathered for a meal, the three generations of the family including Oncle Jules, le papet (grandpa), Anna and their respective houses, a couple of other neighbours and Philippe Noiret, who has come to la Pointe Courte for a short holiday after a twelve year absence. The men do not seem particularly voluble (apart from Jules's regular expletives and demonstrative scenes) but their bodies do much of the talking. From the pushing and pulling the fishermen do when raking the sand to gather shellfish, to the rhythmic movement of their netting shuttles which gives them time to pause, there are many images of their bodies at work. Their constant proximity, their knowledge of eachother's habits and their way of walking with and addressing others testifies to a life determined by the community and its practices. Noiret's character may have grown up there, but several people remind him that he has forgotten about the ways things are in la Pointe Courte. Varda's script manages to capture some of the local expressions (if not the local accent) and her camera often focuses on the bodies of the locals.[6] Varda is keen to recognise their role in making the film happen because their stories form the basis of her script and because the sections in la Pointe Courte rely heavily on their performance. They may not be professionals but because of Noiret and Montfort's acting (which I will come back to), the locals' performance becomes crucial. In *Cinéma 2 L'image-temps,* Gilles Deleuze discusses at length what he calls a cinema of the body and he underscores the notion of '*gestus*' (gest) which he borrows from Brecht (1985: 250–6; see also Bogue 2003: 156). Varda was surrounded by people discussing performance and acting when working with Jean Vilar and his theatre company, and Brecht was certainly a reference at the time. Her directing of Montfort and Noiret is indebted to what she has seen during her years with Vilar's company. As for the sections in the village, they were inspired by and gravitate around the postures and attitudes of the locals who demonstrate in the flesh the social links that exist between them all.

The *joutes* at the end of the film are an important event both for the locals and the couple. This special moment, where we are shown the friendly competition, the concentration and determination of the various teams and the festivities not only serves to celebrate a community but also represents a moment for the spectator to ponder over what he knows of this community. Which are the most representative scenes of the film, the ones focusing on the fishermen and the women at work, or this documentary re-telling of the local festivities? Is this final sequence meant to add to the authenticity of the film or to add to its exoticism for a Parisian audience? Varda's viewpoint is that of an outsider, and her script and directing will impact the portrayal of this place and its inhabitants. As a photographer, she is aware of the partial and biased character of any pictorial endeavour. Even if she has never made a film before, Varda knows that a film with a narrative thread (however laconic) is also a deliberate construction. Nevertheless, because of the coming together of a set of people agreeing to devote some time and effort to a common enterprise, the finished product is the sum of their contributions and therefore a sometimes unexpected patchwork of sights and sounds. While the script dictates some of the events taking place on a narrative level, the bodies of the inhabitants play an important role in that they establish the film as a celebration of the body and a reflection on how it is either restrained or let free by the community it belongs to.

Noiret and Montfort were chosen because Varda knew them from the time they had spent with Jean Vilar's theatre company (le théâtre national populaire or TNP). Sylvia Montfort had appeared in Robert Bresson's *Les Anges du Péché* (1943) and played alongside Jean Marais in Jean Cocteau's *l'Aigle à deux têtes* (1948). Her career was well established when she agreed to take part in the adventure of *La Pointe Courte*. Philippe Noiret on the other hand was less experienced even though he had played with Montfort and Gérard Philippe on stage in *Le Cid* in 1951. One of the difficulties for these two actors was that Varda had required that they 'do not act naturally' (*'jouer raide'* being one of her suggestions). While they stay in the village and mingle with the locals, they remain outsiders. Noiret's character is acknowledged as one who has roots there, but his departure and subsequent transformation in Paris outweigh his former ties with the village. By keeping them unnamed throughout the film, Varda makes them utter strangers to us as much as to the locals. They could be looked at as the archetype of an intellectual couple out of place and in turmoil. Some of Varda's declarations certainly suggest that this was her intention: 'Je voulais que le couple soit une chose parfaitement abstraite...je voulais qu'il soit un homme et une femme qui n'avaient pas de nom, pas de métier, je voulais et c'est évidemment une idée littéraire, qu'ils soient abstraits, qu'il n'y ait pas un dialogue réaliste. J'ai donc fait un dialogue théatral' ('I wanted the couple to be something completely abstract, I wanted them to be a man and a woman with no name, no job, I wanted them-and it was obviously a literary idea- to be abstract, and I didn't want there to be a realistic dialogue. So I wrote a theatrical dialogue') (Varda quoted in Smith 1998: 71). Varda's decision to write theatrical dialogue and to encourage her only two professional actors not to play out emotions in a naturalistic manner gives their situation a certain strangeness.

The fact that they talk to each other a lot (or at least a lot more than the locals) does not provide the viewer with more information. Neither he nor she reveals exactly why they think that they have reached a dead end. We know that they have been married for four years and that he has cheated on her. She says that she has tried to retaliate but failed and claims that she is ready to leave their flat and move on by herself to begin a new life. In the beginning, her impenetrable gaze makes it look like her decision is one that she has thought about long and hard. The fact that she meets him there, however, and her willingness to stay for a few days to explore the place where he grew up shows that she is still undecided. Their long walks become opportunities to discuss their past and present relationship, and the pressure that she feels has been put on her by their entourage in Paris. During these discussions they do not really argue but expose their views. These moments are in fact elaborate joint meditations on what it is to be a couple or to accept to live as a couple once the short-lived passionate beginnings are over. Because both of them are outsiders in la Pointe Courte, they are forced to consider themselves anew. Compared to the dialogue between the locals, their discussions sound literate and verbose as this passage demonstrate:

> Elle: A Paris, il me semble tellement normal de t'avoir comme partenaire. Mais en arrivant ici, j'ai senti l'étrangeté de notre assemblage, je me demandais ce que je faisais dans ce coin que tu as choisi pour naître.
> Lui: Choisi, enfin!
> Elle: Je venais pour me séparer de toi et il y a mieux à faire, je venais pour faire du bruit et c'est le silence qui gagne, quel repos!'
> ('Her: In Paris, it is seems so normal to have you as my partner. But after I got here, I started to feel how strange we are together, I also asked myself what I was doing here, in this village you chose to be born in.
> Him: Chose? Come on!
> Her: I came to be away from you, but there are better things to do here. I came to make a lot of noise, but silence is winning this battle, and how peaceful it is now!)

What some have criticised as the unbearable stasis of the actors encourages the audience to distance themselves from the characters' emotional turmoil. Their performance and calm diction are in direct contrast with what they are expected to experience. This Brechtian approach to acting, no doubt inspired by spending time with Vilar, is meant to trigger reflective distanciation on the part of the audience. One may wonder what the intentions behind this alienating characterisation are. Are these effects meant to force the audience to reconsider their own situation if they are part of a couple (or have chosen not to be), or are they an opportunity to think about the constant interactions between the private and the public sphere, between the individual and the collective? I suspect there is a bit of both in the film. As I explained earlier, I believe that *La Pointe Courte* is a film relying on the bodies of the community, shown most of the time in action and harmony. But this community is not immune to tensions and contradictions. Anna's father, for instance, needs a lot of convincing from his wife and others in order to realise that his rigidity is doing the family no good. At first, he is convinced that coercion and threats will keep his daughter out of trouble, but he comes to realise the necessity of recognising her needs as those of an equal adult-to-be. In the case of Montfort and Noiret, it is the lack of pressure from friends and family that contributes to her taking some critical distance. Her decision to turn the page and accept that they have both changed re-ignites their commitment to each other. In the case of the couple, one could say that it is their isolation from the public sphere that enables them to decide whether they will stay together and accept each other as they are or grow apart to become strangers. Looking at the script's double objective and re-assessing the contrasting performances of the locals and professional actors, it becomes clear that *La Pointe Courte* owes much to the place where it was filmed and to the dynamics of the shoot. Now I want to consider two factors that also affect the finished product but whose impact becomes clear only after the time of the shooting. The sound and editing are critical in determining the way the film works. I will therefore start by examining the soundtrack and its role before moving on to Resnais' editing.

(B) *La Pointe Courte's Musical Patchwork*

There is no doubt that the soundscape designed for *La Pointe Courte* is both radical and original. I mentioned earlier that for practical as well financial reasons Varda and her team did not record any sound on location. Instead notes were scribbled when the locals deviated from the script and Montfort and Noiret, being classically trained actors, were trusted to stick to the director's exacting dialogue. After returning to Paris, decisions were made about the post-synchronised soundtrack. The most striking decision was to establish very different soundscapes meant to emphasise the contrast between the Parisian couple and the locals. In the first half of the film, regardless of the scene setting, the voices of the couple were recorded and added to the images as if the characters were always at the same distance from the camera. In dialogue scenes where the camera stays fairly close to the actors, this will look normal to the audience. But in a sequence where the protagonists start talking to each other up close and then walk into the distance, one would expect their voices to gradually become fainter. In the sections devoted to the couple, there seems to be no attempt to create realistic sound effects. Depth of field and wide angle shots are a fairly common occurrence in the film and are often used to capture the wild seaside landscapes around la Pointe Courte. On occasions then, the audience will see the couple and the landscape in the same wide angle shot and feel that something odd is at work. As Michel Chion explains: 'film as a recording art has developed specific codes of realism that are related to its own technical nature and we as spectators have internalised certain criteria for auditory verisimilitude' (1994: 108).

One of the long conversations the couple have after they drop her bags off is a good example of this anti-naturalistic rendering. In the whole sequence, the sound seems to be at odds with the setting, first because we hear the voices very clearly while the actors walk close and then far from the camera, and second because the sounds of the landscape have completely been wiped out, or rather not reproduced in the recording studio. The train running just next to them, the cyclists riding under the bridge, the water and even the sound of their shoes on the gravel and of the wind in the bushes are absent throughout the sequence. This aural isolation forces the audience to focus on what they can hear clearly, that is to say the dialogue and Pierre Barbaud's accompanying music.

Barbaud was an innovative composer, a pioneer in the field of electronic music, and one of the first people in France to use computers to create music. He collaborated with Varda several times, notably on *Les Créatures* (1966) and when questioned about his composition for *La Pointe Courte*, he underlines his defiant take on composing for cinema: 'J'estime que le metteur en scène doit laisser une entière liberté au musicien, et surtout lui laisser le temps de composer sa musique. La musique de film doit être personnelle, originale. Varda voulait que je fasse un pastiche de Scarlatti. Je ne l'ai pas fait. C'était une partition extrèmement économique: un trio de clarinettes. J'avais envie d'écrire une musique pour trois clarinettes' (1964: 61). Varda did not mind his unorthodox take on the idea of commission, and wrote how much she appreciated his personal contribution (even if her recollection does not match his to say the least): 'Quand j'ai demandé à Pierre Barbaud en 1955 d'écrire un trio de clarinettes pour qu'il soit joué pendant le dialogue du couple, comme un pléonasme à la continuité de leurs mots, c'est en pur dodécaphoniste qu'il l'a traité. Tant d'années après, j'écoute cette musique avec un plaisir extrême, bien plus vif que celui, mitigé et insatisfait, de revoir les images' (Varda 1994 Section: 'en avant la musique').

The slow and melancholy melody played by three clarinets does seem to echo the voices of the actors, not so much their intonation or timbre *per se*, but definitely the way they constantly respond to each other's comments, sometimes almost together in terms of tempo, but most of the time slightly off-key in terms of melody. Because the subject of their conversation is a sensitive one – their love story and separation – one would expect the actors to play with intensity and emotion, but their faces remain calm and placid. The composition of the shots, formal and photographic to the point that sometimes the action seems halted adds to the strangeness of this scene.[7] They

An example of Varda's elaborate photographic compositions. The overlay of Noiret and Montfort shows them as a couple and as separate individuals

walk and look around while talking; they sit down and observe their surrounds more so than their interlocutor, as if in a dream or considering the circumstances, a nightmare. The beauty of the landscape cannot be ignored but it is in clear opposition with the harsh words that the couple exchange. It is only at the end of the sequence, when she sits on a pile of wood and leans forward with her hands folded in her lap that one senses her sadness and resignation and the strain that this conversation has put on her body.

All these characteristics: the restrained acting, the aural isolation of the characters, the unusual music and the composition are intensified by the contrast with the following sequence which takes place in the village. The audience is suddenly thrown back into reality, so to speak, with the close shot of a loud slap that one of the children receives from his mother. The sequence is as important if not more than the one about the couple since it narrates the tragic death of a young child in a series of short alternated images showing his mother with him and the doctor, and striking still life images of la Pointe Courte. Here, words are sparse but they certainly translate the mother's irritation with her other children and the surprise of the physician at finding Daniel so weak. All the sounds are crisp and clear: her angry slap, the wind blowing on clotheslines and slamming shutters, the baby wailing, the cats meowing, the gurgling sound of the tar-soap mixture used to coat fishnets and finally the long and heart-wrenching cries of the grandmother at the sight of the dead little boy, still on the table, in his cot made of a simple wooden box. The sad litany of the grandmother soon attracts the women of la Pointe Courte who gradually obscure the doorway and hide the hunched mother, sat on a chair next to Daniel, her hands now white and empty against the black cloth of her dress, where just a moment before she was holding his frail hand in hers. There is no doubt that the silent grief of Daniel's mother is set against the endless flow of the couple's discussions. The community of women coming to Daniel's house, the groups of fishermen and the impromptu family gathering to discuss Anna and Raphael are all reminders of the equal measure of support and pressure that a community creates, something that the couple are free of in la Pointe Courte. Even after the couple are supposedly reconciled, the music associated with them is different from the community's soundcape based on an array of realistic noises and the music of the local folkloric band summoned for the *joutes* and ball.

Sounds in *La Pointe Courte* can also be enigmatic, aggressive and overwhelming as in the sequence where Noiret picks his wife up from the station. After the spirited tone of the music accompanying him when he walks with a spring in his step over a beautifully graphic junction of traintracks, it is a surprise to hear their dialogue interrupted by a loud, persistent and unidentifiable noise. They walk from the station and stop when he shows her the house he was born in, as well as the shipyard next door. After he tells her that he can never share with her what he has found here, a loud machine-like buzzing sound resonates crescendo. The camera zooms out on Montfort, revealing her confused-looking face and silhouette. At this moment, the spectator cannot be sure whether this sound is that of a machine used in the shipyard, or a sonic rendering of her disarray. When we finally get to see a man working with a sander on a frame in the background, this odd aural intrusion has already had a destabilising impact on the spectators. Similarly, a couple of minutes later, after the couple has walked some more, a train moving towards the camera at a very slow pace appears in the middle of the shot and interrupts the couple's conversation and progress. Its grinding noise is overwhelming and its arrival in the field unexpected. The train is an eerie apparition and a disturbing aural presence. It could be interpreted as a symbol of modernity and as a reminder of the couple's way of life in Paris, surely different from the mundane and provincial life of the locals. The graffiti 'non au CED' written on the side of the train may go unnoticed, but it is a sign that la Pointe Courte is not as isolated or untouched as it seems by politics and modernity. CED stands for communauté européenne de défense (European Defence Community). In August 1954, the French national assembly refused to ratify a treaty that would have established a pan-European military force and debates were raging in the weeks leading up to this decision. This reference may be quick and passing, but it is there nonetheless. Because for an instant the train overshadows the woman's voice and forces her to postpone her confession concerning their separation, one could also associate this aural apparition with the loud noise at the shipyard earlier. Both are indeed associated with a shock and a revelation of sorts. In the first example, she realises that there are parts of him that she will never have access to, and in the second example, she makes him face the fact that their relationship has reached a dead-end. While these two examples can be interpreted as realistic aural intermissions, their intensity, the silent pause they generate in the protagonists and the surprise they cause the audience all point towards a more complex and multi-layered interpretation. In some of the sequences devoted to the couple, sounds are definitely not straightforward. Their intensity and unpredictability disturbs the audience and compels us to re-examine our expectation of a seamless aural verisimilitude. The soundscape of *La Pointe Courte* is complex and unconventional because it experiments with the music, the contrasts between the diction and accents of the actors and the visualised and acousmatic sounds available. It may be disconcerting at times but there is no doubt that it matches the elaborate composition of static shots as well as Resnais' incisive editing, which I want to consider now.

(C) *Alain Resnais' Contribution*

Varda contacted Alain Resnais in 1955 looking for a seasoned collaborator and an experienced editor who would agree to help with her project for free. Resnais, unlike Varda, had been working in the industry. When he moved to Paris in 1939, he started by taking acting classes at the Cours René Simon but soon decided to take the entrance exam for the Paris film school IDHEC (Institut des hautes études cinématographiques) in 1943. He studied there and gained experience on other people's films as an editor and then began to shoot his own films starting with several commissioned short films on art including *Van Gogh* (1948) and *Les Statues meurent aussi* (1953) co-written with Chris Marker.

There is no perfect way to find out who did what or who suggested particular changes when looking at a film. As the two quotes on the music in *La Pointe Courte* demonstrate, one is more likely to come across contradictory recollections and irreconcilable declarations than perfectly matching testimonies. There are, however, many valid reasons for looking at *La Pointe Courte* in parallel with Resnais' filmography and some of his own obsessions. Resnais and Varda are rarely considered together but their background shows many similarities. First, despite his longer experience in the industry in 1954, he belongs to the same generation as Varda and came to the capital as an adult. Like her, he appreciates art and seems to enjoy collaborative projects. He notably worked with Chris Marker on *Les Statues meurent aussi* (1953) and *Toute la mémoire du monde* (1956) as well as with several writers including Marguerite Duras.[8] In the commentary associated with the most recent DVD release of *La Pointe Courte*, Varda remembers her desperate need for a film editor to make something out of the rushes and notes that she had brought back from Sète. She acknowledges Resnais' generosity and declares that he was keen to respect her endeavour, imperfect as it might have been. In the book published for a retrospective of her work at la Cinémathèque française, *Varda par Agnès*, she devotes the section 'Resnais Monteur' to him, and explains that his initial impressions were to guide his editing work: 'Remarquant que *La Pointe Courte* était tourné lent et sans plan de sécurité (ni plan de coupe, ni autre version du découpage, ni gros plans de secours...) il disait qu'il fallait garder au film sa raideur, sa lenteur et son parti pris sans concession' (1994: 46–7). Noting that *La Pointe Courte* had been filmed at a slow pace and that no safety shots whatsoever had been made [...], he declared that he was going to keep the film as it was: stiff, slow and uncompromising (author's translation). So even if Resnais did not immediately agree to take on the project, it is obvious now that he did see something promising in Varda's work and that for that reason he decided to ignore her inexperience.[9]

There are several aspects of *La Pointe Courte* that can be identified in Resnais' films including the use of still shots, the relationship between the material and the invisible, and finally the idea of sensory images. Varda trained as a photographer and her filmography clearly shows that her cinematographic practise has always been informed by the medium of stills photography. Examples of this include *Salut les Cubains!* which was made with photos taken during a trip to Cuba, and more recently her series of photo-video triptychs *Portraits à volets vidéo* (2011). In all these pieces, Varda starts with classic still photos but decides to animate them through a subtle *dispositif*, which is something that Resnais has also explored in his films like *Van Gogh*. In her book length study of Resnais, Emma Wilson highlights this obsession with film form and 'the way cinema orders events' (2009: 3–4). *La Pointe Courte* is on many levels an experiment with film form as well: inspired by Faulkner's novel *The Wild Palms*, built on Varda's knowledge as a former Sètoise and photographer, and informed by her interest in performance and acting. This film is, as mentioned earlier, very particular because of its structure based on two parallel narrative threads: one for the couple and one for the locals of la Pointe Courte. By exploring the way one tells a story: chronologically or not, metaphorically or not, through a straightforward narrative or not, Varda demonstrates that like Resnais, she is interested in experimenting with the way cinema orders events. With a more linear script devoting longer sections to each part of the plot, *La Pointe Courte* would probably have been an easier and more pleasing film. But this is not what Varda and Resnais wanted to achieve, what they wanted was something altogether different. Resnais' editing, which never enables the spectators to immerse themselves completely into a situation or a place, is a perfect match for the script.

La Pointe Courte as a whole is like many of Resnais' films: formally challenging but also accomplished. Having worked with still images like Van Gogh's paintings enabled Resnais to look at some of Varda's rushes and see not a simple celebration of the beauty of still images, but an opportunity to make these images come alive through montage. Many critics mentioned the recurrent use of static shots and contrasted them with the elaborate camera movements like the one immediately following the credits. Neupert for instance writes that 'shots in *La Pointe Courte* begin and end in carefully composed static images, as if Varda thought of the scenes as a collection of photographs that awake briefly before closing up the action once again.' (2007: 61–2). The recurring contrast between still and moving images invites the audience to ask themselves: what is in the end most representative of la Pointe Courte? Could a close up of the convoluted yet beautiful patterns of a log of wood bathed in sunshine and eroded by salt be the best way to evoke the solidity and complexity of the local community? Or is the following sequence exploring the meandering and narrow streets of La Pointe Courte, with its debris, flapping sheets and fragments of conversations more likely to paint an accurate picture of the difficult life of the fishermen and their families? I would argue that the combination of these fragments provides the spectator with the elements to build his own understanding of the place and its inhabitants.

Another way Varda and Resnais both experiment with the cinematographic medium is through associations. In many of their films, they play with various combinations to see how events can be ordered to represent the world. Sandy Flitterman-Lewis's analysis of how *Nuit et Brouillard/Night and Fog* (1955) is simultaneously experimental and associational could be extrapolated to other films: 'Recognizing that the "truth" of an event always exceeds the documented fact, Resnais attempts to locate those other tributaries of meaning and association (social, personal, ideological, emotional, philosophical, ethical/moral, national/cultural) through a metaphoric play of contrasts and oppositions that includes the viewer in the very definition of meaning itself' (1998: 211). In *La Pointe Courte*, the audience is compelled to make important interpretative choices because of the elusive grasp they have of the couple's story and because of the collection of seemingly unconnected snapshots of the community. The spectator will regularly face obstacles even in crucial sections of the film because Resnais refuses to give the audience a smooth ride, a practice he is still attached to years later.[10]

The sequence describing the death of the child Daniel illustrates this perfectly. It starts with the mother slapping one of her children on the threshold of her house and finishes in the exact same place but with the women of the community gradually obscuring the doorway while the child's grandmother is still lamenting inside. It is fairly short, at about three minutes, but it is not continuous; first because we do not stay in the house after entering it with the mother, and, second, because we can assume that some time has elapsed between the slap, the doctor's visit, the mother stricken with grief and the arrival of the grandmother. In fact, the camera spends almost as much time outside of Daniel's home as inside and takes the audience to

 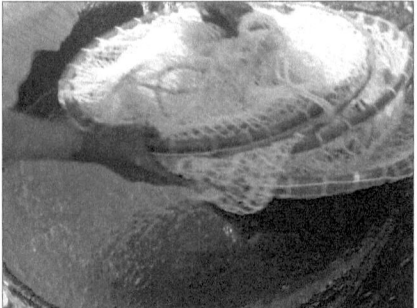

One of Varda's Nature Morte images, a wooden shutter and some clothes drying in the sun (left); the fishnet and tar, as an image of work or death? (right)

places which do not seem directly connected to his situation. Short impression shots show the streets of la Pointe Courte, the wind blowing hard on a shirt and knocking a shutter closed, an empty shed where a cat is sunbathing, baskets with eels and crabs, fishnets being coated with tar and a wooden cart being pushed around. These shots, sometimes forming a mini-sequence, sometimes standing on their own, are inserted in between each part taking place in the house. Because these images cannot be associated with any individual in particular – we can only see the hands and feet of a man stirring the tar mixture and later immersing a fishnet in the bucket, and the frail limbs of two kids pushing the wooden cart – the spectator cannot easily make sense of these images. Some, because of their composition, are reminiscent of still life paintings, like the close up on a wooden shutter decorated with seahorses. Others, however, could be interpreted as forewarning and/or symbolic of the child's future death like the immaculate white fishnet which is vigorously immersed into the bubbling black tar seconds before we see the mother now hunched on a chair and silently grimacing with pain next to the body of her child. This sequence of images builds up a momentum but it does not provide any clear explanation. The audience understands how this drama unfolds by seeing the tired mother, the doctor's powerlessness because he has been called too late and finally the family's shattered existence, but much is left unsaid. By making assumptions and associations, the spectator will approach the confusion and challenges of the family, although there is arguably no perfect way to represent the pain and trauma associated with losing one's child.

Another element which strikes me as similar between *La Pointe Courte* and many of Resnais' later films is the attention both directors pay to the relationship between the material and the invisible. *Nuit et Brouillard* and *Hiroshima mon amour* (1959) may in some ways be very different but both films question what an individual can see and what a camera can show. One could say that what is invisible and always there yet dormant is what animates the opening of *Nuit et Brouillard*. The peaceful landscapes shot in colour are never to be looked at without thinking of what the barbed wire and watch tower were used for. The languid tone and repetition of the commentary by former deportee Jean Cayrol (read in voice-over by Michel Bouquet) are meant to stress this relationship between the physical space that the audience is watching (the material) and the memories of this particular place (the invisible): 'Even an open landscape ... even an open field ... even an ordinary road ... even a resort town with a steeple and a market place ... can lead to a concentration camp.' *Hiroshima mon amour*, Resnais' first feature, is also concerned with the idea of materiality which is evoked through the bodies and documents shown throughout the film. In this impossible love story taking place in Japan, which also establishes connections with World War II through the woman's late German lover, the invisible is like in *Nuit et Brouillard* a crucial element which remains tied either to the past or to another person's experience.

In both *Hiroshima mon amour* and *La Pointe Courte*, there is also a couple remarkable for their minimal characterisation. For instance, we know very little if anything about their respective families, occupations and backgrounds. The conversations between the lovers in both films are prominent because they sound literary and lack spontaneity. The objects and settings therefore become crucial to understanding the films' fragmented and voluntarily incomplete stories. While Varda's film does not deal with any major historical event, it is also concerned with the tensions between individuals and society and with the frictions between certain groups of people and the stories they create to make sense of their circumstances.

The woman played by Montfort in *La Pointe Courte* has made a decision based on her evaluation of the relationship with her partner in Paris. But in this new and mysterious place of origin, she needs to reconsider it anew. She is looking for clues and signs to understand him better and she is also taking distance from their past circumstances. Away from their entourage and from their regular material circumstances, she is given a chance to reassess her role as well as her choices. By coming to La Pointe Courte, one can also assume that she is forcing him to face up to her decision. During one of their earlier conversations, she tells him that to her they have been living a fraud, a parody of happiness, which he does not seem to understand. He admits that he had perceived signs of her dissatisfaction, but he refuses to see their relationship as an artifice or a failure. All this talk about the invisible and intangible feelings which still tie them together seems ethereal because of their acting and almost unreal because it is so distant from the matter-of-fact preoccupations of the locals. Even in their longest conversations away from the village, this contrast between the material and the invisible is established by series of snapshots which show some fishnets left to dry, a discarded tool gone rusty, the buckets of tar used by the fishermen and a crab walking on the beach. Sometimes during the couple's exchanges, one of these images will be used to emphasise one of the character's comments and to make it more concrete. The film's elaborate dialogue and the actor's performance make it difficult to relate to the situation otherwise. Wilson again underlines in Resnais' films his desire 'to represent the complexity of the human process of imagination and recall' (2009: 3–4). How the woman in *Hiroshima mon Amour* comes to remember her visit to the museum or her German lover are instances of such attempts. How to apprehend ideas and emotions and how to show their intensity on screen is certainly one of the film editor's crucial achievements in *La Pointe Courte*. When Montfort tells Noiret that she finds it depressing that the love they used to share has grown old ('Tu ne m'enlèveras pas de l'esprit que l'amour entre nous a vieilli et qu'il y a de quoi pleurer toute la journée'), what we see is the white decomposed corpse of a cat lying on its back with the waves lapping up to it. Not being able to rely on the actors' performances compels the audience to appeal to other means of apprehension. Tapping into realistic details of the scenery and editing them so that they are synchronised with important parts of the couple's dialogue is one way to do so. The concrete world surrounding the characters makes its marks on our interpretation of the situation at hand. Resnais' editing recognises the difficulty in recreating strong emotions and feelings on screen. Authenticity and verisimilitude are not specific objectives here, at least not when considering the couple. Varda and Resnais both attempt to approximate in their films the sense of intimacy one experiences when reading a specific character's thoughts by creating complex individuals who are never one-dimensional.

Resnais collaborated with writers interested in the workings of mental processes like Marguerite Duras for *Hiroshima mon amour* and Alain Robbe-Grillet for *L'année dernière à Marienbad*. Varda may not have known cinema very well when she made this film with Resnais, but what they were both after was a subtle and complex collage of impressions, that she knew well from her experience of reading: 'les collages de Dos Passos, la liberté de ton de Cendrars et l'intériorité de Virginia Woolf ne semblaient pas avoir d'équivalence dans les films dont j'entendais parler' (1994: 38). Varda's idea was to make something different, something inspired by literature. The poetic collages of Dos Passos, the freedom of tone of Cendrars and Virginia Woolf's stream of consciousness were references that Varda wanted to emulate. The emotional turmoil of a separation, the tragic death of a child, the thwarted love of two young people are opportunities to experiment with how emotions can be transcribed on screen. *Hiroshima mon amour*, while dealing with a famous historical event, can also be interpreted as a study of female subjectivity and interiority. As spectators we are exposed to manifestations of the changing and complex thought-processes of the two female characters. The many signs, debris and material traces surrounding the characters add to the complexity of the representation of the lovers' subjectivity and they underline the dialectics between society and individuals. La Pointe Courte is for Noiret's character a place where he can think more clearly and even talk about their future. To her, at first anyway, it is insignificant and disappointing and she says so: 'there is nothing to see'. Their personal visions of this place real and imagined clash at first, until she realises that she can learn from the essence of this village, from its pace and down to earth attitude. The script does not adopt a deterministic viewpoint that would stereotype him as an easy going former provincial and her as a neurotic and intellectual Parisian. But it is clear that the peacefulness of this place and the inevitable reconsideration of what is at stake quells her interior struggle regarding the end of their passion. The local environment in all its materiality is therefore shown as something which critically affects the characters' reactions and impulsions.

In an article discussing *l'Année dernière à Marienbad*, Wilson again remarks that critics often consider Resnais as a filmmaker of the mind (2005: 1), Deleuze being here one of the most influential. This focus on the cerebral in Resnais' filmography unfortunately downplays the connections between the material and the invisible, another important dynamic as we have seen. In this article, Wilson effectively argues that his cinema revels in sensory signs and tactile impressions. It is therefore striking to see the number of sensory images present in *La Pointe Courte*. From the gusts of wind blowing on the drying sheets to the shimmering shades of the shellfish sorted through by women, examples abound. Sometimes these 'stray objects' (Smith 1998: 27) are helping our interpretation of the protagonists and their emotions. When they appear in more realistic situations, they seem to conjure up sensations, like the slipperiness of fish or the softness of seaweed. Varda's declaration: 'le cinéma c'est le mouvement des sensations' ('cinema is the movement of sensations') immediately comes to mind (1994: 62). To access the reality of the fishermen's life without betraying them, Varda uses tactile impressions. Her script could have been built around more elaborate subplots and she could have developed some of the villagers' characters. But instead of this, she has kept those simple and elusive and decided instead to focus on visual and aural impressions of the place.

To the original Parisian audience, this community certainly looked distant and archaic because of its way of life. A sense of nostalgia even permeates sections of the film, as when the fishermen declare that they regret the freedom with which they were able to fish before. This is why sensory images play a crucial role in the film. By privileging experiences common to most of us, such as the loss of a loved one (Daniel), the frustration felt when one is being constrained (Raphael and Anna), and the joy of being together (the *joutes*, the men's meal and ball), Varda makes this community approachable and endearing. The audience may not know the details of the villagers' psychology very well, and some may even disapprove of the decisions they make but by the end of the film, there is a sense that we know and understand better the daily challenges and joys of these people. The fragments of life in *La Pointe Courte* collected by the camera and later edited by Resnais, because they are associated with common sensory experiences, are tangible. Everyone can relate to them.

The final sequence illustrates this both visually and aurally. It takes place during the ball organised to mark the end of the *joutes*. Celebrations are in full swing with Anna and Raphael finally allowed to waltz to their heart's content while the other villagers dance, chat and drink. Very little in the crowds can be distinguished and the band playing a local tune is what ties the sequence together. We see Anna's mother, who remarks that her husband in spite of all his complaining is enjoying himself like a youngster, and the Parisian couple making their way to the station. A cut takes us to Daniel's house where his mother is mending socks surrounded by her brood of kids which are about to be put to bed. Finally, the locals start making their way home by boat while the train to Paris is seen leaving in the distance. The merriment, crowds, and bits of conversation characterise this sequence, which concludes with the band finishing their tune. All these snapshots remind the audience of earlier segments of the film like the death of Daniel, the informal family gatherings and the many stray cats and children seen roaming the streets of la Pointe Courte. They do not erase the difficulties portrayed in the rest of the film and show that the locals are not oblivious to them, but this festive ending wraps up Varda and Resnais' portrayal of la Pointe Courte. It is neither a happy nor closed ending, because many strands of the stories remain unresolved. The outcome of the crisis that Noiret and Montfort experience as a couple remains uncertain. Although the protagonists discuss their problems at length, we cannot be sure whether she can be trusted when she claims that she is now 'résignée, rassurée, ravie' (resigned, reassured, delighted). She may have resolved to embrace their new mature love, but he is still prone to doubting her and says so twice during their last bedroom conversation and as they leave the village. It is a bitter sweet ending which shows the end of some but not all frictions between these individuals and the group they belong to. For the couple, Paris looms on the horizon with its different points of reference and familiarity. For the villagers, nothing is certain either. Will the silence and resignation of Daniel's mother in the end reflect the village's destiny or should we see this festive celebration of being together as the determining tone of the film? The disarming plot structure, the formal experimentation with the soundtrack and the elaborate editing of the film maintain a certain ambivalence. Each spectator will therefore have to decide for himself how he wants to interpret the film and its ending.

In this chapter, I have chosen to write a detailed analysis of *La Pointe Courte* but one may wonder how representative this first feature can really be when compared to Varda's later films. On this particular project, she had to deal with practical and financial limitations but was free to decide on her subject and location. So can one establish whether this unusual work set a trend in her filmography, or whether it was a one off? Being able to look retrospectively at all her films provides some answers. Although she is known for her outspoken attitude, looking at the credits of her films proves that she often engages in long term collaborations with composers like Joanna Bruzdowick (*Sans Toit ni Loi* (1985), *Kung Fu Master* (1987), *Jane B. par Agnès V.* (1987), *Jacquot de Nantes*, etc), cinematographers like Nurith Aviv (*Daguerréotypes, Documenteur, 7p., cuis., s. de b., ... à saisir, Jane B. par Agnès V.*) and film editors like Jean Baptiste Morin (*Deux Ans Après, Ydessa, les ours et etc, Quelques Veuves de Noirmoutier, Les Plages d'Agnès*).[11] Alison Smith underlines Varda's pioneering role when she set up to work with Aviv, the first woman to be recognised as a director of photography in France (2007: 201–2). Despite her lack of technical background, she was thus often at the forefront in terms of technical and aesthetic choices.

In interviews and press kits alike, Varda frequently mentions other people and acknowledges their role in shaping a particular film or exhibition. Christophe Vallaux for example is described as the person in charge of the exhibition design for *l'Île et Elle* in the book (and press kit) published for this event. In *Les Plages d'Agnès*, a film with a decidedly retrospective angle, and in the TV series *Agnès de ci de là Varda*, Varda is also repeatedly turning the camera and focus on the people who enabled her to make these projects become reality. The terms used in the press kit for *Les Plages d'Agnès* are interesting since they highlight the practical and mental support that she has received from her daughter and her assistant: 'I have had two right hand women: Julia Fabry from the first day of location scouting to the last night of mixing, coming along with me on the adventures of my imagination; and Rosalie Varda, my daughter, from the start of this project to its finish, listening to my ideas, reminding me of them at times, and protecting me, with affection'.[12] In her article on cinematic self-fiction in *Les Plages d'Agnès*, Claire Boyle also discusses the importance of collaboration in Varda's work and argues that: 'the way in which the film pushes her towards her collaborators, towards others, [that] can be read as its final operation as an ameliorative and transformative technology of the self' (2012: 70). While her article questions what a cinematic self-fiction can achieve, it certainly demonstrates the importance of collaboration for Varda both off and on screen.

In *Les Plages d'Agnès,* many little scenes turn the camera towards the *'petites mains'* which typically stay in the shadows. The first one is crucial as it introduces the audience to the idea behind the film which was to make a tentative, humorous, and self-reflexive portrayal of Varda. In that scene, Varda walks amid a team of young people and gives them instructions while they carry mirrors on a beach to play with the director's reflection. But what ultimately happens is different from the original plan, as first the wind annihilates many of their efforts, and second Varda herself decides that she should be the one holding up one of the mirrors to show the face of her collaborators on that day: the students of the local École du cinéma in Louvain. The second scene is another irreverent interpretation of the self-portrait as well as a reference to the 1968 political slogan 'Sous les pavés la plage'. Taking place on the rue Daguerre where Varda's home and film company Ciné-Tamaris are located, she performs a funny little scene surrounded by her team who are installed for the occasion on six truckloads of sand, unloaded for two days to recreate their own Paris-Plage.[13] Varda, an ever present commentator in this film, explains that this scene shows how her life and work should not be considered separate since they have coexisted physically in this location for fifty years already. What the scene does, however, is pay tribute to the energetic and dedicated team of her production company. In this quasi-comical performance, we are shown how making a film is a collective and challenging enterprise. The first day of the Daguerre-Plage performance sees the installation and shooting of sections of the first sequence with the content of Ciné-Tamaris's offices (computer, desks, film cans) literally moved outside while the team, a couple of kids and some locals, all in swimming suits, carry on business as usual. The second day could be considered a fiasco since the rain hinders their progress, but Varda decides that they are going to film here anyway while sheltered by her umbrella she pulls on the strings of a set of seagull mobiles installed above Daguerre beach. Here three elements are crucial to the film's enterprise: the director's determination and resourcefulness, the team's willingness to make it happen and chance.

On many occasions Varda has acknowledged that when she films chance is her first assistant and an important if unexpected contributor (see Varda and Boehm 2010). While there is a great deal of preparation and work involved prior to the creation or filming of a particular project, chance sometimes provides Varda with genuine acci-

Varda's version of Paris Plage, rue Daguerre and her office on the beach (left); rain on the second day of filming: a fiasco or an opportunity for poetry? (right)

dental encounters and occurrences. In one of the episodes of *Agnès de ci de là Varda*, for example, Varda gets a chance to film her assistant, Fabry, as she dances, her back to the camera, on one of the musical installations that they have come across. This series in particular (which I will come back to in more detail) is an interesting analysis of the complex dynamics between a specific individual, here Varda wearing her director's hat, artworks that she wants to film or happens to come across as she travels, and the audience and museum-goers that she is keen to keep in her frame from time to time. These examples demonstrate how Varda embraces the collective dimension and chance when making a film or an installation, but they do not help when determining what sort of auteur and filmmaker Varda is. Is this label restrictive or inappropriate to start with? Is it a label that Varda accepts and supports, or rather something she defeats? After filming *La Pointe Courte*, Varda went back to her job as a photographer and even reveals in a long interview published in 1974 that she never thought of herself as a filmmaker (see 1974: 63). If this is really the case, when did a switch occur and how did Varda come to accept the label of director? Analysing how she seems to relate to the definition of filmmaker on screen and off screen will offer some answers and help clarify her position within her time (at various points) as well as more recently.

2. Performing Authorship

In her chapter entitled 'Art cinema, a cinema of auteurs? Low to mid-budget authorial filmmaking', Mary P. Wood debunks many of the myths associated with filmmaking in Europe. She underlines, for instance, that: 'The myth of the unworldly uncompetitive and uncommercial European auteur cinema is an old one which has gained ground since the 1980s' (2007: 24). Some of the filmmakers that she examines in the rest of this section of her book include Eric Rohmer, Manoel de Oliveira and Jean-Luc Godard. The presence of Varda as an additional example of filmmaker who has managed to survive the competition and to carry on creating films for half a century is of particular interest. Wood's chapter only alludes to *Les Glaneurs et la glaneuse* and its international success, but she rightly associates this film with two determining elements which are Varda's unashamedly authorial stance and her ability to exert control on her films (as the owner of her production and distribution company CinéTamaris) (2007: 34–5). Paisley Livingstone and many other scholars share Wood's view on the question of control over a particular body of work: 'authorship, be it successful or unsuccessful given one's artistic values, requires sufficient control over the production of a work presented as the artist's (or artists') own' (2009: 7). In her analysis of *Les Glaneurs et la glaneuse* and its sequel *Deux Ans Après*, Wood considers Varda's use of a cheap digital camera as a sign of the filmmaker's stance against the traditionally 'educated and articulate male' authorial status (2007: 35). Varda's emphasis within the film's narrative on the ease with which the digital camera records situations and testimonies is undoubtedly an invitation to demystify the technical apparatus associated with filmmaking. But is demystifying the filmmaking process necessarily synonymous with taking a stance against the figure of the male *auteur*? Is Varda comfortable with embracing this concept? And is it possible to assess whether Varda's career has suffered or been hindered by the prevalent idea of the great white male *auteur*? One needs to take a look at her career as a whole to get a sense of how to answer these questions. My contention is that Varda has always enjoyed debunking the myth of the all mighty male *auteur,* but that she also knows how to use this myth astutely if this can be to her advantage.

On many occasions, Varda has stressed the difficulties that she faces when she tries to get a project off the ground: 'with each film I have to fight like a tiger. They don't want me.... Oh, I'm a perfect cultural gadget, they have me in all libraries and cinematheques. I'll be unforgotten. But they don't want me to make films... they do films to make money' (1987: 10). Varda's comical re-enactment in *Les Plages d'Agnès* of the kind of conversation she has with her banker to finance a project is a tongue in cheek reminder that things do not get better as she gets older: 'La banque de Nefuso? Il faudrait vraiment nous prêter de l'argent sans intérêt pour qu'on puisse finir ce film un peu confortablement s'il vous plait?' ('Dear Mr Banker, could you please lend us some money interest-free to finish this film comfortably?') At the same time, she is one of the few female directors who has benefited from the label of *auteur* as Vincendeau explains: 'Auteur cinema in France has always acted as a support system to women like Duras and Varda, who have been able to pursue careers, albeit precarious ones…' (1987: 13). Tarr and Rollet agree with Vincendeau and believe that the concept of *auteur* did not help women to gain access to the overwhelmingly male cinematic milieus and institutions in France. But they too regard Varda as an exception (2001: 9–11). So how or why is Agnès Varda such an exception? And how did she and does she negotiate her place within *auteur* cinema?

Vincendeau's effort to pinpoint the restrictions associated with the *auteur* category are an essential starting point: 'Given that the model for the *auteur* is still the individual genius, or at least the artist driven by "internal necessity" towards self-expression, this has had the paradoxical result of pushing French women directors into heightened individualism on the one hand and alignment with male "colleagues" on the other' (1987: 9). From very early on in her career, Varda knew that she was to be a double outsider, first as a novice filmmaker and second as a woman in a male-dominated industry. But outsiders and newcomers can take advantage of both circumstances and labels. Claude Chabrol and Jean-Luc Godard, for instance, who started their careers around the same time as Varda, played up their technical incompetence to create a particular persona.[14] This kind of clever self-positioning shows that there is room to play within the confines of a category, even when this category is far from perfect because it does not promote, for example, feminist awareness or intervention.

When asked about how she prepared for the shooting of her first film *La Pointe Courte* in 1954, Varda explains that her meticulous attention to location and script-writing combined with Resnais' help with montage offset her lack of cinematographic experience.[15] Here, Varda does align herself with other male directors by promoting an image of herself as an individual genius, but she sets herself up as a hard-working and dedicated image maker. Many of her interviews include references to her training in photography and to the time she spent at l'école du Louvre studying painting. This self-fashioning as an image-maker and '*artisan*' is one of the strategies that Varda developed to stretch the *auteur* definition to make it accommodate her work. This image has indeed become a pattern that other scholars have commented on. In her article '*Les Plages d'Agnès*', Kelley Conway rightly notes that Varda represents herself as an active and 'experienced professional filmmaker at work' (2010: 132). When Varda describes herself in the beginning of *Les Plages d'Agnès* as a 'little old woman, pleasantly plump and talkative', she adds another unassuming alter-ego to the many she uses throughout the film and when promoting her work. But these should never be taken at face value since 'Role-playing, staging and a certain degree of caginess on the part of Varda will echo throughout the film. It is clear at this point that Varda is hardly just "a little old lady [...] telling her life story". She is managing a crew on location, composing images and only making minimal references to her past at this point' (Conway 2010: 129). In a similar way, *Daguerréotypes*'s conclusion showed Varda's desire to align herself with the other professionals on rue Daguerre. While she is aware of the special character of her trade, for instance, when she plays with magic and visual tricks on screen, the film closes on the image of the Chardon bleu couple walking home and on Varda's voice-over description of herself as just another Daguerréotype: 'Agnès la Daguerréotypesse.'

Varda's anchoring of her films in the world of work is, however, only one of the images that she employs to represent herself as an *auteur*. Varda creates and recreates herself as an authoring subject in many of her films and in some of the material released and/or associated with her work. To paraphrase Janet Staiger, if these 'authoring statements [...] are part of the subject's authorship and constitute the technique of that self [then] what an author *is*, is the repetition of statements' (2003: 51). Many of the images and visual statements that Varda employs, including some which are decidedly anti-naturalistic, force the audience to ponder the accuracy of representation and the value of labels. *Les Plages d'Agnès*, her television series *Agnès de ci de là Varda* and her DVD box-set *Toute Varda* (2012) offer interesting examples of alter egos which repeatedly downplay through humour the elitism associated with the idea of *auteur*

A cartoonised Varda in her director's chair on the menu of the DVD for *Les Plages d'Agnès*

cinema. Varda's cartoonised version of herself, used on many of the posters for *Les Plages d'Agnès* in Europe, is both facetious and self-derogatory. Drawn by Christophe Vallaux, a professional decorator and friend of Varda's, it shows her as a short and plump old lady, dressed in colourful clothes and seating in a giant director's chair on a beach. Her character echoes the cartoonised Chris Marker/Guillaume en Égypte present in the film, but unlike Marker, Varda has never tried to remain anonymous or to avoid the media's attention. A reproduction of this alter-ego was later included in the DVD case of *Les Plages d'Agnès* alongside another couple of magnets representing a crab and a seagull. Vallaux's drawings of Varda were also incorporated in the catalogues of exhibitions including her *Ping Pong Tongs et Camping* installation. In these, Vallaux's drawings are associated with a sketch documenting the creation of *Ping Pong Tongs et Camping*, so one could consider them as a trace of the 'making of' the exhibition. But what interests me most here is how these drawings highlight a double contrast. Varda is drawn as a little old lady next to her towering male assistant, yet she is not the quiet and inoffensive character one would expect from the physical attributes enhanced by the caricature. On the contrary, a series of hearts illustrate the passion she has for what she does, while her scant but direct speech bubble shows that she is determined and bossy when at work. This shifting alter-ego who is at times unassuming and self-derogatory and at others determined and feisty, is a clever way to position herself. In her big chair on the beach, she is in charge, her own boss and in doing so reclaims the category of *auteur*. But because of the cartoon, the viewer will also probably assume that she is a modest '*petite bonne femme*' (little lady) who does not take herself too seriously.

In appearing as a woman at work, she aligns herself with the many women that she has filmed in, for instance, *Daguerréotypes* and *Réponses de Femmes*. She is simply another one of these workers. When she tries to demystify the aura of the *auteur*, Varda also attempts to make her work as inclusive and unpretentious as possible. She is not interested in being seen as a technically incompetent genius driven by a particularly significant project; she wants to be perceived as a hard-working and modest image-maker driven by passion and dedication. Assigning a label, be it that of art cinema or *auteurist*, is an act of cultural politics; 'knowledge of film history and the ability to understand and classify different forms of cinema practice differentiate a person as a member of a discerning, educated audience' (Wood 2007: 26). Varda's democratic impulse, her attempt to reach out as widely as possible is an attempt to counteract class boundaries and their associated cultural artefacts, as defined by theorists such as Pierre Bourdieu. By using an array of approachable alter-egos and playing with categories and definitions, Varda is not only making a place for herself in French cinema, but also showing that categories can be more than debilitating. When they encourage creativity and feistiness, categories can actually be liberating, so why should she not embrace the *auteur* label, provided this *auteur* is able to discuss taboo subjects like abortion, old age and mourning?

Now that Varda's subversive acceptance of the *auteur* label is established, I want to shift the focus of this section and turn my attention to a series of documentaries where she also questions authorship and artists but in a slightly different way. While her alter-egos stretch the category of the *auteur*, her television series *Agnès de ci de là*

Varda emphasises the idea of a larger artistic community. This series, organised around Varda's journeys in Europe, Brazil, and other places, is definitely turned towards other people and other artists. When this series of five documentaries first aired on the Franco-German channel Arte in December 2011, Varda was already an accomplished *'touche à tout'* and a Jack of all trades in the public eye, so her insistence on the work of others is somewhat puzzling and therefore important to examine. So the main two questions I will address here are: what does this television series tell us about Varda's work and what sort of authorship does this series present?

The series introduction, which is repeated in all five episodes, establishes the premise of the project and explains that all the episodes will focus on a series of journeys that Varda made over two years to meet and talk to a number of artists. Varda's voice-over, an all pervasive guide throughout the series, describes *Agnès de ci de là Varda/Agnes War Da* as a collection of 'fragments, instants, personnes' ('fragments, instants, people'). The prolific nature of these encounters makes this series tricky to analyse, but if one takes it to be a creative *mise en abyme*, a collection of 'portraits of the artists' by another artist, then the series starts to make sense. The choices that Varda makes and some of her comments indicate that this peripatetic series is not just a random collection of fragments but an audio-visual exploration of the puzzles and labyrinths of the work of artists as varied as Chris Marker, Wilfredo Lam, Pierrick Sorin and Ana Vieira (in the first episode).

As she meets people and artists, Varda establishes and discovers connections with her own work. At times, she explores the work of someone who is close to her artistically and/or personally like Chris Marker, who is often paired with Varda as part of the 'Rive gauche' group. Lifting some of the mystery surrounding his closely guarded anonymity, she interviews him in his studio, an Ali Baba-like cave, full of cables, photos and screens. Another of Varda's virtual alter egos, this time in Second Life (a three-dimensional virtual world), descends into Marker's imaginary museum to explore its nooks and crevices. Like Alice in Wonderland, she walks around in a daze and falls into vertiginous spaces, but carries on and eventually finds her bearings on, of all places, a virtual beach. In this sequence, she takes the audience on a very suggestive trip quite typical of the many intricacies of Marker's work. In other sections of the series, Varda presents the work of other creators and interrogates them about their practice. As one would expect, in doing so she also obliquely comments on her own practice, as a photographer, a filmmaker and an artist. These parallels may not necessarily be made manifest by Varda's on or off-screen commentary, but they often become tangible in the editing of the series.

The long section devoted to Miquel Barcelo (in the series' second episode) is a perfect example of how the portrait of an artist can be constituted in a relational way. Barcelo is introduced as a breath of fresh air after Varda has taken her camera to a series of pavilions at the Venice Biennale, a place she knows well since she was there to exhibit her installation *Patatutopia* in 2003. As the sequence gathers momentum, it becomes clear that Barcelo's work is more than a 'painting' respite after a long series of more conceptual installations. The final section of this episode is indeed not what Varda makes it look at first. It is much more than a visual intermission, supposedly

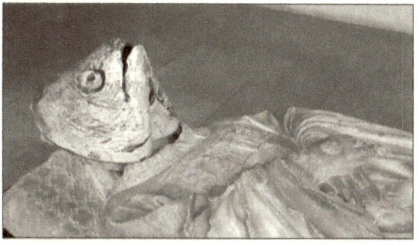 

Miquel Barcelo's original take on a *gisant* sculpture in Avignon (left); Varda's affectionate Daguerreotype of Barcelo in his studio (right)

saving her from a visual overdose or 'vertigo', because Barcelo does more than just painting, as becomes evident when Varda shows us his sculptures. As the sequence progresses, a number of connections between his and her work become clear. After a quick snapshot of the work he showed in Venice, Varda takes the audience first to Paris where Barcelo lives and works and then to Avignon, where he exhibits his work on a regular basis and where she started her career as a photographer. At first, she lets him talk at length about the importance of space and topography in his work. At the same time, she films in close ups the maps of Majorca and Mali that he made with a vegetable material attacked by termites. Barcelo explains that as a teenager he felt trapped in Majorca, a fact that Varda can certainly relate to since she too ran away from Paris for a while after she had moved to the capital after the war. When Varda stands next to Barcelo in front of his huge paintings and when she leans to admire the content of his treasure chest, she documents his artistic praxis. She shows the bizarre tools that he creates, she films him as he mimics the movements he makes to scrape paint into the desired shape and she lets him explain how some of his series originated. Her off-screen commentary underlines his originality, like his knowledge of the animal world or his sense of humour, when he explains with a poker face that the fish head he sculpted for an existing *gisant* (religious figure) in Avignon is perfectly appropriate.

At the end of this sequence, however, what remains is a deep sense of kinship and community between Varda and Barcelo. The continuity between Vivaldi's fifth concerto which accompanies Varda's excursion at the Musée du petit palais in Avignon to see Nicolas Dipre's *L'échelle de Jacob* and the following shot of Barcelo's subversive *gisant* binds them musically. Besides, when he tells her that his numerous paintings of fish are like family portraits, she answers visually with one of her Daguerréotypes. Through this static shot of Barcello, holding up in each hand the head and body of a fish, she asserts this artist's individuality but she also incorporates him into her extended 'artistic family'. While their work may differ in many ways, especially when one considers Barcelo's choreographed performance with clay, the words she chooses to match this sequence and the final shot of Barcelo taking pictures of his audience are telling. Like her, he enjoys playing with the idea of 'performing the artist' and multiplies representations of himself as an artist, as an animal (a gorilla and a dog), as another. The video footage of his choreographed performance may seem worlds apart from Varda's cinema but when he declares that clay is a material with a tactile memory of 'caresses, coup de poings et griffes' ('caresses, punches and scratches'), Varda's recurrent exploration of touch through the use of extreme close ups comes to mind.[16] On the one hand, in this sequence, Varda gives Barcelo a chance to talk about his work and to perform rather than to write his artist's statement. On the other hand, this encounter with Barcelo also demonstrates that when she questions an artist's drive and documents his/her activity, Varda also explores her own relationship to art and to the art world more generally.

Because Varda travels from country to country and as a result immerses herself in different national contexts, the series has a strong comparative dimension. On many occasions, Varda questions the art world and its contradictions or inconsistencies, as she encounters some of its local specificities. Throughout the series, she interviews art buyers, commissioners and curators, she photographs collectors and she asks artists how they feel about their work being exhibited in certain places. Varda is keen on showing what is usually concealed to the average cultural consumer, whether it is extravagant openings like the ones of the Musée Magritte in Brussels and the Pallazzo Grassi, François Pinault's gallery in Venice, or the preparation of exhibitions like one at the Jumex foundation in Mexico City (Episode 5). On many occasions, Varda questions the institution and the spaces in which art works are exhibited. Her promenade in St Petersburg's famous Hermitage museum and her long conversation with Natalia Brodskaia, its head curator, when combined with her footage of the visitors is meant to question what the function of the museum is in comparison to its actual use. While some sections of the series, like the one devoted to Barcelo, can be interpreted as relational, other sections seem more focused on the artist's inspiration and its context. They are explorations of an artist's specific work within its context of production and exhibition. Often Varda will ask the artists retrospectively what in their social and cultural environment may have fed a specific piece. This type of archaeological research brings to light the historical and cultural dimensions of specific artworks. It also justifies the many sequences Varda includes of the country or city that she is visiting. By suturing images more likely to be seen on news bulletins or in documentaries with specific works of art, Varda argues that as conceptual or as abstract as some pieces may seem, they are always anchored in a significant political and cultural context. The long sequence that she devotes to Annette Messager in the third episode of the series is an illuminating example of this type of contextual and pragmatic portrayal of a fellow artist.

What begins as an innocent meal with friends in her home with Annette Messager and her partner Christian Boltanski, quickly becomes an in-depth investigation of the political and cultural events that may have inspired both these artists' work. At the end of a long interview shot at the Grand Palais in Paris, Boltanski acknowledges that the pervading media coverage of Haiti's devastation in 2010 contributed to his installation *Personnes*. Similarly, when Messager tells Varda how her work has evolved over time, she explains that her compositions have always echoed and answered her direct environment. Her piece based on notebooks called 'The Men I love/Les hommes que j'aime', shown both in her studio and exhibited in an art gallery, is described as a reflection on the photos that she selected and cut out of women's magazines to reassemble them on a wall with her incisive commentaries. Messager's transformation of these magazines and of the images of male models they contain sheds a different light

Annette Messager joyfully interacting with her piece 'The Slammer' in Beaubourg

on how people consume magazines. Rather than discarding these as popular culture, Messager's installation defies the viewer's expectation and underlines the importance of considering the cultural and historical role of this kind of media.[17] In case her audience missed the importance of the connections between art and politics, Varda also inserts five short protest scenes following Messager's declaration that she had decided at one point that her work needed to be more pugnacious. Varda's montage establishes a direct connection between Messager's sculptures on poles and the sea of political slogans and radical songs of the French citizens who regularly take to the streets of France. This documentary intermission clearly connects the artist's work with a tradition of political dissent and rebellion.

This sequence is also interesting because it is a departure from the stereotype of the distant and isolated female artist only concerned with personal and/or feminine issues. Messager is filmed in the sanctuary that is her studio, but the meal they share and her comical interaction with her piece 'The Slammer' in Beaubourg enables Varda to show Messager as a personable individual, someone who is eating, laughing, smoking as well as thinking about her work and its context. Varda's selection of Messager's pieces is telling as it goes from the personal to the universal, and from the political to the institutional. At the very beginning of the sequence in her studio, Messager flicks through 'Le petit livre des signatures', a notebook gathering her variations on her signature which she describes as an attempt to demonstrate her originality and versatility. The third piece that Messager comments on, called 'Mes Voeux' (1989) is, however, less personal and more general since she explains that it is about humanity as a whole. Made up of a variety of carefully framed photographic close ups of human body parts, this suspension is gesturing towards the universality of the human body. The next two pieces that I consider significant are 'Les Piques', the set of revolutionary spears which triggers Varda's political/documentary intermission, and 'The Slammer/Le tappeur'. In the last section of the sequence on Messager, Varda asks her how she feels about her work being celebrated after her exhibition at the Pompidou Centre. Her answer is oblique but nonetheless interesting. Commenting on 'The Slammer', a three dimensional animated sculpture repeatedly banging on the window, she explains that she wanted to show that works of art need to be exhibited 'outside' of the museum and that they should not be confined to the gilded cage and places visited by a minority of people. Messager evades the question of her celebrity first by foregrounding the amount of criticism she still receives and second by moderating the importance of cultural institutions.[18] Her conclusion is that what she calls the outside world and real people are an audience as important to reach and touch as the select few who spend their time working in, on or for the art world, a truly anti-conformist and democratic statement.

This conclusion adds to the pragmatic dimension of Varda's portrayal of Messager, but it also resonates with what Varda's televisual project is about. By taking the audience on an entertaining trip around the world and by focusing on various fragments and pieces by very different artists, Varda offers a glimpse of what is 'out there'. Her selection, like any, is partial and subjective, but it incorporates so many different places and works, that the viewers are bound to find something that resonates with their experience. The emphasis Varda puts on the multiplicity of approaches and forms of art available – be it poetry, sculpture, film, photography, installations, popular art – signifies her desire to open the series to as many people as possible within the confines of a four-hour serialised documentary. The fragmented nature of this project therefore makes perfect sense. If you consider art as a means to approach people and to touch them, or as Varda declares in *Agnès de ci de là Varda*, as 'a means to re-present people's emotions', you necessarily need to tap into various forms of expression. The network that is being built in the series connects Varda's work with that of others but the series also tries to establish connections with the audience, with their environment, with their personal experience.

Notes

1. A far more comprehensive analysis of authorship and its lingering use in film studies can be found in Croft 1998.
2. In *Masculine Singular: French New Wave Cinema*, Sellier is clear: '"auteur politics" is also a kind of parthenogenesis, a way of giving birth to oneself by inventing fathers as far away from one's "natural" fathers – namely post war French filmmakers who had suffered the humiliating vicissitudes of history' (2008: 26). It is a real shame that this seminal analysis was translated into English only in 2008.
3. While this documentary film is described by Marker as a collective enterprise made to 'affirm his solidarity and that of those involved with the Vietnamese people in struggle against aggression', it will not be included in this study because very little if anything can been traced back to Varda. For a discussion of the project, see Thomas Waugh's article in *Jump Cut*: http://www.ejumpcut.org/archive/jc53.2011/WaughVietnam/text.html (accessed November 2012).
4. While I would not go as far as crediting every participant as an equal co-author, I agree with Gaut's corrective and more comprehensive stance when he states:

'Rather than rigidly categorizing films by their directors, film should be multiply classified: by actors, cameramen, editors, composers, and so on' (1997: 166).
5 Varda recalls this time as one full of uncertainties for the village too in this interview published in Libération in 2001 http://next.liberation.fr/next/0101395836-les-racines-de-la-pointe-courte (accessed November 2012).
6 To a French native speaker or someone accustomed to the local accent, the voices of the inhabitants of la Pointe Courte are a bit of a surprise, since they are a rather odd mix and match of accents, some quite strong and almost authentic, others far off the mark.
7 Many critics have commented on the diptych of close ups on the couple's superimposed faces saying that the composition of these shots surprisingly pre-dated Ingmar Bergman's own experimentation with faces.
8 Reflections on the relationship between the literary scene and directors associated with the new wave in the 1950s and 1960s form the base of Dorota's Ostrowska's enlightening *Reading the French New Wave: Critics, Writers and Art Cinema in France* (2008).
9 Varda explains why at first he refused to commit to anything: 'Il m'expliquait que ce n'était pas possible: ce cinéma ressemblait trop à ce que lui même rêvait de faire' ('He would explain to me that it was not possible for him because this cinema was too close to what he was dreaming of doing himself') (in Bounoure 1974: 140).
10 Neupert describes, for instance, *L'année dernière à Marienbad/Last Year in Marienbad* (1961) in terms of a 'hypnotic sense of uncertainty' and 'disruptive cinematic language' (2007: 321–2).
11 The bluntness of some journalists is quite amazing today, but their attitude illustrates the way Varda was perceived at the time. See, for instance, Christian Durieux's questions to Varda and Catherine Deneuve in 1966 for *Les Créatures*. http://www.ina.fr/art-et-culture/cinema/video/CAF97061852/agnes-varda-au-festival-de-venise.fr.html (ccessed November 2012).
12 This press kit is readily available online and quite instructive as it describes the origins and making of the film: http://www.cinemaguild.com/beapress/presskit.pdf Accessed November 2012
13 Since 2002, for a few weeks each summer, sections of the riverside thoroughfares become car-free beaches complete with deckchairs, ice cream sellers and an array of generally free cultural events including concerts.
14 In *La Nouvelle Vague et le Cinéma d'auteur*, Philippe Mary devotes a whole chapter to the carefully crafted image of the 'director as creator' who relies on the technical know-how of his collaborators, like Coutard (2006: 166).
15 In the following interview, Varda explains how she gradually gained experience and improved: http://www.egs.edu/faculty/agnes-varda/videos/on-three-early-films/ Accessed November 2012.
16 Textures and touch have always been of interest to Varda. In one of the most commonly commented-on scenes of *Les Glaneurs et la glaneuse*, Varda's digital camera zooms in to explore the texture of her skin and hair. In *7p., cuis., s. de b., ... à saisir* she was already exploring the representation of old age through texture

and touch in the surrealist scene where an old woman sits completely naked in a bathroom covered by masses of feathers.
17 To see to what extent the popular press can mobilise an 'imagined sisterhood', see Reineke's book on Simone de Beauvoir's discourse and her chapter on the concept of femininity (2011; chapter 3).
18 Messager's remark echoes the belief of some of the muralists that Varda had interviewed in the 1980s in America when they claimed that 'art should neither be confined to art galleries nor limited to a selected audience' (Bénézet 2009: 87).

CHAPTER THREE

Varda's Ethics of Filming

My objective in this chapter is to establish that Varda is a striking case of *cinéaste passeur*. The previous chapter aimed to demonstrate that *auteurism* is a valuable method when it adopts an encompassing definition of the filmmaking process. It also looked at how Varda subverts the concept of *auteur* in order to make it her own. In the current chapter focusing on Varda's ethics of filming, my attention is focused mainly on what dictates her decisions when creating a film or setting up an installation. Relationality and connections are concepts often associated with Varda's work. In 'Varda: The Gleaner and the Just', Flitterman-Lewis notices that Varda 'as 'author' sees herself as an 'intermediary who gives voice to those who have none', including the Jewish children whose stories have never seen the light of official recognition' (2008: 219; emphasis added). Jenny Chamarette (2012) also shows how Varda is concerned with the idea of subjective relationality. By drawing on selected examples, I will demonstrate that Varda's cinema is remarkable because in spite of its eclecticism, it is characterised by an unwavering ethics of filming that requires delineation.

The concept of *cinéaste passeur*, which was developed by Dominique Baqué in reference to Raymond Depardon and Jacqueline Salmon, has not been associated with Varda's cinema (2004: 186). A revised interpretation of *cinéaste passeur* however views the filmmaker as a mediator not only between the filmed subjects and the spectators, but also between a specific space and time and the moment of the screening. One of the difficulties when approaching Varda's body of work is the need to take into account both her changing *modus operandi* and the dialectic between the location of shooting and the film.[1] Varda is known for having filmed in a large variety of formats including personal documentaries, short commissioned films, feature films and more recently installations. By discussing contrastive pieces within her filmography as I did in the previous chapter with *La Pointe Courte* and *Agnès de ci de là Varda*, one can determine some of the defining characteristics of her ethics of filming. The two that I will focus on are her genuine interest in the encounter with the other, and her concern with the capture and preservation of images.

1: The Encounter with the Other

(A) *Mur, Murs: A Collective Portrayal*

Sarah Cooper (2006) underlines the dynamics of Varda's films when she describes them as auto/allo-portraits. To demonstrate Varda's understanding of cinema as a cooperative experience and to show that her films are based on encounters, I will focus on the example of *Mur, Murs*, which is the first part of her Californian diptych.[2] In this film, Varda embarks on an exploratory journey to discover the people behind the colourful murals she comes across in Los Angeles. Varda interviews and films many muralists; she also questions their practice, their models, and some of their patrons. She investigates the historical and cultural roots of this phenomenon and its impact on the local communities. Finally, she also incorporates impressive shots of some striking examples of murals like *Moratorium* by Willie Herron. While most of the film focuses on the subject of murals, it also contains a number of digressions that relate more loosely to the film's original topic.

Mur, Murs is an interesting cooperative experience both in its form and in its making. In *Mur, Murs*, Varda's vision of the city is shaped as a collective portrayal. She starts the film by explaining her original surprise and curiosity regarding this artistic alternative to commercial billboards. She then begins to interview locals and artists. Rather than focusing on a single aspect of the city, or a single representative individual, Varda uses murals as her starting point to explore the multiple facets of the city's identity. Echoing

One of the film's murals by Richard Wyatt, *in situ*

the work of the artists she interviews, she creates a portrayal of the city based on the idea of the collective. In the off-screen commentary, she declares that the murals are peopled with typical Angelenos, that is to say 'des noirs, des jaunes et des terres brulées' ('People with black, yellow and dust like red skin'). Varda's colourful acknowledgement of California's diversity exemplifies her attention to the heterogeneous identity of Los Angeles. In fact, both the Chicano and African-American communities constitute a salient presence in the film. This inclusion is hardly surprising considering Varda's longstanding interest in political questions, as evidenced in her earlier documentary titled *Black Panthers* (1968).[3]

To some viewers, the film may be an unsettling experience because of the myriad of images and voices they are exposed to. Despite subtitles indicating the names of some of the participants, it is fairly difficult, if not impossible, to keep track of who appears, when they appear, and who says what. Varda records many of her encounters but chooses to present these in a complex and multi-layered manner. In *Mur, Murs*, Varda does not only assemble a visual patchwork illustrating her encounters with Angelenos, but she also creates a multi-layered audio commentary. Throughout the whole film, she adds a male 'word whisperer', whose voice is superimposed over her own off-screen voice, or over those of Juliet Berto and other participants. This lingering whisper gives the spectator a chance to identify the murals on screen, and to learn the name of their creators. This characteristic of the soundtrack subtly echoes the kaleidoscopic quality of the film. *Mur, Murs*'s almost dizzying assemblage of images is enhanced by the director's play with the voices and music making up the film's soundtrack.

Naturally, some muralists are only interviewed once, while others are allocated several fragments. This is the case of Judy Baca who introduces herself as 'an artist, an educator, and a feminist' and of Ken Twitchell whose work incorporates well-known figures from American popular culture. These sequences help the viewer to find his bearings. Yet, because of the number of participants overall, even these favoured interlocutors undeniably demonstrate that the shape of Varda's film relies on the idea of the collective rather than on that of a single and oversimplified authority.

(B) *Mur, Murs: A Tentatively Comprehensive Portrayal*

The kaleidoscopic and polyphonic nature of *Mur, Murs* is not the only reason why I believe this film exemplifies Varda's understanding of cinema as a cooperative practice based on encounters. *Mur, Murs* is not only a collective, but also a tentatively comprehensive portrayal of the city. Far from presenting a utopian or glamorous vision of the mythic city of Los Angeles, Varda presents a version of the place which includes both its local and lesser known facets. Varda's comprehensive attempt is remarkable because it offers an alternative to the city's bipolar imaginary, as defined by Julian Murphet: 'According to your point of view, Los Angeles is either exhilarating or nihilistic, sun-drenched or smog-enshrouded, a multicultural haven or a segregated ethnic concentration camp – Atlantis or high capitalism…' (2001: 8). In fact, Varda lets all aspects of her interviewees' urban experiences imprint the film. For example, she does not shy away from the practical issues that some of them experience on a daily basis. Violence and gang fighting are, for instance, addressed several times. Rather than assembling a coherent group of testimonies in the editing room, she incorporates in the film several interviews with diverging opinions, which invite the viewer to engage with the debate presented on screen. In doing so, Varda proves that her project is about capturing the multiple facets of the city, however contrasting these may be. The film as a whole is a project open to the different traits and voices generated by this place.

The inclusion of many interviews with artists from the Chicano and Afro-American communities testifies to Varda's efforts to give the viewers a comprehensive representation of Los Angeles. The film includes the traditional have nots or *laissés pour compte* who are not often included in glitzier representations of the city. Flitterman-Lewis's interpretation of *Mur, Murs* as a typical example of Varda's political documentaries confirms this.

> *Salut les Cubains!* marks the first of a long list of political documentary films, both short and feature-length, that Varda has made throughout her career. Her consistent commitment to the Left, and to the struggles against oppression in any form – political, economic, or social – has led her to treat a broad range of topics in these films, from the Black power movement in California (*Black Panthers*, a 1968 film dealing with the Oakland trial of Huey Newton) and the Vietnam war (*Loin du Vietnam*, a collective film in episodes made in 1967), to the situation of Greek exiles in France (*Nausicaa*, a 1970 television documentary using actual Greek exiles in a fictional chronicle), the Hispanic community in Los Angeles (*Mur Murs*, a 1980 'look' at the murals in Los Angeles and their sociopolitical context), photography (*Une minute pour une image*, 1983, a television documentary of 170 ninety-second films, each about a different photograph), and women's liberation (*Réponse de femmes*, 1975). (1996: 230–1)

While I agree that *Mur, Murs* is a politically oriented production, I believe that confining it to the category of 'political documentary' is too restrictive. I would argue that in *Mur, Murs* the notions of testimony and exchange are just as important as those of political engagement and activism. Varda's interest in the city of Los Angeles does not only lie in its politically determined dimensions, but also in its social components. The collective and comprehensive qualities of the film demonstrate that the director is interested in assembling a thorough exploration of Los Angeles informed by her various encounters with Angelenos.

Varda's editing offers further evidence for this interpretation. The focus of *Mur, Murs* is undoubtedly the murals. For that reason, the muralists interviewed by Varda have a specific status in the film. However, many other people on screen have no direct connection with murals. Among these participants, there are teenagers who happen to live in one of the *barrios* Varda films, musicians and singers, an old woman, a baker, a bartender and many passers-by. Because Varda's editing includes these ordinary people, it reveals her desire to make a comprehensive portrayal of the city that gives voice to its various inhabitants. These sections of the film illustrate what De Certeau calls 'the ordinary' and its innumerable 'obscure heroes of the ephemeral' (1984: 256). The presence of these participants cannot be justified *vis à vis* the plot line or the main subject. These interventions illustrate Varda's attention to marginal and atypical encounters. In interviews, she often explains that her approach to filmmaking is intuitive, while her editing is much more controlled: 'When I film, I try to be very instinctive. Following my intuition [...] Following connections, my association of ideas and images [...] But when I do the editing, I am strict and aim for structure' (Chrostowska 2007). A particular episode captures this characteristic of Varda's practice and also shows her acceptance of chance as a potentially generative force when filming. At one point in the film, Varda is interviewing a participant when an accident between a motorbike and a car suddenly occurs. Instead of discarding the footage where the motorbike appears, Varda lets the camera roll and includes the unexpected experience of the crash into the film.

Finally Varda's choice of participants also speaks volumes about her ethics of filming. Even with a focus on Los Angeles's murals, Varda could have opted for more renowned participants. Some of the muralists interviewed have gained recognition today, but at the time of filming, most of them were relatively unknown. Varda did not care about the fame of the artists featured in *Mur, Murs*. She wanted the viewers to meet Angelenos in the flesh, whatever their occupation or origin. This genuine attention to the lives of others is the reason why Varda can rightly be considered a '*cinéaste passeur*', that is to say an artist who truly wants to make the audience share her encounters. Her ambition is to capture the spontaneity of these encounters, which will, once collected and edited, constitute her films:

> En regardant les gens se mettre en scène eux même, en les écoutant parler comme ils parlent, en observant les murs, les sols, les campagnes, les paysages, les routes, etc., on découvre tant de variétés entre le 'à peine vrai' et 'le surréel', qu'il y a de quoi filmer dans le plaisir. En fait on pourrait presque dire que le réel fait son cinéma! (By looking at people acting naturally, by listening to them when they speak, by observing the walls, the ground, the countryside, the landscapes, the roads etc., you discover the incredible variety there is between what is 'almost true' and 'completely surreal'. And all this generates real pleasure when you film something!) (De Navacelle *et al.* 1988: 46; author's translation)

(C) *Mur, Murs: A Portrayal Focused on the Encounter of and the Exchange with the Other*

While *Mur, Murs* has been interpreted with reason as a political documentary (see Flitterman-Lewis 1996: 230–1), the fact that it reflects overlooked experiences and tells unconventional stories about Angelenos shows that this film is more than a mere snapshot of California's muralist movement in the 1980s. In fact, I would argue that Varda's encounters form the core of the film, and that her focus on these encounters echoes the practice of filmmakers who engage fully with the film's participants, like the pioneers of *cinéma direct* in Québec, Claude Jutra and Pierre Perrault. Vincent Bouchard's study of the poetics of relation in the work of Jutra and Perrault is particularly *à propos* when one examines Varda's films: 'Le tournage est l'expérience d'une rencontre avant d'être un événement cinématographique' ('Shooting a film is above all the experience of an encounter. And that even before it is a cinematographic event') (2005: 86). In *Mur, Murs,* the testimonies of Angelenos prevail over a deceptively objective presentation of the city. The dynamic of the film is determined by the encounter and the relationship between the filmmaker (or her alter ego on screen, Juliet Berto) and the participants. The participants seem to lead the director from one neighbourhood to another and from one idea to another. By association and jumps, the spectator is led through the city, discovering new spaces and listening to the voices of locals. *Mur, Murs* can therefore be seen as a collection of valuable images that testify to the collective experience between Varda and the participants.

The experience of meeting and filming Angelenos is simultaneously presented as precious and fragile. This experience is shown in its variability: things may happen that the director has neither planned, nor hoped for, as well as in its fugacity: people may die, or not be present when she assumed they would. This is the case with the muralist John Wehrle who she wanted to film, but could not in the end meet. In the off-screen commentary, Varda explains that because she was unable to film Wehrle, she decided instead to use the recording of their conversation over the phone. By including traces of her research, Varda reinforces the spectator's attention to the tentative quality of the film. There is no certainty whatsoever when a project is still a work in progress. The film relies on financial means as much as on circumstances which vary according to the director's exchanges with others. Often in Varda's films, what matters the most is the recording of the fugacious moments which testify to her connection with others. As Froger writes: 'Le film est le moment et la trace d'un don et d'un abandon où l'image, en tant que donnée, importe moins qu'en tant que chiffre d'un acte qui atteste du lien à l'autre' ('The film is both a special moment and the trace of a gift and abandonment, during which the image, as an indexical document, matters less than as the trace of a connection with another person') (2004; author's translation). Varda's attempts to establish a special relationship with her participants is visible in her documentary films such as *Mur, Murs, Daguerréotypes, Les Glaneurs et la glaneuse* as well as in some of her installations like *Les Veuves de Noirmoutier*. When filming these encounters, Varda favours cooperation and spontaneity and makes the choice of revealing hiccups and surprises.

In *Mur, Murs,* Varda is a '*cinéaste passeur*' insofar as she records the unique character of these encounters. The old woman who out of the blue starts singing when she is asked what it was like to grow up in the local neighbourhood is a brilliant example of the unexpected yet cooperative dynamics typical of Varda's work. These moments of exchange make the connection between the filmmaker and the filmed participants tangible. This woman's response certainly took the director aback when it happened. However, its inclusion in the final cut illustrates Varda's acceptance of unplanned events and spontaneous reactions. This type of moment makes the supposedly strict boundaries between documentary and fiction vacillate. Some of the questions spectators are faced with are: is Varda really telling these people's stories, or does she fictionalise her interviews? Do her interventions undermine our reception of the film, or does her presence facilitate the transmission of that particular experience? I would argue that the dialogues we see on screen, and the questions Varda leaves open prove that she neither imposes an omniscient point of view, nor pretends that she is completely objective. She recognises that cultural productions are affected by the artist's subjectivity. In the opening of *Mur, Murs*, she makes this point clear by stating that the film originates from her curiosity about murals. At the same time, the diegesis quickly departs from this subjective stance in order to follow a journey dictated by the hints and suggestions of the locals. In her analysis of Varda's work, Cooper confirms this when she writes that the director privileges a 'position of non-knowledge' and refuses a 'hierarchical separation from her subject' (2006: 88, 89). The way the participants respond to Varda's project is formative. Varda will let these encounters and discoveries lead her in different directions. As a consequence, *Mur, Murs* gains a multi-layered quality that may, as mentioned before, leave the spectator in a state of uncertainty, speculating once it is over what the film was really about. *Mur, Murs*'s openness and its constant referral to others encourages us 'to relate to the bodies on the screen by evoking our own history' (Mai 2007: 143). The few scenes in which Varda records ambient sound or uses music as opposed to interviews are often full of action and movement: children running and playing with firecrackers, groups of people dancing and rollerskating. There is a definite invitation to make the spectators engage with either the recorded words of Angelenos or with their embodied experiences. Varda's enterprise is not only about meeting locals, it aims to make us share these experiences.

One of the many musical scenes in the film. Here, dancing rollerskaters in Venice

RESISTANCE AND ECLECTICISM   77

Some of her comments on *Les Glaneurs et la glaneuse* make obvious the importance she attributes to the encounter and to its passing on:

> this kind of film has two very important things for me: it really deals with the kind of relationship I wish to have with filming: editing, meeting people, giving the film shape, a specific shape, in which both the objective and the subjective are present. The objective is in the facts, society's facts, and the subjective is how I feel about that, or how I can make it funny or sad or poignant. Making a film like this is a way of living. (Varda and Anderson 2001: 26)

2: *Capturing Time and Images*

(A) *Mur, Murs and the Preservation of Images*

Varda's particular affection for art history's classical iconography and her debt to photography is visible in films like *Salut les Cubains!* whose motto is 'When Photos Trigger Films' (Chrostowska 2007: 124) and *Cléo de 5 à 7*.[4] My objective here is to expand the corpus traditionally favoured by scholars to establish Varda's consistency throughout her career and to analyse selected examples in detail. The concept of trace mentioned in Froger's quote cited earlier is central to understand Varda's ethics of filming. Unless the director keeps a visual or written diary during the shooting, the film that the spectator watches is the only material trace of these encounters.[5] Jean-Louis Comolli,

Roderick Sykes and Susan Jackson in conversation in St Elmo's village

a prolific analyst of documentary films, explains that cinema is supposed to bring back to life (for the spectator) the 'here and now' of the meeting between the filmmaker and the documentary's participants.[6]

In *Mur, Murs*, Varda films the 'here and now' of her encounters with many different Angelenos. She films her meetings with muralists and passers-by; she also films some of the locals involved in the painting of these murals. She does not hesitate to linger when dealing with specific places. For instance, she devotes a full sequence to St Elmo's village and its festival. In the mid-1960s, visual artists Roderick and Rozzel Sykes decided to rent some of the dwellings on St Elmo Drive and to transform this environment into an art space, where they could organise exhibitions and welcome local children and adults to explore and develop their creativity through art. This project provided locals with art workshops and underlines the vital connection between a specific space, its inhabitants and art. All these examples show how fundamental spending time with, listening to and speaking to Angelenos is to Varda. The fleeting but frequent images of children also confirm that live recording and local shooting are vital qualities for Varda.

In filming the 'here and now' of these encounters, it is obvious that Varda means to lay emphasis on the fleeting nature of this 'being together' and on the question of time more generally. An interesting parallel can be drawn between her encounters with Angelenos and her discoveries of murals, since they share a certain transient quality. The fact that murals are an ephemeral art form, that they are frequently destroyed or erased, and finally fade into oblivion make the collective experience of painting them, and their public enjoyment (for the time they are visible) the main point of the murals. During the course of the film, Varda underlines this particularity several times.

Among the artists interviewed many, like Arthur Mortimer, acknowledge this ongoing process: 'Mural painting is ephemeral by nature, murals fade, they are mutilated, they change with time, and this is all part of their beauty.' But to him and other artists, it is more important to paint 'vital art', where it is most needed, than to produce collectible pieces. This is precisely where Varda's project accomplishes the unexpected, since she literally lends these murals a lasting value for as long as copies of her film are available for screening. She truly becomes a *'cinéaste passeur'*, because her film keeps material traces of the murals, even if their preservation is uncertain. By documenting these murals, Varda freezes them in time and anchors them in history. By making their appreciation possible for thousands of potential viewers, she makes them durable. The mural that opens the second opus of Varda's Californian diptych, *The Isle of California* painted by Victor Henderson and Terry Schoonhoven, only exists now as a faint shadow because it was painted in enamel on stucco. The irony is that this particular mural represented the city in ruins, and that Schoonhoven's work is concerned with destruction, time and death. 'The L.A. of Schoonhoven's imagination has collapsed its own future into its present; that future has the iconographic properties of various possible California apocalypses, but in the end it is beyond questions of right and wrong, being simply, in the romantic American mode of Poe and Whitman, *Death*' (McClung 2002: 219).

The Isle of California by Henderson and Schoonhoven before its destruction

When Varda films her personal experience in Los Angeles, she returns to the essence of cinema, or at least to one of its essential characteristics, as Comolli puts it: 'le cinéma filme du temps, fabrique des durées, les fait expérimenter, c'est à dire vivre par le spectateur' ('cinema captures time, constructs durations, and it enables spectators to experience these moments') (1997: 36). Varda indeed films time as it is passing by, and as it is affecting murals and changing people, in short as it is mechanically recorded on film, in its inherent irreducibility. Several examples come to mind, which all evoke this idea of fugitive time. When she shows certain murals like *The Great Wall*, or *Bride and Groom* by Twitchell, the long process it took to paint them is mentioned, sometimes even illustrated by still photos made during their execution. Of course, what is visible at the time of *Mur, Murs*' shooting is only the end result, but by detailing the step-by-step composition of these murals, Varda highlights the notion of time and the efforts that were necessary to make these projects happen.

In other cases, Varda privileges ordinary people (and not artists) to illustrate the idea of time. The sequence devoted to Betty Brandelli is brief yet telling. Betty is interviewed standing in front of a particular mural, a configuration repeated several times throughout the film. On Mortimer's *Brandelli's Brig*, Betty and her husband are represented standing side by side in front of their bar in 1973. Since then, Betty has changed physically and her sitting in front of this image makes for an unusual collusion of times. Her husband's absence, combined with the towering presence of the mural, makes her look frail and isolated. Her candid look at the camera and her explanation that her husband has passed away are direct reminders of the time elapsed between these two moments. Following this revelation, the camera zooms out and reveals a wider shot showing Betty surrounded by the lights and microphones that are being used to film her. Looking a bit lost, she visibly hesitates about what to do next, and finally gathers her things before leaving the set. This almost brutal episode is a striking example of the way Varda makes the viewer realise the ephemeral character and the fragility of any artistic practice, and of those who partake in their elaboration. This sequence seems to echo some of Varda's preoccupations in her later installation *Les Veuves de Noirmoutier* (2005). 'Time and mortality are central themes to [Varda's] work' (Beugnet 2004: 286) and this type of sequence shows that many points of convergence exist among Varda's otherwise eclectic films. She knows that she cannot change time, however manipulative and ingenuous she may be in her editing. Nevertheless she can decide to link sequences in a certain way, and to point her camera towards subjects outside of the dominant commercial trends. *Mur, Murs* is a case in point of her desire to collect images of a specific time and place. An analysis of her attention to capturing images of the margins is therefore called for to fully understand her ethics of filming.

(B) *Capturing Images of the Margins: Ethics and Praxis*

Varda's work has been associated with many different categories including *la nouvelle vague*, the political film (see Tyrer 2009) and *auteur* cinema. When interviewed, Varda often questions rather than confirms the labels that critics and spectators apply to her

Betty Brandelli as she is being interviewed in front of Mortimer's mural *Brandelli's Brig*

work. Martine Beugnet notes that Varda's work denies 'the divide between a subjective approach and her exploration of social issues' (2004: 287). In other words, Varda's subjective perspective cannot be separated from her interest 'in depicting marginal subjects and in portraying disenfranchised areas of French society' (2004: 288).

O'Shaughnessy describes this attention to the margins as typical of a new wave of political film in French cinema.[7] But Varda's attention to the margins of society is truly remarkable because it runs through most of her films including her fiction works. Mona in *Sans Toit ni Loi* is probably the quintessential figure of marginality. The large number of analyses of this film show that scholars have deservedly paid attention to the themes of marginality and exclusion (see, for instance, Wild 1990, Rachlin 2006 and Déchery 2005). While it is discussed in *Sans Toit ni Loi*, this concern dates back much earlier in Varda's career. As early as 1958 with *L'Opéra Mouffe*, Varda made a point of including images of homeless, drunk and marginal people.

Filmmakers invite their viewers either to discover new worlds and dimensions, or to revisit the world they think they know. Many of Varda's films prompt a re-assessment of familiar spaces and figures. Giving the marginal centre stage and an active role in the film's narrative is a recurring practice in Varda's cinema. By using a selection of examples, I will demonstrate that Varda is a *cinéaste passeur* determined to capture images of those whom cinema often rejects. Varda's method when depicting the margins requires specific attention. In fact, by analysing specific examples, one realises how Varda's ethics of filming defines her praxis. The examples I will draw on belong to films shot at different times and in different places and these variants confirm that there is a strong constant running through Varda's production.

In *L'Opéra Mouffe*, subtitled *Carnets de notes d'une femme enceinte*, Varda films among other things people chatting at the market and drinking at the local bar in Paris's 5th Arrondissement. This subjective diary is full of associations and metaphors. The film, shot in black and white, runs approximately fifteen minutes and includes separate sections introduced by intertitles. *L'Opéra Mouffe* recalls silent cinema, because its sections are introduced by intertitles. At the same time, *L'Opéra Mouffe* does not try to mimic silent films since Varda uses a changing musical soundtrack throughout, rather than adopting a musical performance or a *bonimenteur* to accompany the film's images. The film's various sections do not all seem to be related to one another. One of them focuses on a couple named '*les Amoureux*', another one, '*Les angoisses*', relates the anxieties of a pregnant woman. The two most interesting sections through which to discuss the depiction of marginality are '*Quelques autres*' and '*l'Ivresse*'. '*Quelques autres*' is a selection of close ups on various faces, while '*l'Ivresse*' shows the silhouettes of people sleeping on the pavement and inebriated individuals. The juxtaposition of these sequences with the more idyllic love scenes seems to illustrate the contradictory feelings and anxieties experienced by the pregnant woman of the title. As mentioned earlier, it is important to underline that Varda's diary of a pregnant woman echoes her subjective experience: '*L'Opéra Mouffe* was a short film about the contradictions of pregnancy. I was pregnant at the time, told I should feel good, like a bird. But I looked around on the street where I filmed, and I saw people expecting babies who were poor, sick, and full of despair' (Varda and Peary 1977).

Émilie cannot bear her friend's questions and breaks down, alone and desperate

In another of Varda's films centred on a woman's experience, *Documenteur*, several fragments focus on homeless people sleeping rough in bus terminals, drinking coffee or wandering the city of Los Angeles. In the first part of this film, Émilie, the protagonist, spends most of her time trying to find a place for her son and herself after separating from her partner Tom. This process seems long and difficult although very few details are provided as to why. Until she finds a new place to live in, Émilie struggles with her new condition as much as with her overpowering emotions. She is, to borrow Varda's words, 'poor and full of despair'. During the film, Émilie's frail figure is seen in

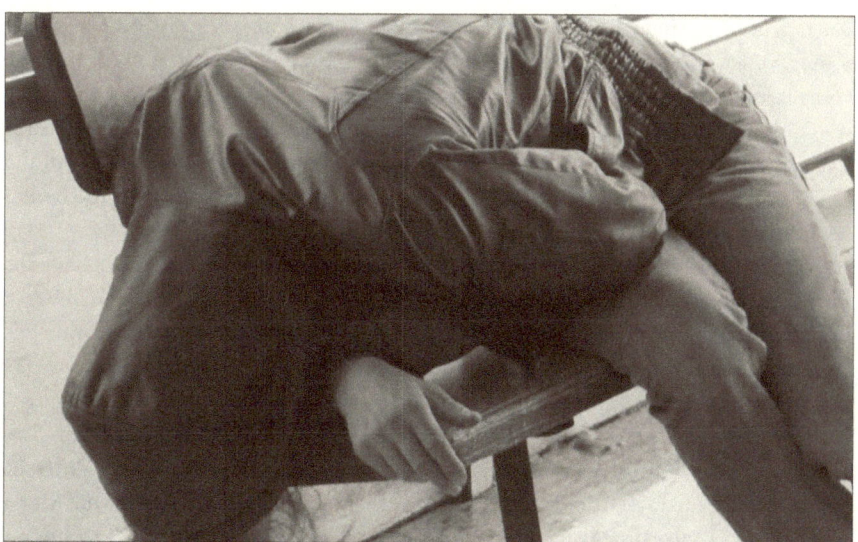

A rough-sleeper in Los Angeles, one of the many images of homelessness

a variety of public places, like a laundromat, a bar, a phone booth and a bus station. In all these places, people physically surround her, move around her, while Émilie is static, almost out of touch. The fact that Varda chooses to have her talking to very few people makes her isolation look even more intense. When Émilie is not filmed in a static and meditative position, the fact that she cannot seem to settle down illustrates the fluctuating character of her emotions, and the uncertainty that oppresses her. At some point, she bluntly tells her son Martin that until they find a 'home', they are disturbing their friends' lives. This being literally 'out of place' is visually paralleled by the numerous shots of beggars and homeless people. Émilie is a double outsider who does not belong anywhere because she does not have a home, and because as a French person in California she does not seem to feel at home. This marginal status makes her akin to the many anonymous faces that the director films. This collection of close ups on homeless Angelenos reflects Émilie's marginal position.

This darker take on the city is a complex counterpart to the colourful and upbeat *Mur, Murs*. *Documenteur* revolves entirely around Émilie's subjective experience. Her interior monologue is a crucial indicator of her estrangement and isolation. Her voice does not tell the spectator much about her material conditions, but describes her feelings in detail. While voluble about her emotions, Émilie says nothing of the marginal figures of California. The spectator cannot even say for sure if these sections are subjective shots. Does Émilie see these people around her, or is she oblivious because of her focus on finding a place to live? Do these shots belong to the narrative, or should they be assigned another status? They definitely do not fit easily in the diegesis. As none of these sequences are glossed over, they are left for the spectator to interpret. In fact, these sequences have three functions in the film. First, they illustrate what Émilie's difficulties could lead to. Her new status as single mother makes it difficult for her to do everything, including work to make ends meet, find a new house, and a new school. Second, they give the spectator time to ponder Émilie's monologue and to assimilate new information. And third, by inserting long takes focusing on these marginal people, which could be compared to what Noël Burch calls 'pillow shots' (1979: 162), Varda forces the spectator's engagement to shift from the fictional to the documentary and in doing so, she points 'offscreen to the embodied viewer's concrete and intersubjective social world' (Sobchack 2004: 284). So these passages do not only testify of the reality of Los Angeles in the 1980s, they also encourage us to engage with the bodies onscreen by evoking our own experience.

Varda's focus on the margins of society is manifest in at least two other films for which she received critical and popular acclaim, *Sans Toit ni Loi* and *Les Glaneurs et la glaneuse*. Despite their differences, these two films share many traits. Both films gravitate around fragments of testimonies and stories. In *Sans Toit ni Loi*, Mona's corpse triggers reactions and generates an *a posteriori* portrait based on the personal account of those who met her, and on the sections showing her before she dies. *Sans Toit ni Loi* is an impossible portrait in the sense that the locals have very different opinions on Mona. At the end of the film, there is no consensus on who Mona really was, and no consensus on what she wanted or on what drove her to life on the margins of society. In *Sans Toi ni Loi*, Varda does not provide any answer. She refuses closure and linearity in favour of fragmentation and indeterminacy. What she intended to make with *Sans toi ni loi* was an impossible portrait of Mona: '*Vagabond* is really constructed about different people looking at Mona – like building together an impossible portrait of Mona' (Varda and Quart 1987: 6). The world she presents is full of people with certainties such as 'les filles comme elles on les connait, toutes des allumeuses!' ('girls like her are all the same, she's just another tease!'), but soon Mona's existence and her mysterious death forces the people who criticised her to question their certainties. Eliciting the spectator's participation is a common practice in *Sans Toit ni Loi*, as well as in *Documenteur*. The film contains many sequences similarly shifting from fiction to documentary. While long takes are certainly used to situate Mona within the landscape, they also give the spectator the opportunity to relate the film to his own embodied experience. Because of Mona's silence and of the questions her death provokes, the spectator looks for clues in Mona's body language as well as in the space surrounding her. He is compelled to consider the landscape in a more subjective way. This characteristic probably adds to the spectator's impression that the narrative is fragmented and incomplete.

A real story inspired Varda when she started working on the project of *Sans Toit ni Loi*. Headlines depicting the death of homeless people because of particularly cold winter nights are not uncommon in France. This choice of a somewhat common subject coupled with the formal construction of the film is meant to hold the mirror up to Varda's fellow citizens. When Varda chooses Mona as an evasive and missing protagonist, she makes her fellow citizens reconsider this apparently unremarkable event. For a film concerned with homelessness, Varda's film is remarkable because it is neither didactic nor 'donneur de leçons'. Rather, it is simply teaching the spectator to look beyond appearances and stereotypes at the bodily experiences of marginal individuals. It captures the coldness, hardships and solitude experienced by individuals who, like Mona, refuse to follow social conventions. Varda never romanticises Mona's character, she is not an intellectual *flâneuse*, which is not to say that she does not reflect on her own choices in the film. Her character is presented in such a way that it is not easy to feel overwhelming empathy towards her. In the presence of other marginals, Mona can be puzzlingly as prejudiced or abusive as the so-called normal people of the film. On several occasions, Mona refuses the help of well-meaning people, with no clear reason to justify her attitude. Varda does not build up a black and white portrait, nor does she create a totalising narrative of marginality. Using a real story as a starting point, she invites the spectator to engage in a reconsideration of his certainties, just as she did when she started working on this film: 'Around '84, the newspaper [sic.] were talking a lot about the *new poor* ... The words *new poor* always made me think of the *old poor*, those who from time immemorial until today, beggars or not, have hung around the towns or roamed across the countryside' (translated by and quoted in Smith 1998: 148).

Now, the last piece in this section concerns another film that undermines the idea of a single totalising narrative of the margins. In *Les Glaneurs et la glaneuse*, Varda undertakes an exploration of the idea of 'gleaning'. Varda seems 'as interested in creating fascinating fictive "vagabonds" as in exploring the ways in which her culture encodes and defines excluded insiders' (Rosello 2001: 29). Her research on and exploration of gleaning takes her to various places where she interviews a variety of people whose complexities and contradictions she makes no attempt to conceal. Sometimes she follows people who look for food in the bins of supermarkets, while at other times she reflects on the legal meaning, or artistic renderings of the activity of gleaning. In this film, she accumulates and juxtaposes fragments that make *Les Glaneurs et la glaneuse* a subtle *bricolage*. Ruth Cruickshank associates the idea of *bricolage* with Varda's film, because it is 'part of a tissue of texts, made up of provisional differing and deferring meanings' (2007: 127). Interestingly, Varda also describes her practice in *Les Glaneurs et la glaneuse* as a subtle *bricolage* mingling documentary interviews that are later edited into a fiction.[8]

Both these analyses of *Sans Toit ni Loi* and *Les Glaneurs et la glaneuse* show that in editing her collection of interviews, stories and testimonies, Varda becomes a *cinéaste passeur* who prompts the spectator to reconsider what is usually left out of mainstream cinema. The people filmed by Varda are for the most part neither young, nor beautiful. They do not form a coherent group, partly because the wide variety of reasons for their gleaning. Besides, Varda's exploration of the term 'gleaning' is wide ranging. I would argue that this opening to possibilities is characteristic of her practice. Several critics including Cruickshank (2007: 124) and Rosello (2001: 33) have commented on a passage in *Les Glaneurs et la glaneuse* in which Varda forgets to turn off her small digital camera and films the dangling lens cap. In *Mur, Murs,* as mentioned, the sequence where she accidentally captures and incorporates the aftermath of a road collision into her film illustrates her acceptance of chance. So while Varda's attention to the margins is related to Cooper's description of the director's ethic, which involves a privileging of others over the self (2006: 89), it is also important to note that her practice is always self-reflexive. In *Les Glaneurs et la glaneuse,* Varda never separates her observation of gleaners from her personal concerns about, for instance, the art of making films, or the ineluctable passing of time. They are weaved together in Varda's subtle editing which establishes potentially meaningful connections for the viewer.

Notes

1 Varda's poetics of space will be addressed in the following chapter.
2 The films are two separate entities but were made and released at the same time. Many consider them together including myself (Bénézet 2009: 85–100) and Michel Mesnil who calls the diptych *Varda 81* (Bastide 1991: 108).
3 This particular film was shot during her first stay in America and dealt with the pivotal Free Huey rally held on February 17th, 1968, at Oakland Auditorium in Alameda, California.
4 For details on the power of images see Smith 1998: 12–59.
5 Some directors are fond of this practice, one can think for instance of Luc Dardenne's *Au Dos de nos Images, 1991–2005*.
6 My translation of: 'le travail du cinéma est avant tout de ressusciter pour chaque spectateur l'ici et maintenant de la rencontre filmée' (Comolli 1997: 22).

7   For a detailed analysis of this phenomenon, see O'Shaughnessy's *The New Face of Political Cinema* (2007).
8   'J'utilise la technique du documentaire pour refabriquer une fiction avec des interviews documentaires dedans. C'est un bricolage assez subtil qui me plait beaucoup.' ('I use various techniques of the documentary genre to fabricate a fictional account made of documentary interviews. I really enjoy making this subtle kind of bricolage.') Part of Varda's intervention during the Q&A section of the conference Le Cinéma et au delà at the university Rennes 2, recorded by Radio France and broadcast in April 2008.

CHAPTER FOUR

Poetics of Space

Space is a fundamental aspect of Varda's cinema, and one that both critics and the director herself have underlined very early on. Alison Smith, for example, devotes a whole chapter to 'People and Places' (1998: 60–91) and Kelley Conway more recently identifies geography and emotion among Varda's perennial preoccupations (2009: 212). Varda has always been fascinated by space and writes that her work consists in capturing the light on inhabited landscapes to offer it up to the spectators of her films. 'Entre [...] dans mes films, c'est ouvert, il y a de la lumière, du moins celle des paysages avec figures que j'ai filmés' ('Come into my films, the door is open, there is light, the light captured on the inhabited landscapes that I have filmed') (Varda 1994: 6). This tripartite emphasis draws our attention to the landscapes and their inhabitants, the uncertain capture of light onto film, and the director's inner desire to offer these to us, the audience.

In each film or artistic project undertaken by Varda, there is a specific *modus operandi* which is determined by the location she focuses on. Her filmography shows that she enjoys working in a variety of places, maybe because Varda's youth was characterised by geographical movement. Scholars have often privileged her Parisian films (see, for instance, Mouton 2001, Forbes 2002 and Morissey 2008) even though recently her peripatetic, provincial and expatriate works have been the focus of more intense scrutiny (for more details see Bénézet 2009, Powrie 2011 and Boyle 2012). In this chapter, I will straddle this divide and discuss an apparently eclectic corpus of films to see how Varda understands space and how she uses it in her cinema. In her work, space is neither objective nor topographic. It is not a blank canvas or a *tabula rasa* on which the filmmaker can build anything that she wants. As I have written elsewhere (Bénézet 2009: 87), Varda's perspective is close to that of cultural geographers who argue that space is socially constituted through the interaction of boundaries, representations and practices (see Davilà 2004: 75). Varda attended some of Gaston Bachelard's lectures in Paris and although she claims she did not understand much, her practice seems to be steeped into a phenomenological and relational understanding of space that I will examine through a set of particular cases. In *Poetics of Space*, Bachelard distinguishes between abstract space and lived space and recognises that in the second half of his career he moved from a rationalist to a phenomenological approach (1969: xi–xii). Like her professor, Varda believes that lived or inhabited space is known phenomenologically through participation in or inhabitation of the world. How Varda renders this experience of space on screen is what I examine in this chapter. How is Varda approaching space when she films or sets up installations? What is she looking for in a particular space? And are there common elements that she focuses on in her otherwise disparate filmography? These questions form the core of this chapter. To cover as much ground as possible, this chapter will be organised around two main sections discussing, first, the notion of emotional geography and, second, the relational *modus operandi* of Varda's work.

1: Emotional Geography

In Varda's films, as soon as space is observed or physically experienced (by being walked through, for example), it becomes invested by someone's presence and by his or her embodied subjectivity. This space may remain mysterious and uncontrollable to the subject but its depiction changes drastically. In *L'Opéra Mouffe* discussed in chapter one, the many experiences of the pregnant woman of the title influence the cascade of free associations that the spectator is exposed to. While we cannot be sure how many subjectivities invest the film (is it just that of the pregnant woman or a collection of female experiences including those of the lover?), this work illustrates that Varda will not, even in a short film portraying la Mouffe in 1958, separate her documentary images from the visual notes and impressions of an individual, whether it is herself, an alter ego, or more simply a set of characters. The term 'subjective documentary' that she coined to talk of *L'Opéra Mouffe* demonstrates how in this particular case La Mouffe cannot be separated from the woman of the title and the director.

This is also true of Varda's fictional works. *Cléo de 5 à 7* chronicles ninety minutes of the life of a rising pop singer who is waiting to hear the results of a biopsy. The progress of Varda's Parisian heroine has been analysed by many scholars in terms of space, most following in the footsteps of Flitterman-Lewis's analysis (1996) interpreting the protagonist's journey as one of self-discovery. Varda's exploration of the connections between a specific environment, here the city, and a character is an obsession that she openly acknowledges but she also emphasises that it is the dialectic between an embodied subject and a specific space that she is interested in: 'This question of space and people on film concerns the body in film because it is also made by people's bodies. I don't think we can talk about Cléo without remembering, all the time, that she's a beautiful, tall, blond woman who is in danger, who is attacked by fear and by illness. We cannot forget either that Mona is a woman, maybe hidden under these strange leather rotten clothes that she is wearing' (Varda *et al.* 2011: 190). In *Cléo de 5 à 7*, the spectator is taken in an array of places, from Cléo's hyperfeminine boudoir where she performs for her lover and composer to the café Le Dôme where she observes and listens to the people around her.¹ Her itinerary is not a fixed one as she is mobile and able to change her mind whenever she wants to. She is, for instance, taking a taxi with her assistant Angèle at the start of the film and then using public transport with Antoine, a soldier on leave from the Algerian war that she meets in Parc Montsouris.² The incoherence and unpredictability of the city are here inspirational and celebrated.³ When Cléo leaves her flat upset and starts the unaccompanied walk that will ultimately take her to the hospital to hear that she does have cancer, she 'ceases to be an object, constructed by the looks of men, and assumes the power of vision, a subjective vision of her own' (Flitterman-Lewis 1996: 269). She is finally by herself and in charge, willingly soaking up the changing and fleeting sights of the city and opened to chance encounters. The idea of movement and change is essential in this section of the film as suggested by Özgen Tuncer: 'The female protagonists who are on the move not only constantly elude fixating and sedentarising powers, but also trigger a transformation in the territories they travel through' (2012: 114). Cléo is literally on the move but as she leaves her flat, she is also escaping the diva and starlet stereotypes that her entourage seems keen to associate with her. She is making the choice to leave and go wherever chance will take her, whether it is the sculptor's studio where her friend Dorothée is posing, or the local theatre for a cinematographic interlude. The changing interaction between Cléo and her environment and the discussions (open or veiled) about time and death can be regarded as the two founding principles of the film. Thus looking at the dialectic between the varied landscapes and Cléo's evolution provides the audience with a better understanding of the emotional landscapes that Varda's films construct.

Another eloquent film literally built on this dialectic between space and characters is *Plaisirs d'Amour en Iran*, which was meant to be screened before *L'une chante, l'autre pas*. Varda made this six-minute film with two usual suspects, Nurith Aviv and Sabine Mamou, in Teheran, Ispahan and Cairo during the summer of 1976 and used the characters of *L'une chante, l'autre pas* played by Valérie Mairesse and Ali Raffi. The film is unapologetically presented like a fiction when it opens with the off-screen voice of a woman saying: 'Il était une fois un homme et une femme qui étaient amoureux à Ispahan en Iran' ('Once upon a time there was a man and a woman who were in love in Hispahan in Iran'). As she speaks, the spectator sees a series of long shots of a beautiful mosque visited by tourists and locals including a young couple. The narrator explains that the couple is astounded by so much beauty and amazed to see and feel for the first time the effects of the total harmony between architecture and nature as well as between their environment and their body ('l'harmonie entre nature et architecture, entre corps et décor'). Two conversations between the lovers follow this establishing scene, the first begins with a medium close-up of the two protagonists but continues off camera while we see images of the contours and details of the surrounding building. The second is different because its setting is more private as the couple sits on the edge of a fountain in a little shady courtyard (maybe their hotel). The subject of their exchange shifts slightly from the description of their erotic sensations, when they are off screen, to the declamation in the courtyard, on screen, of two love poems, the first learnt by heart by the man, the second audacious and improvised by her in response to his ceremonious declaration. The scene closes on their embrace even if he jokingly proffers that she does

The two lovers of *Plaisir d'Amour en Iran* embracing in the private courtyard

not understand men at all while she answers that the feeling is mutual ('Him: Tu ne comprends rien aux hommes; Her: Et si c'était réciproque?'). The film then shifts to a series of close ups on Persian miniatures representing a couple embracing followed by groups of men and women who are described and linked to the story of the couple by the female narrator's voice-over. The last miniature by Behzād (1488) showing the couple Yusuf and Zulaikha in a huge and sumptuous palace provides a link back to the royal mosque's architecture in Ispahan. The narrator carries on explaining how this space where nature and culture and profane and sacred art meet is a truly sensational

Behzād's version of the lovers Yusuf and Zulaikha

place for lovers even if they are fictional characters ('C'est un lieu troublant entre tous pour des amoureux même s'ils sont les personnages d'un film').

Although made over thirty years ago, this film exemplifies many of the elements that Varda requires from the places that she incorporates in her work. What she seems to be looking for above all is an evocative space which will be able to trigger and generate associations and new images in the spectator's mind. In a statement published for one of her recent exhibitions, Varda explains that she aims to make images with the potential to surprise, provoke and trigger thoughts and *rêverie* in her audience: 'Je voudrais que ces images, fixes ou animées, créent des surprises, éveillent des pensées et suscitent des rêveries'.[4] *Plaisirs d'Amour en Iran* achieves this by meshing the couple's thoughts with the ornate details of the mosque as well as the miniatures and by establishing connections between three different love poems with very different tones. The film is permeated by their joyful celebration of sensual love, but it also translates a sense of admiration for art, whether it is architecture, poetry or visual art. The domes of the mosque take on a surreal existence when she compares them to pairs of breasts, and we start to realise that things may not always be what they seem. From then on, the audience will be more likely to look for *risqué* hints both in the couple's dialogue and in the images that they see. The landscape is not a simple exotic background; it literally takes on a life of its own and changes according to the content and intonations of the couple's intimate conversations. Interior and exterior worlds become bound through the combinations of the images and dialogues on screen. We know, for instance, that the lovers listen to their drives when they say that they are hungry or thirsty, and in so doing they explain how this particular space has an impact on them.

From the moment we hear them talk, lightness and sensuality seem to pervade the sacred place of the mosque. The lavish motifs and shapes on the mosaic walls evoke a garden where love flourishes. From the shady courtyard with its small trees and flowers to the ornate designs of the miniatures, gardens are an important element of the film connecting the lovers with their environment, the miniatures and poetry. In the first poem that he recites to her in Arabic and then translates, the poet compares his lover's body to a garden. The quote from Paul Éluard's poem 'Je ne suis pas seul' ('I am not alone') read by the voice-over narrator synchronised with the miniature of a poet alone in a garden, is also significant.[5] In the final lines of his poem – 'Je parle d'un jardin, je rêve, mais j'aime justement' – Éluard makes it clear that he is not just describing an imaginary garden but that he is alluding to the woman he loves. The garden's flowers, the fruits, the sun and the rain summon her beauty and her material presence. They enable the poet to feel as if she was here by his side. The space he is in becomes entangled with his memory of her and his proclamation of love. In Varda's film, the lovers' experience of space, their enjoyment of sensual love and their aesthetic response to architecture and poetry also become intertwined.

If the two lovers were the spectator's only guides, the film would be a parodic portrayal of intercultural misunderstanding or a simple vignette about the tribulations of love. In fact, she is enjoying his company but seems unaffected by his love of grandiosity and performance; while he clearly finds her directness titillating but also a little bit shocking. When she writes her love poem on a toilet roll and describes him as a man-bird with a gentle and proud tail, he cannot refrain from telling her that she cannot be serious and uses one of the most clichéd statements about the inability of women to understand men and *vice versa*. The narrator, who could be considered the director's alter ego, is the one perfecting the surreal symbiosis on screen. The landscapes and gardens, their artistic representations and the lovers' embodied experiences become inseparable thanks to her suturing of these fragments. We are watching more than a comical and sensual evocation of love and its misunderstandings; we are offered a chance to think about what sensory and intellectual apprehension is beyond or rather through artistic representations. The emotional landscapes that Varda creates are not only subjective and contested but also self-reflexive. As Powrie concludes in his article on *Les Glaneurs et la glaneuse*, Varda is keen to show how the process of filmmaking becomes a 'vehicle for transforming the everyday, for revealing what the surrealists called the marvellous' (2011: 75). This idea of transformation through connections is one that I want to elaborate on because it almost seems to become a method for Varda when it comes to space. Analysing the connections created between space and various other elements will also help to establish the originality and consistency of Varda's poetics of space.

2: A Relational Modus Operandi, or How Space Establishes Multiple Connections in Varda's Films

In the film that she said would be her last, *Les Plages d'Agnès/The Beaches of Agnès* (2008), the beach is a common thread which enables Varda to connect an otherwise often disparate set of memories. This work was described as an autobiographical film and as a cinematographic self-fiction (see Boyle 2012). What I find particularly interesting in *Les Plages d'Agnès* is that Varda presents her own identity as determined by the ever-shifting relationships that she has had with the beaches of her life. The philosopher Frank Kausch rightly calls it a '*portrait en creux*' and foregrounds the elements that are in contact with and transforming Varda's identity.[6] Varda's *modus operandi*, her way of establishing connections may be more apparent in her recent projects, but I would argue that she was already using a similar strategy in earlier works (including commissioned projects).

(A) *Du Côté de la Côte, O' Soleil, soleil and Eden Toc*

Du Côté de la Côte (1958) is a fruitful example of Varda's approach when it comes to space. This film was commissioned by l'Office national du tourisme (the French tourism office) and was supposed to promote tourism on the French Riviera. It was made with a small team, on a decent budget and with material that Varda was happy to experiment with, like tracking rails. She spent eight weeks on site and ended up editing a very personal vision of this region. The film was finally released in June 1959 in Paris and screened with Resnais' *Hiroshima mon amour*. Unlike *Plaisirs d'Amour en Iran*, *Du Côté de la Côte* is presented as a documentary. From the beginning, the off-screen male narrator explains that tourists and crowds are going to be the film's main subject, not the locals: 'Notre propos n'est pas de cinématographier les indigènes, toujours vieux et charmants [...] notre sujet c'est la foule, les touristes, les curieux...' ('Our purpose is not to film indigenous people, who according to custom are always old and charming. [...] Our subject is the crowd, the tourists, the curious people...').[7] This declaration of intention almost sounds like a disclaimer explaining why the filmmaker does not embrace a more discreet *cinéma direct* approach that would focus on the locals rather than on their seasonal counterparts.[8] At the same time, this tongue-in-cheek opening also reminds us that the documentary we are about to see is decidedly subjective. And why should this not be since, as the narrator explains, there is no consensus about who invented, created and perpetuated the set of images generally associated with 'La Côte d'Azur'? Out of this abundance what Varda does in *Du Côté de la Côte* is to juggle with the garish images and clichés about la Côte, some archival footage and reproductions and her own often Tati-esque footage to assemble an original and exuberant picture of the Riviera. This film which is as much an essay as a travelogue operates *vis à vis* space in two ways that require attention. Two types of connections will be then investigated: I will look first at how Varda addresses the mythology surrounding the Riviera and how she introduces the marvellous and poetic. The second set of connections are the ones she establishes between herself as a visiting outsider and the audience.

From the very beginning, *Du Côté de la Côte* simultaneously focuses on two things: the roots and 'constructedness' of the idea of the Riviera, and the current practices of space exemplified by the tourists. The credits accompanied by a collection of panoramas and vintage promotional posters showing the sights of Cannes, Antibes, St Tropez and Menton immediately establish that the film is not going to limit its attention to one city. These colourful images are synchronised with the song of a *bel canto* tenor who praises each location by repeating 'la più bella' (the most beautiful) after each poster so that the sequence resembles a list of the top places to visit found in most travel guides.

Opening credits of *Du Coté de la Côte* (left); vintage promotional posters for St Tropez included in the opening (right)

Gorbman interprets this musical opening as 'tourist music' even if it was 'composed by Georges Delerue to Varda's lyrics' (2012: 48). 'Imitating the sunny tunes of itinerant musicians who circulate among tables in Mediterranean dining spots, and [...] accompanied by guitar and mandolin', she labels the lyrics as '*du toc* – fake Italian or perhaps fake Provençal – successively proclaiming each coastal town (Nizza, Canna, Antiba, Saint-Tropez, Mentona) *la più bella*, the most beautiful of all' (ibid.). From then on, it becomes evident that Varda is going to be a rather unorthodox guide that I would describe as an inquisitive anthropologist. First we learn how much tourism impacts on the demography of small cities like Cannes and St Tropez, and who were the first figures to put this particular area of France on the map of seasonal tourism. The male narrator mentions Cornelia Salonina (the wife of a Roman emperor), the Cardinal Maurice de Savoie (on his honeymoon) as well as Lord Brougham and Queen Victoria, while the female narrator whispers the name of each of the locations (respectively le Cimier's water spa, Nice and finally Cannes).[9]

Varda's perspective can be compared to that of a stroller-historian as defined by Sylviane Agacinsky:

> The historian takes possession of the past by interpreting traces, whereas the trace of the past happens to the stroller and takes possession of him. Let us not claim, however, that nothing happens to the historian; undoubtedly his desire also involves an anticipation, a curiosity with regard to what will come to him from the past, what he will discover in the shadows and encounter. There is often a stroller at the heart of each historian, a part of him that is trying to let himself be touched by the traces. (2003: 52)

Varda shows curiosity, a desire to capture and make sense of traces of the past, and a willingness to be touched by what she encounters during this summer of 1958. Although anchored in the past via an array of eclectic references to historical figures and artists like Picasso, Valéry, Colette and Matisse, the film is also interrogating the way people currently inhabit the region, whether they are famous like Brigitte Bardot, or anonymous like the crowds of the opening. The mythology associated with the Riviera is made tangible through black and white footage of Bardot and Sophia Loren, and a long sequence on the architecture of palaces such as the Negresco and the exuberant private villas. We are told how these sights are magnets for tourists and how their attention naturally shifts from these unattainable ideals to far more easily consumable places like the gardens, museums and beaches of the coast. There is humour and irony in this portrayal of the coast. Tourists and buildings alike are prone to changes in

L'hôtel de la mer, an example of the local architecture and its bright colours (left); bright colours are fashionable too when it comes to swimsuits in 1958 (right)

fashion: 'yellow and blue are in one year', though green seems to be the colour of choice for Germans. Delerue's use of the brass, reminiscent of the music matching the gesture sequence in *L'Opéra Mouffe*, turns a successions of sunbathers coming in and out of the same tent on the beach into a comical ballet. Tati's similar use of human movement in space in the modernist architecture of *Playtime* (1964) comes to mind. The artificiality associated with what Varda calls 'l'Eden toc' (the fake or gaudy Riviera) comes to the fore on many occasions. This array of sights leaves the camera dizzy and the spectator uncertain that there is any essence behind these colourful surfaces. With the pomp and luxury of hotels and villas, Varda contrasts the more democratic spaces of the beach, the camping site and the cemetery. Although space is also at a premium in all these places, there is a sense that they reveal as much if not more about the Riviera as the glossy images usually associated with the region. More than an idealised or promotional 'idea' of the Riviera, these are material places which are truly lived in or which resonate with the living.

The long section at the end of the film documenting the carnival in Nice is another significant sequence, especially since the narrator provides only very sparse commentary. In this passage, we see very little of the streets or buildings because the camera focuses on the revellers and on the giant *papier maché* puppets and masks which are paraded for twelve days through the city. The dancing, the fireworks and the burning of the king's figure accompanied by loud brass band music create the frantic atmosphere and topsy-turvy universe where hierarchy and inequality have supposedly no place. One could say that in Nice the carnival has become more inclusive since it has

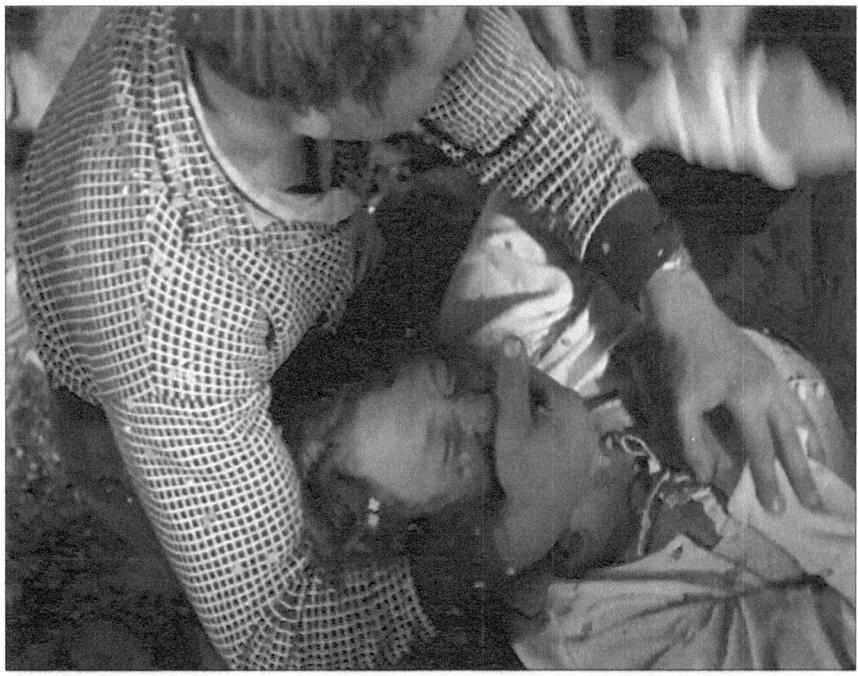

A close up on one of the women held captive during the carnival in Nice

evolved historically from a set of private balls and receptions in the thirteenth century to a boisterous celebration for all. But when Varda's camera lingers on several women who are repeatedly held captive by a group of men to be covered with *confetti*, we come to the conclusion that the carnival is only a temporary safety valve and that inequality and divisions between the sexes are still manifest. Whether it is the dream or the celebrations that tourists are after, it is clear that these are manifestations of a shared need for escapism and utopia. In *Du Côté de la Côte*, Varda deconstructs some of the myths the Riviera is built on, and sheds light on the lingering gap between the more and the less privileged. The egalitarian ideal associated with the carnival can neither live on nor change things radically. The only two comments of the male narrator heard just before and after the carnival sequence confirm that it should be looked at as a temporary and limited event: 'De la nostalgie naît le carnaval' and 'le Carnaval brûle […] le carnaval est mort, le silence va régner' ('Nostalgia gives way to the carnival' and 'The carnival burns […] the carnival is dead, silence will reign').

Even if the carnival will neither resolve tensions nor appease longings, the ending of *Du Côté de la Côte* suggests that all is not lost because 'l'Eden existe' ('Eden exists'). The paradisiac island where a naked man and woman nap undisturbed is beautiful and peaceful, an improbable sight after the crowds that Varda's camera has favoured until now. The gentle melody of the flute matches the slow movements of the camera caressing the waves, the sand and the branches, before it finally lingers over the couple's back. The close up of their hands marks an important switch since it is the female narrator who takes over for the conclusion. In this final sequence, her sober and melancholy voice explains that fantasies ('les rêveries collectives') are only ethereal ideas, whether one thinks of a perfectly manicured garden, the Riviera or Eden. As a series of gates and beach umbrellas are closed against grey skies, a song about the fleetingness of the summer starts which says how sad and silly the end of a party and of summertime can be ('le soleil de la fête, il est démaquillé, c'est triste et bête, la fin de la fête, la fin de l'été'). This is a melancholy, poetic and sensible conclusion to this vertiginous travelogue. After showing the fakeness and illusive quality of 'la côte d'azur', Varda acknowledges her own desire to make this place more beautiful and dreamlike. Her unorthodox deconstruction does not result in a completely cynical 'so what'. On the contrary, the comical, poetic, and unexpected connections that the film establishes between the spaces of 'la côte' and its tourists create a vivid and joyful picture of the Riviera at its peak, that is to say in the summer. Varda's unorthodox connections suggest that the fabrication of the Riviera opens up endless avenues to her imagination and that of her spectators who are invited to dream of many more. Her travelogue may be dizzying at times because of its eclecticism but by transforming the everyday and mundane (like hats and parasols) into something marvellous (flowers and crowns), Varda proves that she is a relentless 'enchanteuse du quotidien', a true enchantress.

Since the film was conceived as a promotional assignment, it is not surprising to find references to the dazzling glamour and widespread attraction that this region has over people in general. Through her presentation of the history and fabricated myth of the Riviera Varda also tries to establish visceral connections to the spectators and to touch them. People who saw *Du Côté de la Côte* were, apart from the film buffs and journalists who attended the film festivals of Tours, Obenhausen, Brussels and Berlin, either the ones who went to see *Hiroshima mon Amour* in 1959 or people living in the half million (or so) French households who owned a television in that same year.[10] At that point in her career, Varda had not made a feature, so she was not well-known. *Du Côté de la Côte*, contrary to some of her other more fictional works, does not contain characters *per se*, so it does not lend itself to easy effects of identification. As remarked earlier it does not rely on a simple talking head either, but on an unusual duo and on Delerue's music. It almost feels like one is playing a game of hide and seek when trying to locate the director's presence. But there are moments where she surfaces, and during these occurrences, Varda, the outsider, establishes connections with the audience throughout the space of *la côte*.

In *Du Côté de la Côte,* the Riviera becomes a giant stage ready for its many performers; it is lived in, animated and embodied through colourful characters. These may be anonymous bathers and tourists, but they make the experience of the coastal beaches tangible well beyond dreams of fame and limelight. Varda's editing combined with Delerue's music and the narrator's commentary are conceived to trigger reactions in the audience. In the beginning of the film, for instance, we see a long row of bathers on the beach lying down in tight rows like sardines in a box. The end of the tracking shot reveals a surprise when the couples give way to a mismatch of women and children, with one woman in particular wearing a stripy bathing suit who caresses a dove, while three others rest on her belly and towel. The commentary which describes the subject of *Du Côté de la Côte* matches these images of the symbol of freedom: 'les passagers qui découvrent un jour cette côte et s'y assemblent pour épuiser leur temps de liberté' ('the temporary occupants who one day discover this coast and decide to flock there to use up all their free-time'). After a momentary pause on the lady with the doves, a pirouetting movement of the camera mimics the effect of this vertiginous array of bodies on the beach and the caustic nature of the commentary hits you: why is it that people come to this overcrowded region in the first place? And why do they keep on coming? The paid vacation granted to French workers for the first time in June 1936 has just been extended in 1956 from two to three weeks and the seaside's popularity shows no sign of abating. The sea, the sun and the aura of movie stars remain favourites. Varda is not completely cynical, since her film simultaneously shows the artifice and some of the Riviera's artefacts on screen. In her conclusion, she embraces the natural beauty of the region and even acknowledges its appeal on herself. In a way, she recognises the longings associated with 'la côte d'azur' from the very beginning, a place that seems so close: à côté (close by) so to speak, but also distant and pure with its incredible Azure landscapes.

Varda is not a local and the film does not suggest at any point that the director or narrator know more about the region than the spectators or tourists. The film comprises much information but it always feels tentative and inquisitive about its findings rather than purely didactic. To keep the viewers on their toes and trigger their reactions, Varda alternates between brief fact-based sections and cascades of free associations often characterised by humour. Some of these sequences are clearly built like colourful ballets of bodies. There are casual walks on the promenade akin to fashion shows, close ups of

Sunbathing on the Riviera; an example of Varda's humorous collages

tanned and burned skin, and shots of napping beach lovers captured at an angle which gives the comic impression that their head has been replaced by that of a toddler or a dog. Varda repeatedly inserts amusing vignettes into her flow of images and edits the footage in such a way that realistic images are defamiliarised and turned into something different and new. Effects of collage are used to make the audience laugh as well as to make them think about their own experience of 'holidays at the seaside' or their aspiration to some. However small the experience may be, like the itchiness of a hand-knit swimsuit, the oiliness of sun lotion or the warmth of the sun after a swim, they are all ways to connect the spectator, then and now, to the seasonal tourists of the Riviera. In *Du Côté de la Côte*, the questions 'Qui sont-ils?' and 'Où sont-ils?' ('Who and where are they?') are only rhetorical ones because Varda's insistence on sensations keeps reminding us that we could very well be them. The film may lack the 'interview' dimension of other documentary projects like Edgar Morin and Jean Rouch's *Chronique d'un été/ Chronicle of a Summer* (1960), but an important portion of the film is dedicated to the daily sensory experiences of these people, to their longings and to their interactions with the sights and the locals. Through sensations and laughter, Varda tries to engage the spectator at a level other than purely intellectual. For instance, she enjoys pointing to the silliness and repetitive nature of routines and situations. Her deadpan comparison between the campers who are just as crammed in their respective lots as the occupants of the tombs in the nearby graveyard is a reminder of Varda's unwavering wit. By giving attention to these excesses and at times irrational longings, she is turning the mirror towards both herself and ourselves and asking us to consider the question: what sort of tourists would we be? There are many possibilities in the film since she is careful not to lump all vacationers into one single group. Her derision is equally divided between all groups as she flags the contrasts between the different types of people enjoying the Riviera. The rich tourists who are looking to buy or build the most delirious villas are just as comic as the working class tourists. When they are handing the keys of their fancy cars to the hotel doorman, they do look the part of success and wealth, but at the same time Varda often contrasts their swimming trunks, bare feet and nonchalant gait with the ceremonial elegance of the doorman. The juxtaposition of these vignettes makes it obvious that even if all these people share a common space for the holidays, they indeed live very different lives. What unites them is this particular place that they all seem to fantasise about and the sensual experiences of the beach and seaside.

The emphasis on sensory experiences is not the only way that Varda connects with her spectators. Although the figure of the doorman underlines the different spheres that tourists occupy, it also makes reference to something that Varda and her audience have in common, their love of cinema. In the beginning of the sequence about doormen the camera focuses on their attention to their customers. It is their body language and gestures that we are invited to scrutinise: 'Au baromètre de sa familiarité, on est quelqu'un ou pas' ('His friendliness indicates whether you're a somebody or a nobody'). In this series of images, there is no way for us to really differentiate between the doormen, or to single one out. The second part of the sequence, however, is quite different as Varda's zoom on the direct gaze and face of a Buster Keaton lookalike who is said to have been a doorman at the Grand Hotel in Cannes for twenty

Cannes, its Grand Hotel, and one of its real (or imaginary) doorman?

years suddenly takes us from reality to fiction and from the present to the past. As the camera slowly zooms out, the eeriness of the scene submerges the audience as they come face to face with a building site where the doorman continues to greet people in spite of the chaos around him. So where is the Grand Hotel? Does this place exist, is it an invention of Varda's, or a real building renovated at the time she was filming? Originally built in 1863, soon after the boulevard de la Croisette, the Grand Hotel was torn down in 1957–58 before being rebuilt by its new owners. So what Varda does here is to show us that reality and fiction are never separate entities. The mythical palace of the Grand Hotel is a dream that is being re-built, echoes of the dream factory, i.e. cinema, can be found just around the corner in the flesh and all that the audience needs to engage with these images and ideas is to be both curious and open-minded. In *Du Côté de la Côte*, Varda goes well beyond 'the spirit of old postcards found in a musty album' (Gorbman 2012: 47) as space becomes an opportunity to tell stories, to introduce unexpected connections and to connect through sensory experiences with others. We are not presented with an emotional geography associated with a fictional character or the director's alter ego, but instead, in this work, it is the fleeting impressions and vivid sensations associated with the Riviera that Varda is summoning up for us.

This attention to sensations when examining the potentially conflicting perceptions associated with a specific place is a constant throughout Varda's work, including her recent installations. So to round up this chapter on Varda's poetics of space, I thought it would be informative to probe into three of her installations which deal one way or another with the beach and seaside: *Ping Pong Tong et Camping*, *La Cabane de l'Échec* and *Dépôt de la cabane de pêcheur*. The first two installations *Ping Pong Tong et Camping* and *La Cabane de l'Échec* were displayed in 2006 on the ground floor of the Fondation Cartier in Paris. *Ping Pong Tong et Camping* and *Dépôt de la cabane de pêcheur* were also exhibited together in 'Y'a pas que la mer' at the Musée Paul Valéry in 2012 and I will take into account as much as possible the respective scenography of these two exhibitions.

(B) *Deambulations in the Space of Varda's Installations*

In her article on feminist beachscapes, Fiona Handyside analyses 'the sheer multiplicity of connections Varda makes between different ideas, images and cinematic representations of the beach' in *Les Plages d'Agnès* (2011: 86). In the two exhibitions mentioned earlier, the seaside is also a place where ideas and images can come into contact and give rise to unexpected results. Varda, who is 'a flâneuse on a beachscape' (2011: 87), enjoys surprising her audience with mental zig-zags and associated twists no doubt influenced by her passion for surrealism. The three seaside installations *Ping Pong Tong et Camping*, *La Cabane de l'Échec* and *Dépôt de la cabane de pêcheur* are quite different in the way they present beachscapes, but they all invite the visitors to step into an unconventional space where our senses are brought to the fore.

La Cabane de l'Échec, later modified and renamed *La Cabane du Cinéma* (2009–10) for the Biennale de Lyon, was made of two separate elements in Paris.

On the one hand, Varda and Christophe Vallaux had conceived a shack inspired by the temporary huts erected in Noirmoutier and along the coast, often made with pieces of wood, metal and discarded material. On the other hand next to this 'hut of failure' made of a metal structure covered with old film strips from the commercial copies of Varda's unsuccessful *Les Créatures*, stands a professional mixing table projecting an inverted copy of the film. The hut is big enough for several people to stand in, and with its walls permeable to light, it looks like a rudimentary miniature of the bigger and glass-filled room where it stands in the Fondation Cartier. In both the exhibition's catalogue and on the description of the installation, Varda emphasises the commercial failure of *Les Créatures*, the fact that it was shot in Noirmoutier (partly in her house, a restored windmill), and the famous actors involved in the project: Michel Piccoli and Catherine Deneuve. In doing so, she anchors this fragile edifice in the island of Noirmoutier (l'île in *L'Île et Elle*) and connects these artefacts with the career of her actors and the cultural memory and capital that goes with it. What should be pointed out in relation to the concept of a poetics of space is the director's experimental play in this installation with light, scale and time. This architectural structure made of recycled film is a sculpture of light, a frame where strips of ageing 35mm celluloid, now greyish and red, echo the sheets of metal covered with rust. The capture of light and movement on film is arguably the essence of cinema, so that when Varda plays with light and perception here, she is going back in time and questions what one sees when watching a film in normal conditions versus non-traditional ones. The premise of this installation is the same as René Clair's *Entr'acte* (1924), a film meant to underline the idea of threshold (between the stage of the theatre empty of its dancers during the intermission and the spectators) and of dynamic inversion.[11] The light shining through stained glass windows in churches is supposed to encourage contemplation and meditation, and here visitors can take advantage of the static nature of images (and of the relative silence) to come as close as technicians do to the celluloid material of the film. Piccoli and Deneuve are recognisable icons of French cinema, young and famous but also small and partly visible because of the decaying film, their real strength being the fascination they hold for film-lovers.[12] The visitors have a participatory role in observing the installation, they can move around and out of the hut, go back at their own leisure and even watch the film's topsy turvy and at times comical footage. Cinema as an artistic medium has changed; moving from the analogue to the digital world. The mixing table nearby could very well become a relic, the trace of a different time and a proof that technological changes can impact our perception. Freed from the constraints of traditional screening, the reels of film become a material in their own right like wood and metal, which can be manipulated at will.

Varda's ingenious recycling shows that they are neither lost nor useless since they become a self-referential and malleable material. The visitors' experience certainly differs from that of Varda who was personally involved in the making of the film (the possessive 'ma cabane de l'échec', 'my hut of failure', is significant here). But the installation as a whole is a reflection on memory and on what we can (and cannot) share as spectators in the time we have together, and what remains and changes after

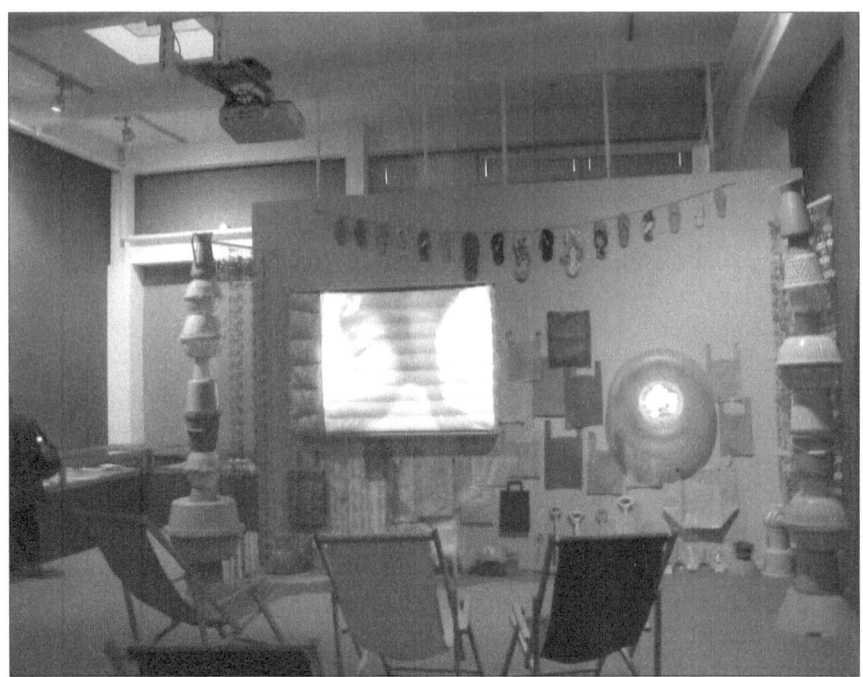

The colourful set up of *Ping Pong Tong et Camping* in Sète (photo taken in April 2012)

we have parted. The temporary nature of any screening, the vintage character of the table and Varda's experimentations throughout *L'Île et Elle* with photography, cinema and sound show that she wants to explore the new encounters that can occur in and out of the gallery with people who are willing to embrace this tribute to her work. Chamarette explains that 'Through filming, refilming, exhibiting and re-exhibiting, mourning becomes a dynamic and recuperative gesture between film, filmmaker, exhibition space and viewer' (2011: 45). I would add that the spectator's mobility and sensory engagement in space necessarily needs to be considered to understand Varda's practice as a site of resistance and creativity. If *La Cabane de l'Échec* is moving, it is not only because we feel part of a community of strangers, but because it makes us realise that our bodies (and minds) are intertwined in time and space alongside those of others. Varda's cinematic promenades can only be effective if they take visitors on a challenging walk through memory and space.

The second installation I want to turn my attention to is *Ping Pong Tong et Camping* which, like *Du Côté de la Côte,* is unapologetically colourful and exuberant. In 'Spatial and Emotional Limits in Installation Art: Agnès Varda's *L'Île et Elle*', Jordan accurately describes the cornucopia of sounds and colours that the visitors face when they encounter this 'jubilant study in fluorescence [...] framed by stacks of bright plastic buckets, jugs, bags, and colanders' (2009: 583). In between the two symmetrical columns of buckets and jugs and the garish plastic curtains which make this space feel a bit more enclosed, there are two pseudo-screens. On the left hand side of the wall, a six-minute film which shows close-ups of children's bodies as they play is projected on an inflated mattress, while on the right a child's buoy serves as a second lower frame within which is projected a sequence of elaborate still images of flip-flops. In front of these two screening surfaces, there are five colourful deck chairs waiting for visitors to take place.[13] The soundtrack that accompanies this piece is rhythmic and joyful and includes electronic noises, piano scales and the noise of children playing and shouting in the distance. This collection of sounds semi-orchestrated by Bernard Lubat is meant to summon the joyful mood associated with the camping site of the title.[14] The soundtrack as a whole is fabricated in such a way that it invites the visitors to consider what they hear as an evocative soundscape for the whole installation rather than as a narratively-driven score matching the video projected on the mattress. The scenography of *Ping Pong Tong et Camping* evokes a camping site or a family's spot on the beach, left empty as its occupants have gone for a swim. The double screen, which looks as if one is for the grown-ups and one for the children, is reminiscent of the family slide-show often organised after a holiday, a ceremony as important as the siesta (or quiet time) that Varda's camera captured in the camping sites of the Riviera in *Du Côté de la Côte*.

On the slide show and video here, one element is particularly important: there are no visible faces and therefore no way for the visitor to identify a particular participant. Our attention is firmly directed towards the ping pong balls and colourful clothes and buckets, as well as on the actions and gestures that we see. Varda has taken the definition of camping that she provided in *Du Côté de la Côte* as 'the airiest form of freedom' and turned it into an installation inviting the visitors to engage with the objects and sounds meant to summon the joy and freedom experienced at the seaside.[15] The profusion of plastic, a cheap material *par excellence*, may make the installation look like an endlessly recyclable scenography, but the carefully placed chairs and garlands of flip-flops and the attention to detail testifies to the elaborate process that has gone into organising this farandole of colours and sounds. This evocation of how vacationers spend their everyday also shows 'the subtle beauty of both the mundane and the commodity' (Chamarette 2012: 123). But are these objects speaking any real truth or is this installation a beautified fantasy? The flimsy quality of the plastic and the slide show of unconventional photographic still lifes remind us that holidays are only a temporary parenthesis, and that we are viewing a carefully prepared installation in a space with conventions different from those of the space it represents. The preparatory sketch included in the exhibition catalogue for Sète and the press kit for Paris highlight the development of the project. The reproduction of the compositions projected on the buoy are also telling. Flowers and fruits, classic elements in still life, are used as a background for the flip flop(s). Varda's interpretation is both topical and comical as she chooses a form of art traditionally considered lower (yet popular) and uses round and oblong shapes (with olives, peas, cherry tomatoes and tulips) to reproduce the round frame of the buoy. These still lifes are also subtle *memento mori* or 'reminders of death' meant to underscore the joyful yet transient character of life.

In the Musée Paul Valéry, *Ping Pong Tong et Camping* was fittingly installed at the very end of the exhibition next to the glass cases holding traces of Varda's epistolary exchanges with the late local painter Pierre François. Varda's description of these objects from their personal collections: 'un plaisir des yeux, un sourire qui virevolte en couleurs, des moments sporadiques de contacts' ('a visual feast, a colourful and twirling smile, sporadic moments of contact') could equally be applied to *Ping Pong Tong et Camping*. Varda calls attention to the transient nature of the experience of the beach while emphasising its sensory dimensions. The holidays and their freedom may be an illusory respite but they offer endless material for a comical and sensory re-appropriation. One could speculate as to how viewers feel when required to engage with such a space after they have seen the darker and more contemplative *Les Veuves de Noimoutier* and *Dépôt de la cabane de pêcheur*. Contrary to the Fondation Cartier where these pieces were on different floors, the path that we have to take as a visitor in Sète is undeniably finishing on a more positive if not upbeat note with *Ping Pong Tong et Camping*.

Despite the title of the exhibition in Sète: 'Y'a pas que la mer!' (which literally means 'There is much more than the sea'), the beach constitutes a recurrent presence in Varda's work.[16] In her provocative *Dépôt de la cabane de pêcheur* (2010), Varda's vision of the beach is quite different from the colourful vision she elaborates in *Ping Pong Tong et Camping*. This is proof that the beach, like other spaces that Varda uses, is a highly malleable starting point to play with, an opportunity to engage with the set of stereotypical images associated with a place, and a chance to defeat her audience's expectations and preconceptions. The '*cabane*' of the title here (the hut) is not a refuge and looks open to the elements and the potential fury of the sea. To see this piece the visitor needs to enter a separate room, as a wall isolates it from the rest of the gallery; there is, so to speak, a threshold to cross to encounter this installation. Upon entering, one soon realises that this seaside scene is meant to feel different because the room is not only much darker, but also strewn with disparate objects often piled against each other including fishing nets, plastic and wooden crates, ropes, life buoys, rusted sheet metal, large wooden sticks and tarpaulins. This is not a touristy place, but a working shipyard or a harbour that may have been abandoned. The wall in front of the visitor where a looped video is screened is not flat but obstructed by rods and its double angle makes the video look oddly segmented. Against the opposite wall, visitors can sit or lean for a moment on a small pile of crates covered by a cushion or on a couple of basic beach folding chairs. The video entitled 'La Mer Méditerranée avec 2 r et 1 n' is a rollercoaster in terms of content and rhythm. It starts on a quiet beach, with the camera embracing the horizon as well as a group of random-looking walkers. On the left hand side, we see a long line of poles planted in the sand, symmetrical and graphic. On the right hand side, there is a (blue) screen in the shape of a sign where various images (including some of the same beach empty) are screened. In between these two, the walkers move away or towards us. The video incorporates scenes from Varda's filmography like the naked lovers embracing in a hammock on a beach and the gigantic whale that Varda had built for *Les Plages d'Agnès*.

What is striking in 'La Mer Méditerranée avec 2 r et 1 n' beyond Varda's use of her work as an endless source of striking audio-visual fragments is that the segments on the beach are contrasted with a mismatch of mostly amateur documentary footage, of the kind weather and news channels use to testify of the strength and horror of natural disasters and human conflicts. This section which immediately follows a close up on the giant whale and its scary stone head is frontal, violent, and surprising especially if one knows that Varda has a very strong fear of violence (see Varda and Adler 2010). Its editing to a sonic crescendo, and the poor quality of most of the images makes it hard to know what is really going on; in successive waves, we see fires, tsunamis, tanks, vehicles and bodies flicked away like grains of sand, and everywhere destruction and distress. After this short yet intense interlude, we go back to the calm lapping of the waves, to the poles on the same beach and to the walkers. The main difference with the first segment is that apart from the father carrying his young daughter in his arms, all the people we see, once they have walked past the screen, give the spectators a wave and are shown in close up on the blue screen in the right hand side of the wall we are facing. This acknowledgement by a gesture or a direct gaze of our position as a witness and onlooker is reminding us of our own position: we are in a comfortable gallery enjoying an artistic installation in a protected environment. This *mise en abyme* adds to the layers of meaning and does not obscure our understanding of the piece.

The multiple screens and fragmentary nature of this video and its mysterious nature attest that Varda is fully aware of the imperfect nature of any representational attempt. 'Varda has no illusion about the limits of representation, but she plays with 3D possibilities to destabilize viewers, in and out of the comfort zone of their viewing practices in art spaces' (Barnet 2011: 104). She knows that our time and space cannot, at the moment that we are experiencing this piece, match the confusion and despair that characterise the documentary footage that she has pieced together. This oscillation then between love, hope and beauty and the distressing admission that the world is not well is what makes this piece particularly effective. In a way, this installation is like an essay on the powerful nature of art. As in many of Varda's works, her motto here could be summarised as: take a space, build up mental associations, refuse romanticising *clichés* and confront the audience by forcing them to engage with what they see, what they hear and what they feel. Contrary to the melancholy ending of *Du Côté de la Côte*, the part of 'La Mer Méditerranée avec 2 r et 1 n' that addresses our place within this elaborate artistic installation shows us that if there is only one thing that is still possible in the face of chaos, it is human connection. The cheeky goodbyes or hellos that the participants are sending us are proof of the fragile yet potentially significant connections that we can establish with others. The visual and material chaos in this hut and on the looped video and the fleeting emotions we are invited to experience are conceived as complementary rather than incompatible. What the artist decides to leave us with is the sense that in an age of ubiquitous visibility, images of human connections are still worth seeing and contemplating. While in cinema, space often explains or confirms the psychology of a fictional character, in installations as well as in unconventional works like 'La Mer Méditerranée avec 2 r et 1 n', *Du Côté de la Côte*, and *L'Opéra Mouffe*, it serves a different purpose. Space is a creative crossroad, a potentially endless source of connections and an opportunity of being with and feeling with others.[17]

Notes

1. In the alphabet book section of the volume she published on the occasion of her retrospective at the Cinémathèque française, she devotes a section to Bachelard which reads: 'L'épistémologie n'atteignait pas ma compréhension mais il parlait de beaucoup d'autres choses, de Jonas par exemple bien installé dans sa baleine, ou des maisons depuis la cave humide jusqu'aux greniers qui sentent la pomme' ('I did not understand epistemology but Bachelard was talking about a lot of other things. He talked about Jonas, for instance, and his comfortable set up in the whale and about houses which smelled of apples from their humid basement to the attic') (Varda 1994: 11).
2. Antoine Boursellier who plays Antoine in this film is the father of Varda's older daughter Rosalie. He played in *L'Opéra Mouffe* in 1958 and was an active theatre actor and director until he died in May 2013.
3. For more detailed and enlightening readings of Cléo's journey, see Jim Morissey's 'Paris and voyages of self-discovery' (2008: 99–110) and Valerie Orpen's excellent *Cléo de 5 à 7* (2007).
4. For details on her first exhibition in Sète in the spring of 2009, see http://www.languedoc-roussillon.culture.gouv.fr/fr/0index/01actu/CRACSETEAVRIL2009-VARDA.pdf (accessed January 2013).
5. I am copying here the whole poem from the book *Médieuses* to enable readers to get a sense of the text as a whole: 'Chargée, De fruits légers aux lèvres, Parée, De mille fleurs variées, Glorieuse, Dans les bras du soleil, Heureuse, D'un oiseau familier, Ravie, D'une goutte de pluie, Plus belle, Que le ciel du matin, Fidèle, Je parle d'un jardin, Je rêve, Mais j'aime justement.'
6. 'Le prologue, mettant en place un réseau de miroirs déroulant une série infinie de points de vue [...] souligne que le portrait est ici en creux, dissimulant toujours ce qu'il révèle en portant l'attention non sur une identité, mais sur ce avec quoi elle est en relation, donc en transformation' ('The prologue with its ensemble of mirrors creating an infinite number of viewpoints [...] emphasizes the fact that we are watching an "anti-portrait" which reveals as much as it hides and which focuses not on Varda's rigidly fixed identity but on what her identity is connected to and on how it changes') (Kausch 2008: 15).
7. There are two voice-over narrators in *Du Côté de la Côte*: one female and one male who take on different roles as the film progresses. This is why it is important to specify who is saying what at all times.
8. Claudia Gorman in her analysis of Varda's early travelogues underlines the significance of this choice as well: 'At the very opposite end of the scale from *cinéma-vérité*, which purports to give unmediated images of brute reality, *O Saisons ô Châteaux* and *Du Côté de la côte* arrange, reframe, and frankly denature any preconceived notions of their subjects' (2012: 56).
9. It is interesting to note that this is very similar to the way Varda proceeds in *Mur, Murs* twenty years later when she uses a male whisperer to associate her images of murals with their title and creators.
10. The first time that the Office de Radiodiffusion Télévision Française (ORTF) broadcast something in colour was in 1957 and as time went on they looked

for more and more programmes in colour and developed some in their studios of the Buttes-Chaumont. On the website of Varda's production company, one learns that *Du Côté de la Côte* was used as a film-test screened on television daily for two months. http://www.cine-tamaris.com/films/du-cote-de-la-cote (accessed February 2013).

11 *Entr'acte* is a classic of *avant garde* cinema. It was commissioned by the Ballets Suédois's director Francis Picabia who wanted an intermission for the ballet *Relâche* (1924). Its orchestral score composed by Erik Satie and loose narrative thread underscore and test the potentialities of the cinematographic medium and remind us today of the exciting adventures of the Dada movement in Paris at the time.

12 Piccoli was a household name even before he acted alongside Brigitte Bardot in 1963 in *Le Mépris* (1963), one of Godard's most famous films. As for Deneuve, she had played in Demy's *Les Parapluies de Cherbourg* (1964) and many other memorable films including Roman Polanski's *Repulsion* (1964).

13 Interestingly enough, on the day I visited the exhibition in Sète, I noticed that while many visitors took the time to sit down and pause in front of the other installations where sitting was provided (in the shape of a chair or a bench) only children dared to use the deckchairs, often comparing the answers they had given to the quiz provided as a guide for the exhibition and chatting about what they had seen before their parents caught up and shooed them off.

14 I use the term 'semi-orchestrate' because the composition is a real team effort. Varda was inspired when she saw him play his 'musical table' and asked him to take part with this unusual instrument. The footage of the recording in Uzeste, however, makes it clear that even while she is shooting his hands tapping away, Varda is also indicating her approval and encouraging him, with two assistants throwing balls when she gestures them too. A partial clip of this happening can be found online at the following address: http://www.dailymotion.com/video/x80ji1_bernard-lubat-agnes-varda-uzeste_creation#.UVkeKhysiSo (accessed March 2013).

15 In *Du Côté de la côte*, Varda's allusion to camping as the ultimate form of freedom is quickly overturned, however, when the overcrowded sites full of happy folks are compared with the campgrounds of happy dead who have also been attracted by the peaceful shores of the Mediterranean: 'Le camping étant la forme la plus aérée de liberté et de cérémonial, […] ces camps surpeuplés de bon-vivants qu'attire ce rivage latin préfigurent bien les camps de très bons morts que ce rivage appelle.' ('Camping is the airiest form of freedom […] campgrounds crowded with happy folks attracted by the shore mirror the campgrounds of happy deads on the same peaceful shores.')

16 Fiona Handyside's article on the beachscapes in the work of three important female directors, including Varda, testifies to the need to analyse space in cinema in a way that incorporates more options than the simple dichotomies between urban and rural locations.

17 For an illuminating take on Varda's attempts at being-with in *Jacquot de Nantes* (1990), see Laura McMahon's discussion (2012: 15–20).

CHAPTER FIVE

Cinécriture and Originality

'Cinécrit par Agnès Varda' is a caption that appears in many of her films and in an interview with Barbara Quart, she explains why for her this expression encapsulates the many possibilities of the cinematographic medium: 'what I call in French *cinécriture* [...] means cinematic writing. Specifically that. Not illustrating a screenplay, not adopting a novel, not getting the gags of a good play, not any of this. I have fought so much since I started, since *La Pointe Courte*, for something that comes from emotion, from visual emotion, sound emotion, feeling, and finding a shape for that, and a shape which has to do with cinema and nothing else' (Quart and Varda 1987: 4). In this passage, Varda asserts the specificity of cinema and declares that it should be considered in its own right rather than conceived as a derivative or hybrid form of other artistic media like literature, painting and photography. Looking at this this quote, one also realises how much Varda has strived to maintain an exceptional position that she began with her first project in Sète.

Varda's reluctance to follow pre-set production standards, and her desire to experiment with images and sound contribute to her originality. She has made commissioned films like *O Saison O Châteaux* (1957) and advertisements but she has also managed to remain independent thanks to the establishment of her production company Ciné-Tamaris in 1954. Other scholars have underlined Varda's uniqueness historically (see Sellier 2008: 217), but what I want to examine here is the unorthodox quality of her *cinécriture* in order to see whether it matches her theoretical conception of cinema as 'the movement of sensations'. To do so, I will survey a number of works and focus first on the unconventionality of her subjects and praxis to develop on to an examination of what Kate Ince calls her 'carnal cinécriture'.[1]

In the introduction to her book on subjective cinema, Laura Rascaroli explains that one of the difficulties she faced when writing was to resist overtheorisation when discussing 'the unorthodoxy of technical formats, of subject matter, of aesthetic values, of narrating structures and of practices of production and distribution' of the essay films in her corpus (2009: 2). I would be reluctant to categorise Varda's entire filmography as essayistic, but many of the issues mentioned in this quote are pertinent when thinking about her work. This is why this chapter will begin with a section establishing Varda's unorthodox subjects and practices of production. To keep this chapter to a reasonable size, I will restrict my focus to four films that illustrate her unique praxis: *Elsa la Rose*, *Uncle Yanco*, *Les Glaneurs et la glaneuse* and its follow up *Deux Ans Après*.

1: Deceiving Expectations, or Why Unorthodox Subjects Matter

Elsa la Rose was originally conceived as a diptych on Elsa Triolet and Louis Aragon; two famous and charismatic authors who had been living and writing together for thirty eight years when Varda filmed them. Inspired by the principle behind *Les oeuvres croisées d'Aragon et Elsa Triolet* (a joint publication of their complete work started in 1964 and illustrated by artists including Matisse), Jacques Demy was supposed to make a film showing Triolet's vision of her lover's childhood while Varda was to create one presenting Aragon's imaginary version of Elsa's childhood in Russia. When Demy abandoned the project, Varda decided to carry on with her half but modified the project by shifting the focus from Elsa's childhood to their recollection of the day they met and their relationship from then on. Elsa Triolet and Louis Aragon were well known in France as a very public, political couple. Aragon was a journalist, art critic and prolific novelist and poet who was involved in the French Resistance movement and the French Communist Party. He was also well travelled, having toured Europe with Nancy Cunard, a rich British heiress and former lover. Elsa grew up in Russia and lived in Tahiti with her first husband André Triolet before getting divorced. This stay triggered important life changes and when the writer and political activist Maxim Gorky read some of the letters she had written to Victor Schklovsky from Tahiti, he encouraged her to become a writer. She also lived in London and Berlin before moving to Paris in 1924. She translated Russian literature into French and was the first woman to be awarded the *Prix Goncourt*, a prestigious French literary award, for *Le Premier accroc coûte 200 francs* in 1944. Aragon and Triolet regularly appeared on television together and Aragon often reminded journalists, critics and readers in his poems and interviews that Elsa, his muse, wife and intellectual partner had saved him from himself and enabled him to carry on writing.[2] They met in 1928 at la Coupole in Montparnasse, a key meeting place for expatriates and intellectuals like Jean Cocteau, Man Ray, Josephine Baker, Simone de Beauvoir and Ernest Hemingway. It is also the café where Cléo listens to her song on a juke-box in *Cléo de 5 à 7*.

In *Elsa la Rose*, their meeting is re-enacted almost hypnotically with Elsa pushing the cafe's swing door open in a fur coat and hat like the ones she was wearing on that day. Aragon acknowledges from the very beginning that his attempt to remember that day can only be tentative, and he tells the audience that even tiny details will never be able to match '*l'infixable*' (what escapes him and what cannot be pinned down). Aragon has always been interested in playing with versions of his life on the page and in reinventing himself. He is a strong opponent to the fantasy of the origin, maybe because he was an illegitimate child who later as a writer would not let his absent father impose a name on him.³ *Elsa la Rose* is in a way a similar project of re-invention and re-creation with a pair of accomplices: Agnès and Elsa. Both women have a significant role in shaping the film. Triolet's eloquent wit is obvious when she tells us what she remembers of the first time that she laid eyes on Aragon. His black suit 'as shiny as a piano' and his almost too good looks made her think he was a professional dancer ('un danseur d'établissement') rather than a writer or poet. In this film about memory and creation, Elsa will not let herself be relegated to a silent shadow over Aragon's shoulder; she is much more than the mythical rose of the title. Both her voice and Varda's voice take part in the polyphonic whirlwind of the film, which is also inflected by Michel Piccoli's recitation of Aragon's verse and Alain Ferrat's song 'Que serais-je sans toi?' (composed in 1966 by Ferrat but based on Aragon's poem).

Instead of making a classical biographical documentary, Varda embraces the idea of a documentary like a six hand piano composition which is complex and multi-layered. The film is not about Aragon's work even if by the end of *Elsa la Rose* the spectator gets a sense of the content and style of his writing, and that in spite of Piccoli and Ferrat's contrasting styles of delivery. Nor is it a fictional and rosy-looking opus on love and poetry. Many surrealists, including André Breton (a close friend of Aragon) idealised and glorified women, as if they were divinities. Many of Aragon's love poems depict Elsa as beautiful and inspirational, but there are glimpses in the film of some of the material compromises that he had to make, like becoming a journalist to earn a decent wage after too many poor and *bohème* years in Montmartre. Aragon is clear about the fragile nature of love in 'L'Amour qui n'est pas un mot', a poem recited by Piccoli, when he writes: 'c'est miracle que d'être ensemble' ('It is miraculous that we are together'). Love is fragile and precious but above all it is a collection of down to earth decisions and material events. When asked whether the poems that Louis has written for her make her feel loved, Elsa is unequivocal: they do not. It is daily life rather than poetry which makes her feel loved. The final section of the film is explicit when it comes to this utopian idea of love. Aragon's voice tells us that we might see this film as a modern fairy tale, but it also reminds us that fairy tales are only malleable and ever changing fictions with artificial resolutions like 'Ils se marièrent et vécurent longtemps heureux comme dans tous les contes' ('they got married and lived happily ever after, like in all fairy tales'). Aragon's commentary at the end of the film is honest: this film is only one of the possible versions of Elsa, the lover he has imagined for the last thirty eight years, but this version is not representative of Elsa the imaginative creator of characters and fiction who has been working alongside him for all these years. If the film was turned over its head, as Aragon suggests at the end ('Si, si... If, if...'), then he would probably become one of the minor characters of her books and as an audience we would experience something altogether different.

From the start, the whole enterprise is not about the pure knowledge of someone else, but about the exploration of multiple versions of a single event and about the passing of time. It is an essayistic piece shifting between fiction, documentary and aesthetic experiment. The re-enaction of the day they meet is, for instance, much more of a self-reflexive performance with a slightly comical twist than an attempt to recapture the past magic of that event. How many times can we see Elsa going through the swing

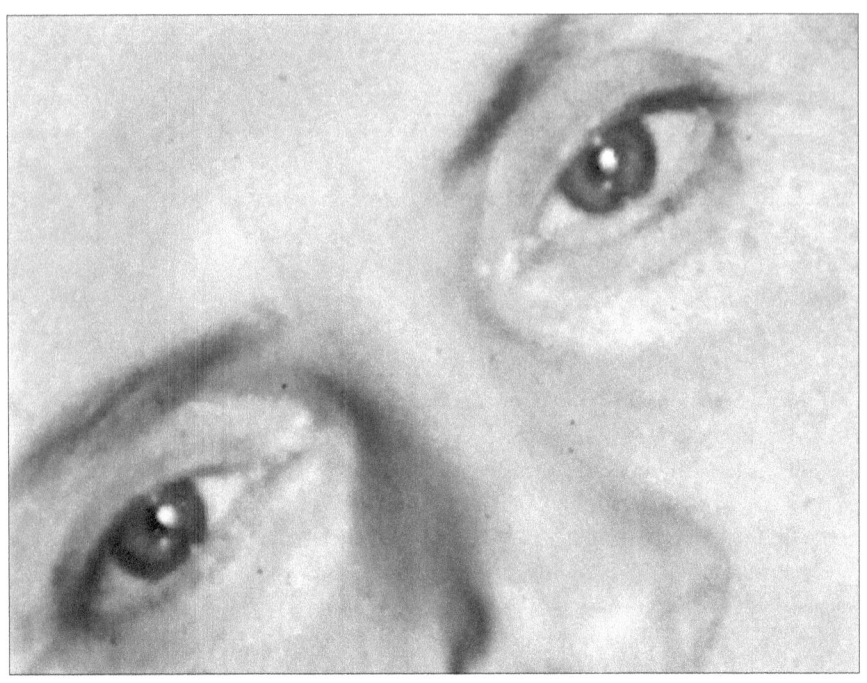

One of the many close-ups on Elsa's face, here the focus is on her beautiful yet mysterious gaze

door and Louis playing with a dice at the bar before it becomes clear that no representation can ever be truthful? Luck plays a part in their meeting, as Aragon mentions that they had missed each other in Berlin a few years earlier. The revolving door they go through several times, separately and then together becomes a symbol of time, chance and change. The mirrors and photos inside their home and Varda's attempt to capture the vitality of Elsa with multiple close-ups of her face and eyes reinforce the idea that our true selves often remain a mystery to others. The fast-paced editing of a number of photos of Triolet shows that however close they are, Elsa remains a mystery even when Aragon asks her on camera what she is thinking about. Seeing Elsa and Louis's gestures towards each other when together reveals their enduring affection. At the same time, misunderstandings are often played out. During an interview, he mocks the fashion sense of her sister's lover, the famous futurist Vladimir Mayakovsky. She answers that the photo of him on the wall is out of date and that to her he looked like an extremely tall Jean-Paul Belmondo, handsome and impressive. Anecdotes are part of the narrative, but the film as a whole does not concentrate only on the personal. Many of the changes that affected the couple are correlated with important historical changes. The year 1933–34 associated at first by Aragon's voice-over with the beginning of his career (and salary) as a journalist is connected visually with Berlin and the fire of the Reichstag. The long travelling sequence during one of his walks in sunny Paris with Elsa on his arm is in strong contrast with the short scenes that follow where violent demonstrations, Hitler and battles appear. Aragon was involved in politics and he was a supporter of communism and Stalinism, two movements which turned out to be a terrible deception for many intellectuals in France. Aragon's passionate love for Elsa is juxtaposed with the cruel conflicts in Germany and Spain. The vertigo of love is the one the film concentrates on, but these short sections also justify some of his decisions and positions in the past, making sense *a posteriori*. Here, he is a passionate and immoderate individual both in love and politics.

In *Elsa la Rose*, images and words are assembled in a vertiginous way to mimic the entangled layers of lived experience and one of the innovative and surprising choices in the film is the way it invites the audience to inflect the narrative. In the last long interview with Elsa in the garden, we are left to decide what to make of the shadow and presence behind her, of the handwritten captions 'Vous prenez tout cela pour une allégorie, vous ne m'entendez pas' ('You think all this is an allegory, you don't hear me') and of the silent sequence that follows where we see Elsa and Louis chatting, smiling and simply enjoying time together. Piccoli's hurried recitation does not help us, he is not a literary *bonimenteur*. The poems he reads add to the dense layers of images and ideas that we are exposed to. They do not clarify the images but intensify our attention, or if lost for sense make us cling to what we see as potentially more reliable. This continual exchange between the performers, creators, and audience is what makes *Elsa la Rose* unorthodox and impressive to this day. Refusing to freeze Elsa into a silent muse or to pin her down as the ultimate rose, Varda plays with Aragon's text like she did in *L'Opéra Mouffe* with vertiginous cascades of free associations, between, for instance, a rose, an artichoke, a sea urchin and a gypsum rose. This film is not a classic biographic documentary since it incorporates contradictions and abounds in sponta-

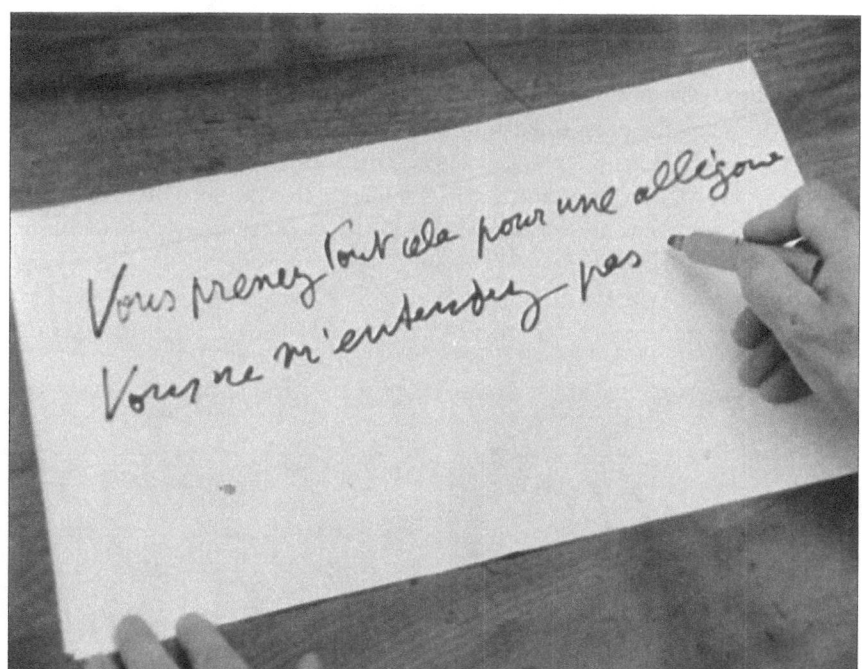

Aragon's handwriting interlude, or a trace of his inability to communicate with his interlocutors

neous digressions. It is a free spirited invocation by Aragon of 'mon univers, Elsa, ma vie' ('my universe, Elsa, my life'), as well as a fragmented and poetic attempt to engage the audience through images, music and emotions.

2: Unorthodox Structures and Practices of Production

Uncle Yanco and *Les Glaneurs et la glaneuse* were made many years and many miles apart, but they both demonstrate Varda's unusual and at times surprisingly spontaneous conception of filmmaking. *Uncle Yanco* is a twenty minute film shot over three days (October 27–30 1967) in Sausalito Bay before Varda has to fly back to France. She had heard about Jean (or Yanco) Varda from Tom Luddy whom she had met at the San Francisco Film Festival. Her reading of Henry Miller's profile titled 'Varda the Master-Builder' had also made her curious to meet this potential relative.[4] Yanco Varda was a painter and a teacher who lived with many others in a houseboat community full of strange and wonderful constructions. He is indeed a distant relative (since he is the cousin of her father Eugène) and one that Varda adopts very quickly by referring to him as 'Uncle Yanco' as if she was a kind of prodigal niece. Beyond these family ties, it is obvious that Yanco and Agnès share a mutual love of stories, colours and fantasy. The film is a joyful celebration of their reunion and experience together. Like *La Pointe Courte*, *Uncle Yanco* portrays a specific community, but in this film there is no Parisian counterpoint; the film gravitates around the central, patriarchal and hospitable figure of Yanco. He seems open to new encounters and glad to interact with people from all walks of life. He happily gives the director a nautical tour of the extraordinary houseboats near his own and invites her to a communal Sunday meal in his house. Varda is keen to leave traces of the making of the film like in *Elsa La Rose*. She re-plays with visible pleasure their first meeting in several languages and enjoys performing their first embrace behind various colourful filters in the shape of hearts. Here again there are multiples references to the place and time of the shooting, i.e. California at the height of the hippie movement, like the footage of demonstrations against the Vietnam war and love sit-ins. Hippie culture rejected materialism, competition, militarism in favour of communal love, illicit drug-induced ecstasy and non-Western philosophies and spiritualities (see Starr 1985: 238–41). San Francisco was in 1967 at the centre of this counter-cultural movement and the place where the

Varda's playful use of filters during the re-enactment of her family reunion in red (left) and an embrace with Yanco in yellow (right)

Yanco draws a family tree and establishes family connections for both Varda and the spectator

'Summer of Love' took place. In *Uncle Yanco*, the filmmaker decides, however, to refer to this movement obliquely. She is not filming sit-ins or demonstrations like in *Black Panthers*. It is when she films Yanco taking a big group of young people on his boat for a pleasure cruise, or when he walks around and stops to show her how this house is a place where love, music and art is made and discussed, that we clearly see how he belongs to that particular place and time.

Many sections of the film are funny and irreverent, like when Yanco appears as a modern day Pythia behind a bright red window that a child opens every time he comes up with an unexpected prophetic prediction. Agnès and Yanco's free-flowing dialogue seems to alternate between his musings on various subjects including art and politics and her questions that he either answers or laughs off. When she remarks that her father never talked of his family and had probably forgotten that he was Greek altogether, Yanco draws an ornate family tree for her. In a reciprocal movement, Varda inserts two shots of their daughters, establishing a continuity and parallel between their lines. Having elucidated their bloodline, they start to explore their imaginary lineage and Yanco explains that he can never be '*un oncle d'Amérique*' (an expression in French which refers to a wealthy, distant relative who is willing to pay off your debts or help financially). Dressed up as a caricature of a cowboy, with a white hat, red tie and jacket, he looks like a comical version of himself especially since we have only seen him wearing bright pink and yellow clothes until now. Agnès and Yanco's status as accomplices telling a story together is obvious when he shoos her off to have a nap, his sign 'Do Not Disturb Siesta Time' in full view. Even in the sequences where he is supposedly having a rest on his bed, he agrees to address her questions. During one of these conversations, he remarks that she should stop worrying about questions bigger than herself. His semi-cryptic answer using Cocteau's opinion on life and death is to say the least personal: 'La vie, la mort, c'est comme les catastrophes de chemin de fer,

Yanco dressed up as a rich American uncle (left); Yanco in his usual attire (right)

comme Cocteau a dit, ça ne s'explique pas, ça se sent' ('Life, death, like railway catastrophes, as Cocteau said, they can't be explained, they can only be felt').[5] Yanco's reference to Cocteau shows his rejection of over-intellectualism in favour of sensual experiences both in work and life, an interesting point when paralleled with what the film achieves. Varda's colour filters and close ups on Yanco's bright paintings, the patchwork of rock'n'roll and traditional Greek music, and Yanco's oftentimes cryptic maxims are combined to produce a sunny documentary celebrating imaginary families, which is both unorthodox and radical.[6]

While *Uncle Yanco* was made urgently as a personal tribute to her uncle, *Les Glaneurs et la glaneuse* is a more elaborate project/film in which time was obviously invested to offer an inclusive and dialogic result. Because this film was produced by her company Ciné-Tamaris, Varda was able to take her time and to take to the road on numerous occasions to meet people in different locations including the North of France, Beauce, Jura, Provence, Pyrénées Orientales and Paris and its suburbs. It is a truly peripatetic road movie if one looks at the regions it covers. *Les Glaneurs et la glaneuse* was very successful and received many critical awards. It is also notable for its popularity with an audience that did not know Varda's work before seeing this film. One can assume that it benefited from the fact that at that time documentaries were making a 'comeback' in France and that a return to realism and to the political was also apparent (see Powrie 1999).[7] The defining characteristic of new realism, identified as 'an [...] engagement with social realities, inhabiting an uneasy middle ground between the ethnographically dispassionate and the dramatically compassionate' (Powrie 1999: 16) is evident in *Les Glaneurs et la glaneuse*. Varda's interest in modern day gleaners testifies to her lingering interest in those considered by society as outsiders and misfits. In this film she seeks out ignored individuals to allow them to share their experience with those who are less in need. But there is another side to this project which offers a counterpoint to these images of suffering. For Tyrer, they form 'the other side of the film's structural dialectic, constituting a discourse of digressions [...] moments in which Varda discovers 'beauty' in the lives and looks of *marginaux* [...] in the heart-shaped potatoes that she gleans [...] and of course in the various works of art that she encounters' (2009: 170). As exemplified by this passage, Varda's film also generated a number of scholarly publications, some interested in the politics of the project (see Tyrer 2009), others in different aspects such as the portrayal of old age (see Beugnet 2006, Rosello 2001). When Beugnet describes *Les Glaneurs et la glaneuse* as 'a hybrid of essay, documentary proper, road movie and diary' (2006: 4), she points to the difficulty one encounters when trying to categorise Varda's work. In this section, I will restrict my focus to Varda's unorthodox structuring of her film(s) and her constant consideration of the audience and participants since they are manifestations of her original *cinécriture*.

When Varda started shooting for this project in September 1999, very little was planned in advance and she spent eight months on and off the road to find gleaners willing to take part in this adventure. When asked about the making of the film, Varda recognises that luck played a huge role in the shooting schedule because she did not have a list of gleaners handy (see Varda and Meyer 2001). She asked her assistants and acquaintances to tell everyone they knew about her intended project and to contact any peasant, fruit grower, farmer or owner who might know some gleaners. Sometimes this quest almost turned into a detective story, where Varda would track a particular individual she had heard about like François, the defiant and charismatic gleaner who claims that he has managed without buying any food for years. Her scouting is also meticulous if scarily un-selective. When she drove, she would look for trailers and occasionally stop to ask people for someone who did not exist. She would carry on until this odd conversation starter would lead to an invitation to sit down and maybe have a drink or a coffee. She would then look around and explain that she was a documentarian and that she would like to chat with them for a little longer, and maybe even record them, either on that day with her little digital camera or at a later date with her team (see Varda and Anderson 2001: 24–7). Many people answered positively and these wide-ranging fragments of conversation ended up being part of the material she had at her disposal when she decided to edit the film into a coherent whole.

Some encounters led to unplanned scenes during the shooting of the film. In the beginning of the film, her interview with a group of potato farmers makes her realise that many end up dumping important amounts of perfectly edible potatoes, because they do not fit the commercial gauge, or were cut by machines during the sorting process. When these farmers tell her that people regularly follow their trucks to pick some of these discarded potatoes, she is no doubt hopeful and not ready for the letdown of reality: only one person is there on that day and he is there purely by chance. Ignoring her bad luck, Varda starts filming this man, suddenly interrupts him and enters the frame to grab a potato in the shape of a heart which will become for many the symbol of her film. She then proceeds to pick as many as she can and brings them back home to film them from up close, when abruptly, in one of her typical puns, she realises that these would be great for people going to 'les restaurants du coeur', a charity which provides meals for people in need. So she calls them up and tells them where the dumping site is for aesthetic and politic reasons so that they can collect hundreds of kilos of potatoes and she can film a group of people gleaning food together. As these volunteers (who are also beneficiaries) pick the potatoes, she asks them questions that will feed into the movie. This expedition would never have occurred had she not followed on a whim the tractors and trucks, and had she not stayed with the isolated gleaner who found her first heart-shaped potato. This chain of events makes visible how decisive time and chance are when Varda undertook this film. With a set schedule and detailed script, this could not have happened. For this lucky break to occur, one that also leads her to meet Claude M. (who lives all year round in a trailer with no electricity, and to whom she devotes a long sequence) Varda needs flexibility, openness and a fluidity in her approach. She is happy, for instance, to leave heavy material to film at home and scout with a small digital camera. Her willingness to abandon high-end film equipment in favour of low-end digital video is unusual since one could expect a filmmaker of her stature to be more selective or demanding. She justifies this decision in interviews by saying that the development of cheap and functional digital cameras prompted her to try them out in the hope that it would give her as much freedom as she had when she worked independently on projects like *L'Opéra Mouffe*: 'The third reason which pushed me to begin and continue this film was the discovery of the digital camera. I picked the more sophisticated of the amateur models (the Sony DVCAM DSR 300). I had the feeling that this is the camera that would bring me back to the early short films I made in 1957 and 1958. I felt free at that time. With the new digital camera, I felt I could find myself, get involved as a filmmaker' (Varda and Anderson 2001: 24).

After it was released, the film was so successful that Varda started receiving letters and presents as modest as potatoes shaped like hearts and as elaborate as artistic collages. A lot of people did not seem to mind her personal or aesthetic digressions in the final cut of the film (the diaristic and self-reflexive parts on aging and cinema) but felt compelled by them. It seemed that she had found a perfect balance between the objective and the subjective, two supposedly opposite tendencies of cinema that she tries to reconcile in many of her films: 'Her inquisitive corporeal presence in front of and behind the camera endows her films with an aura of subjective honesty. Her conspicuous physical involvement in the image-seizing process evinces cognition beyond that of distracted and anaesthetized spectatorship' (Chrostowska 2007: 130). This success led to the making of two corollary films: *Deux Ans Après* and *Post-Filmum* (2002) which need to be considered as they were made as a response to the audience of *Les Glaneurs et la glaneuse* and as a follow up to the experience of Varda and the participants.

Deux Ans Après was made two years after *Les Glaneurs et la glaneuse* but was not conceived as a money-making sequel meant to milk the success of the first film. Like *Les Glaneurs et la glaneuse* it proceeds by short bounds, by fragments, separated by intertitles. These sections can be watched chronologically but they can also be accessed from *Les Glaneurs et la glaneuse* by clicking on the blinking heart-shaped potato button located in the top right corner of the screen. This ingenious device gives the viewer the option to travel in time and space (unfortunately only forward) to see what has happened to some of the participants after the release of the film. In its introduction, Varda quickly glosses over the awards and prizes ('ces machins') that the film received and declares that she wants to acknowledge them in order to move on to more meaningful rewards: the letters and gifts. From the folder full of letters she received, she takes out a few and thanks everyone. She then selects an elaborate collage made with the paper case of a train ticket, and a cinema and tube ticket and asks: 'Qui donc m'écrit dans un wagon?' ('Who's writing to me from a train?'). In an instant, as if by magic, she is off with a train ticket of her own to meet the couple who wrote to her and capture their impressions in the flesh and on film. Reviving the tradition of the *ciné-club* (but on an intimate scale), a practice at its peak when she started making films, she meets Delphine and Philippe in Trentemoult, listens to them talk about their work as art workshop leaders, asks them questions about the film and spends the day with them. The filmed interview focuses on their dialogue, on their hands and smiling faces, on their hospitality and thoughtfulness. After this sequence, Varda returns home to more letters and tells us that many people were touched by the situation, and by the choices made by François F. She still sees him regularly, often offering him a coffee after he has gleaned at the market. In the interview that follows, she incorporates his dissonant and opinionated views. François does not sound bitter that his situation has not changed and he even seems genuinely surprised that more people have bought the Big Issue-type of magazine he sells at Montparnasse station, presumably recognising him. Varda explains that he was paid sporadically by theatre owners to come and talk with the audience at the end of screenings of *Les Glaneurs et la glaneuse*. What follows is an animated debate about the merits of the film between him, Varda (as she is filming) and a lady who was about to enter the station and caught their conversation. François liked the film but did not appreciate Varda's self-reflexive vignettes and tells her that he found them unnecessary. The woman starts arguing with him and tells him that in her opinion Varda remains unobtrusive and a welcome addition which increased her pleasure when she rewatched the film recently. The discussion moves on to his activity as a volunteer literacy teacher and ends on a more peaceful note when the woman tells him that she is grateful for the opportunity to see people like him, who make her want to be better and to pay attention to others ('Ça nous donne envie d'être meilleur, de faire attention aux autres').

This section and those that follow repeat the *modus operandi* of *Les Glaneurs et la glaneuse* where Varda is gleaning impressions and experiences one after the other. In this second opus, she is still keen to present the work of artists like Macha Makeïeff and Michel Jeannès (Monsieur Bouton) but alternates these sequences with sections where she chats with some of the gleaners that she had filmed in *Les Glaneurs et la glaneuse*. In doing so, she accomplishes two unorthodox things. First, inspired by the effusive mail she received, she offers her spectators a paratext (or rather parafilm), an addenda that lets us see how these people are doing, how they have changed, and what they have experienced since the film has come out. Varda films Gislaine and Claude M. whom she had met in their trailers. Both still live precariously, and both still drink though according to them only occasionally. Gislaine says that she can go without a drink for five or six days; compared to her previous consumption of ten to fifteen bottles of rosé a day, this is an achievement. Like a shy schoolgirl, she also reveals that she has fallen in love and that if things are not perfect, they have nevertheless changed for the better since they last met. She feels better and more in control, rather than lost and powerless. The second unusual achievement of *Deux Ans Après* is the shape of the film itself, which becomes a contemporary *cadavre exquis* (exquisite corpse), a game created by the Surrealists. The principle of this game was to gradually collect images and words that would be assembled into an unexpected surreal whole. Through images, music and spoken words, Varda elaborates a rich and touching film, in which she incorporates her own experience of aging, grieving and sharing. When she follows François, who is running the Paris marathon with thousands of others, or when she films a demonstration against the Front National (an extreme right wing political party then led by Jean Marie Le Pen) 'the movement of the film is decisively into the public arena' (Corrigan 2011: 75). By reaching outward and by expanding on questions and issues evoked in the first film, Varda demonstrates her willingness to learn from others and to embrace chance while remaining true to herself, that is to say politically engaged and emotionally sensitive to the world and people surrounding her.

The DVD of *Les Glaneurs et la glaneuse* is a perfect example of Varda's atypical conception of cinema, a conception open to new avenues and presented with humour. Besides *Les Glaneurs et la glaneuse* and *Deux Ans Après*, the DVD includes a set of additional *boni* full of surprises: a 'Petit musée des Glaneuses' (little museum of gleaners) which contains paintings and drawings often commented on, a section with legal texts about the practice of gleaning (from the Bible to the Napoleonic code), a short tribute to Zgougou, Varda's cat who was given to her by Sabine Mamou, and a *Post-Filmum* or final instalment of the director's 'wandering road documentary'.[8] The *Post-Filmum* piece subtitled: 'Les derniers arrivages (un peu cassés), patate ultime-sublime et fin' lasts less than a minute and could be interpreted as a conclusive audio-visual triptych. In a slow tracking shot to the right, Varda films the latest gifts that she was sent: (three gleaner motif plates, two of which are cracked) laid on a red tablecloth while we hear bird song including that of a nightingale. Is the use of these songs intended to suggest the renewal that spring brings about or to suggest through the date (July 2002) that we should enjoy summer for the few weeks that it lasts? This certainly depends on how optimistic the viewer is. A fade to black marks the transition to the final and sublime heart shaped potato ('la patate ultime-sublime'), all dried up and shrivelled against a dark brown and earthy looking fabric. Finally Varda's unmistakable voice proves one more time that she has a way with words as she gives us her version of 'That's all folks!': 'Cette fois-ci, c'est tout à fait fini!' As in the rest of Varda's project, this final instalment, which takes the shape of a pastoral, meditative still life does not provide definitive answers or solutions. Neither didactic nor utopian, *Les Glaneurs et la glaneuse*, *Deux Ans Après* and *Post Filmum* offer the audience an opportunity to witness a wide range of gleaning practices and raises political and aesthetic questions; it opens a dialogue between the people involved and the public sphere and expands outward encouraging us to reconsider the humanitarian and ecological issues it tackles like homelessness and overconsumption.

3: Varda's Carnal Cinécriture

While the previous section focusing on *Uncle Yanco* and *Les Glaneurs et la glaneuse* intended to underline Varda's unorthodox production practices, it also established the director's desire to converse with the spectators of her films. To touch the spectators, Varda does not resort to easy processes of identification with charming protagonists, whose psychology is transparent and straightforward. She likes her characters to remain nebulous, independent and potentially surprising, and says so frequently.[9]

Mona in *Sans Toit ni Loi* and Viva in *Lions Love (…and Lies)* (1969) are perfect examples of characters who remain until the end of the films puzzling and obscure. Many of Varda's protagonists, as Hayward remarks, defeat categories and stereotypes: 'Mona assumes her filth just as she assumes her marginality, she answers to no one and thanks no one. In so doing she creates her own image and simultaneously destroys "the Image of Woman"' (1990: 271). So what does Varda do to make us react and to move us? What elements are key to her *cinécriture*? In 'Soi et l'autre: Les Glaneurs et la glaneuse', Claude Murcia explains that *Les Glaneurs et la glaneuse* inscribes the most marginal of the gleaners into an egalitarian and democratic patchwork which is valuable because of its diversity (2009: 44). She explains why reciprocity goes hand in hand with equality and comments on the importance of the bodies of participants as a means to make the other exist on screen: '*Les Glaneurs et la glaneuse* est un film qui fait exister l'autre. Dans son corps, dans sa parole, dans sa 'vive voix'. […] Dans le film d'Agnès Varda, chaque protagoniste existe dans sa corporéité et dans sa singularité' (Murcia 2009: 46). The corporeality and singularity of each participant is central to this project but it also resonates with other films by Varda. Corporeality is at the core of what I would call Varda's cinema of interpellation. Like other forms of enunciational address, such as the direct gaze into the camera, an offscreen voice or intertitles, the bodies of the people on screen call our attention. Looking at the forms of address and the bodies calling for our attention in three very different films: *Ydessa, les ours et etc.*, *Réponses de Femmes* and *7p., cuis., s. de b., … à saisir* will help in defining Varda's carnal *cinécriture* which I believe is based on an embodied vision of the world.

(A) *Interpellation and 'Conversation croisée' in Ydessa, les ours et etc.*

When Varda saw Ydessa Hendeles's exhibition 'Partners, The Teddy Bear Project' in 2003 at the Haus der Kunst in Munich, she was taken aback by the scale of the project. Almost immediately she decided that she needed to meet the person behind the show, and to interview visitors to discover whether their reactions matched the intensity of hers. Varda's curiosity and original shock thus compelled her to make the documentary *Ydessa, les ours et etc* I will argue that this initial reaction and the time she spent with Ydessa in Toronto are precisely what Varda, the director, wants us to experience. Through her editing of fragments of conversations with Ydessa and the visitors, and an embodied vision of the show, Varda proposes a perceptive visit and a reflection on art as a means to experience and understand the world.

Ydessa Hendeles was born in Germany in 1948, the only child of Jewish parents, both Holocaust survivors who emigrated to Canada when she was six. She is a passionate and charismatic Canadian collector, artist and curator who talks of her work in terms of 'curatorial composition' (Hendeles and Ferrando 2012). She is particularly sensitive to space and always thinks of a particular *mise en scène* for the objects she exhibits in her gallery and other museums.[10] For that particular show, Ydessa had purchased and collected, over several years, hundreds of old photographs of people with a teddy bear and displayed them from floor to ceiling in two rooms whose atmosphere was reminiscent of a library or archive room. The visitors therefore started with documentary

A general view of *Partners in Munich* with the vertiginous display of photos and the bears (left); the sculpture in the final room of the exhibition (right)

pieces: the photographs (generally grouped by affinities) and the display boxes with rare specimens of teddy bears. Each object contributes to the narrative that Hendeles is forging but it also holds a place in the composition as a whole. The visitor is free to watch the photos at her own pace, to ignore the ones that are either too high or too low, and the profusion of photos and saturation effect they create certainly encourages an intermittent attention. One thing that is set, however, is the order in which the visitor discovers the Teddy Bear Project. After the two rooms filled with photos, the visitor enters an empty room, in which the very realistic statue of a little boy, seen from behind, kneels in front of a bare wall, a work by Maurizio Cattelan called 'Him'. It is then a great shock to find that the little boy's face once you get to see it is that of Adolf Hitler. Now, the visitor must turn back and look at all he has just seen with new eyes. The teddy bear, a symbol of comfort and protection, has lost its innocence and the visitor must now reconsider the reasons behind the grouping of certain photos, the significance of juxtapositions, and the logic driving this exhibition, set in a museum opened in 1937 and built to Hitler's orders to exhibit Nazi-sanctioned art.

Varda's film, like Ydessa's exhibition, defers this final revelation and only discloses the content of the last room in the second half of the film. Until then Varda alternates between scenes and interviews in the first two rooms, conversations with Ydessa about her approach, still close ups of photos selected from the show, and mobile shots gliding over the photographs on display that suggest movement and mobility. The visit to Ydessa's exhibition we are invited to join in *Ydessa, les ours et etc* is based on the director's subjective recollection, it is a reconstruction of Varda's impressions after the fact but based on clips and close ups. Varda and Ydessa's sensibilities collide in the space of the gallery and in the film, and their ongoing conversation offers the spectator an opportunity to think about the idea of indirect or inherited memory. For Ydessa, the concept of inherited memory and family heirloom are particularly meaningful. Like many descendants of emigrant or deported Jews, Ydessa owns only one photo that pre-dates World War II (that of her grandmother) and she says that she misses this sense of visual roots and all the mythology that goes with family albums. On screen, she stresses the fact that she is not a survivor, but she states that she has inherited her parents' and grandparents' history. She cannot escape this legacy and her identity is bound for ever to her family's displacement and later immigration to North America. Like the visitors at the end of their journey trapped in the white room, she is defined by her past. The fact that the only photographs with a caption in these two rooms are those of Ydessa with a teddy bear and her parents identified as Holocaust survivors might have alerted some of the final shock to come, but this could also have simply been a way to point to the origin of the collection.

Varda's experience of World War II is different from Ydessa's. Her family emigrated from Belgium to Sète during the war, and when questioned about that period of her life she claims that she was unaware of what was happening, too young to even understand the activities of the resistance. Varda started working with Jean Vilar in Avignon in 1948 at the age of twenty, and trained previous to that as a photographer in Paris. So during these years (before she moved to rue Daguerre in 1951), Paris, a city still feeling the impact of the war and occupation, must have been an eerie experience for a young woman used to the quiet village of Sète. In her films, many Parisian characters (like Cléo or the pregnant woman of *L'Opéra Mouffe*) feel overwhelmed by the big city. The only war evoked in Varda's filmography though is that taking place in Algeria. In 2007 the French government asked her to conceive an installation commemorating in the Panthéon 'Les Justes', those French citizens who risked their lives to save Jewish people (often children) during the war. *Ydessa, les ours et etc* and this installation are therefore her only frontal confrontations with experiences and memories of war. Regardless of her personal circumstances or professional choices, Varda understands the haunting quality of World War II's emotional trauma if only because as someone who lived and worked in France at the time, her life became inextricably entangled with the legacy of the war and the memory of those who died.

Thomas Weski, the curator of the Haus der Kunst, speculates about Ydessa's initial motivation when collecting personal photos, and suspects that she was trying to compensate for her lack of personal mementos. Varda sounds less naïve underlining the fact that Ydessa has gone well beyond fashioning a fictional substitute. Rather, she sees Ydessa's photos as a giant panorama so rich and diverse that any visitor will be able to engage personally on one level or another with Ydessa's collection. A German visitor echoes her view when she says that she feels that the artist has assembled a monument to humanity's collective memory, and indeed how could we not see any links between ourselves and these figures of the past? But this fantasy of ourselves as sharing the same collective memory is allegedly hit hard by the last room's content. Forced to face the deeds of our recent history through such a potent figure, what will be our reaction? How will we turn back and face all these images again? What will this unexpected figure trigger? The visitors that we hear immediately after this revelation express disarray, discomfort and malaise. Varda illustrates this feeling of physical and mental oppression by superimposing their faces with that of the statue, which becomes an unforgettable and daunting shadow regardless of the nationality of the interviewees (French, German or American).

Varda trained as a photographer and she has never lost her eye for still images and composition. As her recent exhibitions show, she has not completely abandoned photography either, but continues to experiment with movement and stillness within and around the frame.[11] Ydessa is fascinated by the potential of photos, not just as works of art but as triggers and as meaningful artefacts of a time which is now past.

Her meticulous attention to assembling a series of photos is no doubt similar to that of Varda who worked on projects where still images gave rise to animated and moving sequences like in *Salut Les Cubains!* (1963) or *Ulysse* (1982). In the first conversation filmed between Ydessa and Varda, Ydessa is clear, she thinks of meaning and narrative when acquiring objects and artworks: 'What meaning can I pull out when I work with the objects that I choose [...] to make articulate visual contemporary art statements?' Like Varda then, she is a provocative story-teller and an animator of objects. She wants her gallery (or the museum she exhibits in) to become a space infused with discursive and emotive potential. Like Varda who constantly thinks of her spectators, she wants to trigger reactions, questions and debates. The provocative figure of Hitler is one means to get the visitors to react and engage with the material that they have viewed. To trigger reactions, Ydessa tries to build bridges between the visitor's mind and the works that she curates, between their bodies in the gallery and the space itself (as well as its history if there is a special one attached to it), between the past and the present. Varda and Ydessa are both '*passeuses*' and '*enchanteuses*' although I would argue that the tone of their works often differs. Ydessa is outspoken and determined when she presents what she does to Varda: 'My show deludes them [the visitors]: I create a fantasy world where everyone is happy, where everyone feels secured and has a teddy bear.' When she deludes her audience, Ydessa does what storytellers do whatever medium they work in. She takes various elements, assembles them in a particular, sometimes beautiful, sometimes challenging way to entice the viewer to look at reality differently, to affect them and move them.

In *Ydessa, les ours et etc.* Varda takes the role of a *bonimenteur*. She lets Ydessa speak but she also frames her, editing sequences carefully and modifies 'Partners' to engage the audience via purely cinematographic means. After a suspenseful journey to track down Ydessa, the mysterious 'woman with a name fit for a novel', she films a striking (and at first silent) slim, black figure against the white walls of her gallery in Toronto. Varda selects a series of photos from the show and time and again suggests narratives: 'Once upon a time, there was a brother and a sister'; 'in grammar school, all the boys were in love with their teacher'; or asks questions: 'like Jules and Jim maybe, who knows?' Varda even inserts herself in the Teddy Bear project by adding a photograph of herself as a child in a series of photos of little girls wearing bows in their hair. But she is quick to point out that she never owned a teddy bear and that this is a fantasy of hers, a *mise en abyme*. While she takes into account the reactions of various visitors, she also imposes her narrative and experience on the film.

Varda does not only encourage the spectator to listen to her stories, she also wants her to feel things alongside her by using fluid camera movements and close ups in and out of the exhibition that recreate her own sensations. To illustrate this point I will turn to two scenes which significantly frame the film. In the beginning of *Ydessa, les ours et etc.*, just after the credits, the camera takes us on a short un-narrated tour of the first two rooms of the exhibition. Isabelle Olivier's atmospheric harp music perfectly matches the slow and fluid movements of the camera, mimicking the gaze of a visitor which finally comes to rest on a display case containing a big, inoffensive looking teddy bear, sat on a chair under a light, a vignette that seems to say: 'lights –

camera – action!' This brief sensory-rich respite allows us to experience for ourselves what Ydessa's show feels like, right at the beginning of the film. In the rest of the film, Varda intends her voice and commentary to be both a guide and a reference, but here she voluntarily leaves us for a moment to invest this particular situation on our own terms. In the other scene, at the end of the film, we are in Ydessa's house while she works on a book based on her exhibition. Varda films Ydessa's busy activity in her huge kitchen and the dozens of photos lined up on the floor, and suddenly she becomes disoriented and dizzy. Like Alice in Wonderland who cannot find her bearings once she has stepped out of her familiar environment, Varda feels lost in front of this vertiginous project possessed by Ydessa's obsessive energy and her haunting exhibition. A series of high angle shots of Ydessa ordering her images over the geometric tiles of her kitchen and under lines of hanging kitchen utensils looks increasingly bizarre, like a sketch by Escher. The numerous shots at odd angles and the crescendo pace of editing refuse us any clarity until an increasingly unsteady and fast moving camera glides over the path of the images assembled on the floor, finally taking us to a similar series of straight lines, this time on the ceiling of the Haus der Kunst. Olivier's harp provides a sound bridge to the space of The Teddy Bear Project, its melody synchronised with the unsteady camera, thus evoking Varda's final word '*vertige*' (vertigo). When the camera eventually stops moving, this feeling of vertigo has not completely receded because the low lamps placed over the display cases and photos are still swinging in mad circles, forming a surreal ballet of luminous pendulums. The reference to Alice in Wonderland is certainly intentional on the part of Varda who has just presented to us another aspect of Ydessa's personal art collection full of oversized and tiny objects scattered around the massive mansion that she occupies by herself. The return to the walls of the gallery may bring the camera to a halt, but this stasis will not give us easy answers or any sense of a resolution. In this dreamlike and vertiginous sequence, built on masterfully edited sensory images and music, Varda reframes Ydessa's project and makes us experience her emotions as well as some of those expressed earlier by the visitors to the exhibition. This revisiting of her impressions combined with an appeal to our senses shows how Varda's films depend on a *carnal cinécriture* based on an embodied vision and on a network of corporeal images ('des images qui naissent dans le corps') (Varda quoted in Bastide 2009: 18) that need to be elucidated.

In this documentary, we are called to take part in a sensory 'conversation croisée' (or double dialogue) where Varda and Ydessa are partners and directors of their own work. Both try to guide the viewer and both are interested in provoking and shocking her with unusual assemblages of images that will affect her physically. Soliciting the spectator via movement and stasis around the images, informing us how we see, or temporarily ignore what we see is part of their common objective. How could we not notice the guns and weapons held by the children, the soldiers, and the sports team reminiscent of those who filled the ranks of the army and the ghettoes? Varda has the final cut of *Ydessa, les ours et etc.* so it might be hard to see this documentary as a collaboration between equal partners, but it is definitely a striking and provocative conversation, a moving reconstruction and an invitation to let complex works of art affect us intellectually and physically. Via this sensory exploration of different times and spaces, Varda endeavours to connect us with a history that may not be our own, to touch us and to encourage us to re-think our engagement with art and its multiple narratives. In the end, we may not be sure about what to answer when asked at the end of the film 'Qui regarde qui?' ('Who is looking at who?') but we have learnt that we can and should all engage productively and creatively with the mystery of the still and moving images surrounding us both inside and outside of the gallery.

(B) *Manifesto, Interpellation and Action in Réponses de Femmes*

In 1968, a group of French film directors including Chris Marker, Alain Resnais and Jean-Luc Godard decided to take revolutionary action by making short black and white silent films that would be numbered and anonymous yet highly personal (each director was to self-produce and self-edit). Those short films were militant in their message and distributed outside of the commercial circuit to like-minded audiences. Many were filmed during the demonstrations and events of May 1968 and most opposed the vitality of young militants to the old conservative bourgeois order epitomised by De Gaulle's government. They were conceived as an alternative form of news, a new form of agit-prop and an encouragement to this momentum of change. Varda was not in France in May 1968 so she did not contribute to this corpus. She may have been friends with Marker and Resnais but as mentioned earlier she was a bit of an outsider and her prior involvement in a group project (with *Loin du Vietnam*) did not amount to much.[12]

So what is exactly *Réponses de Femmes* which is described in the credits as 'un cinétract d'Agnès Varda'? This eight minute film was made for Antenne 2, a French television channel, to celebrate women since the United Nations had decided that 1975 would be International Women's Year. Its description as a *cinétract* is deceiving since, however militant, it is produced well after the canonical corpus of French *cinétracts*. *Réponses de Femmes* is therefore an unorthodox *cinétract* both in its form and in its content. Formally it deviates from the 1968 corpus since it is shot in colour, relies heavily on the participants' voices, identifies categorically Varda as its author and is made for television.[13] In terms of content, it is also different for two reasons: first it focuses on the experience of women in the mid-1970s (and does not focus on 1968 as a foundational date), and second, it is blunt and provocative in its approach to the body, women's rights and female experience. In the 1970s, activists had won important battles like the legalisation of birth control in 1967 and the de-criminalisation of abortion in January 1975 but many feminists thought the conditions and rights of women in France could still improve. At the time, Varda was involved in the feminist movement and signed in 1971 the famous 'manifeste des 343', one of the texts that generated outrage but initiated debates and changes in the legal system. It is therefore important to underline that feminism constituted a pervading topic during this decade and a personal preoccupation for Varda.

The instigators of the television series 'F comme femme' had asked Varda and several other women including lawyers, historians, sociologists, and filmmakers: Qu'est ce qu'être une femme? What does it mean to be a woman? Very quickly Varda

The cast of *Réponses de Femmes* includes a wide variety of participants: some young, some old, some naked and some dressed

decided that she wanted to make a pragmatic rather than theoretical film about 'Notre corps, notre sexe' ('our body our sex'). To drive the point home, Varda filmed a variety of women, often but not always naked, an element that some found excessive.[14] In this *cinétract*, there are many naked bodies, some young (including an infant) and some old but, like Orpen I would not call any of these nudes 'titillating' (2007: 71). The women we see are staged and often posing for the camera in elaborate compositions. When they move, which is rare, the blank space of the studio behind them, the recurring intertitles and their gaze at the camera make it impossible for the viewer to ignore that their bodies convey a message. What in retrospect seems more shocking to film and feminist studies specialists today is the essentialist view that Varda seems to endorse. Kate Ince pinpoints this when she writes: 'For the majority of critics writing in the 1970s and 1980s, the very notion of a "feminism of the body" was biologically essentialist, and rendered problematic Varda's evidently positive pleasure [...] in representing the gestating or artistic female body' (2012: 13). The opening question in *Réponses de Femmes* and its immediate answer: 'Qu'est ce qu'être une femme? C'est naître dans un corps de femme' ('What does it mean to be a woman? It is to be born in a woman's body') seems to be in direct opposition with De Beauvoir's influential phrase: 'On ne naît pas femme, on le devient' ('One is not born, but rather becomes, a woman') in *The Second Sex*. I would argue, however, that the questions evoked through the body in this very short film such as 'Do all women want to become mothers?' are timely and discerning. These questions address and challenge the ways in which the female body is perceived, represented and treated by society and the media. The bodies on screen force spectators to question their views and their position in society: are we objectifying women on a day to day basis? Are they oppressed by stereotypes and if so how? When do we, as a society, start imposing reductive and retrograde *clichés* on children, and is formal education an accomplice? Are legal changes adding challenges for women by separating reproduction and sexuality? Why is it that people react so strongly to the naked bodies of pregnant or older women? And are things really changing in the public arena? In this film, Varda is not ignoring Simone de Beauvoir's work but she wants to remind the viewers that the female body has never been and will never be neutral: it carries certain values, it is taught by various discourses and gestures how to behave, it is managed and controlled.[15] One of the crucial questions to consider is whether the female body can be set free, and if so, by whom? Varda does not present women in the 1970s as free, liberated and unhindered by society; the women she films are able to speak out but like the little girl who is heard repeating the same sentence twice, they can only hope that 'Maintenant ça va changer!' ('From now on, that's all going to change!').

Having established the feminist bias of this *cinétract,* one also needs to consider how it compares with other representations of the female body on screen. Antoine De Baecque summarises in his essay 'Écrans' (2006) how the cinematographic representation of the body has changed over time. Determining where Varda's film is situated on a historical continuum is an important question. In its early years, cinema represented bodies as spectacles and as sources of burlesque entertainment as in the films of Charlie Chaplin, Buster Keaton and Harold Lloyd. Then Hollywood started to create, control and promote a glamorous type of body through the figure of the *femme fatale* and its many incarnations on screen. It is later in the 1960s that modern cinema broke away with earlier and more traditional visions of the body. This modern body is different from its earlier sugar-coated and tamed versions. This unruly and liberated body becomes for new wave filmmakers and others a means to denounce the pseudo-realism of films made in studios. *Réponses de Femmes* is a fine example of modern cinema in that it presents women of all sizes and ages: the slow and silent tracking shot that gives us a chance to watch the participating women's faces (each '*tête de femme*') and the vox-pop section at the end of the film add to this impression of variety and uniqueness. At the same time, the film experiments with its own 'artiness' and draws attention to its construction with the sound of the clap and lingering presence of a technician in the frame. The particular style of delivery of the non-professional participants and the film's carefully scripted dialogue also points to Varda's careful *mise en scène* and *mise en texte* (script-writing). All these traces and markers tell us that we are watching a carefully crafted and polemical film, one that tosses ideas around and expects the audience to respond one way or another.

To interpellate the viewer, Varda does not only rely on bodies, she also experiments with the voices of the participants who repeatedly tease the audience as well as their interlocutors on screen: a fairly large and silent group of men identified at the end as 'Messieux les pères, les amants, les maris, les patrons, les mecs et les copains' ('dear fathers, lovers, husbands, bosses and buddies'). In the film, individual or choral delivery of statements like: 'Je ne suis pas limitée aux points chauds du désir des hommes!' ('I am more than the hot points of men's desire!') or 'Qu'est ce qu'un corps de femme si on doit toujours rendre compte de nos poids et mesure?!' ('What is a woman's body if we must always account for our weights and measures?') alternates with several off-screen voices, including that of Varda and an unidentified man. This man plays the role of the devil's advocate and has a hard time coping with the consequences of the feminist revolution of the 1970s: 'Continue comme ça! Plains toi! Bientôt tu cesseras de nous plaire!' ('Go on, keep complaining! Soon we'll no longer desire you!'). His reluctance to change does not bode well for the future, but in a last minute poetic twist Varda concludes on a more hopeful note. At the end of the film, she edits an unusual face-off between the group of men and the group of women, all dressed now, who having complained about their objectification declare that things need to change. The most radical of them then says 'je suis une femme, il faut réinventer la femme' ('I am a woman, women must be reinvented'), and the male off-screen narrator answers 'Alors il faut réinventer l'amour' ('Then love must be reinvented'). To this peculiar reworking of Rimbaud who claimed that love must be reinvented, the women answer in unison 'D'accord' ('Agreed').[16] By shifting the focus onto the ideological travesty of love, the director implicates society as a whole and suggests that joint responsibilities must be taken for significant changes to happen. *Réponses de Femmes* is split in terms of space between the perfect space of the studio and the chaotic building site behind the silent men. For things to change, the political ideals of women need to be debated by society as a whole including men. It is only through these animated discussions that a balance will be reached in the public sphere, away from the messiness of the building site and the all-too-perfect studio. This debate and issues are therefore a work in progress and as Varda concludes: 'À suivre donc' ('To be continued').

(C) *Sensations and Emotions in 7p., cuis., s. de b., ... à saisir*

The last film I want to discuss is like, *Ydessa, les ours et etc.*, a film that came about as a reaction to an exhibition. In 1984, in the building of Hospice St Louis in Avignon, Louis Bec was given free rein to set up an exhibition that he called 'Le vivant et l'artificiel'. Varda, remembering her reaction to the show, says that she was mesmerised: 'Un désir immédiat en découvrant l'exposition Le vivant et l'artificiel qu'avait organisée Louis Bec à Avignon et dont je me suis servie tout autant comme prétexte que comme motif, matière et décor. J'ai filmé comme on rêvasse' ('I was seized by a sudden desire when I visited Louis Bec's exhibition in Avignon 'The Living and Artificial Life' and used it as an excuse, a motif, a set of material and a film-set. I filmed it as if I was daydreaming') (Piguet and Varda 2007). Bec and his collaborators (Danièle Sanchez and Hervé Mangani among others) had made a unique use of space and brought unexpected elements into this former hospice including stuffed bears in the corridors, live lamas in the courtyard and turkeys in the kitchen. Anatomical wax models from the collection of the self-proclaimed doctor Pierre Spitzner which toured the fairgrounds of France and Belgium in the 1920s and 1930s were also displayed in various rooms, including his famous sleeping Venus. Inspired by her original experience and gut reaction, Varda makes a puzzling film which uses both this exhibition and the space of the hospice as starting points for an experimental *rêverie*.

Summarising *7p., cuis., s. de b., ... à saisir* is a challenging task even if the obvious common denominator between the sections of the film is the building of the title which is at first described in terms of an excellent real estate opportunity ('*à saisir*' is the explicit subtitle of the film). The offscreen voice of an estate agent talking about this house and its previous owners, a doctor and his wife, are the first elements we learn about, as a staircase and massive closed doors welcome us. The rest of the film will see many doors opening on a variety of vignettes, some narrated by the estate agent we never see, or by former occupants of the hospice, while some are performed by a family and their servant at different times of their life. The film is also punctuated by mysterious short tableaux which do not necessarily relate to the family plot but which evoke emotions associated with the building's various rooms. Based on the idea that these walls have a soul ('ces lieux ont une âme') and that in empty rooms, you can write your future but also get a sense of the past, Varda experiments with layering a number of vignettes through which we learn about the frustrations, love stories and daily life of the family and former occupants. In two separate episodes which I call 'conversations in bed', the doctor and his wife discuss what their life as young passionate parents feels like, and later how distant from each other and unsatisfied with their lives they have grown over the course of a decade. Scenes about their family life and brood of children are played by a mix of actors, non-professional participants, and wax figures. Yolande Moreau plays the last of the family's maids, while earlier servants are shown as a couple of wax figures presumably killed by syphilis or a disfiguring disease. Louis Bec assumes the role of the older doctor and is, I suspect, also the narrating estate agent. As a whole, the film is an unusual and provocative piece which I would describe as a kind of hallucinatory *rêverie*.

What I find of particular interest in relation to the rest of Varda's production and the notion of carnal *cinécriture* is the experimental layering of emotions and sensations that the director uses not only to tell an elusive set of stories, but to shock the spectator into reflection. In *7p., cuis., s. de b., ... à saisir* emotions indeed run high since the family goes fairly quickly from an idyllic unit to conflict and havoc, with at the centre of the dispute a rebellious young girl Louise (who has just turned eighteen) and her father Louis who is both authoritarian and uncompromising. Louise wants a job rather than family ('ce qu'il me faut c'est un métier et pas de famille'), and as she looks out the window she imagines the other life that is waiting for her outside ('Derrière ces platanes, il y a la vraie vie'). On the opposite end is her father, a former epicurean who has become a self-centred and conservative patriarchal figure who cannot bear the thought of his children being independent and autonomous outside of his control. The mother, although not inarticulate, does not seem particularly supportive of her children, partly because she too feels trapped in a life that she did not want.

This conflicting set of emotions is not easy to navigate because the vignettes are short and often cryptic. Like Spitzner's sleeping Venus, the mother looks calmly alive but there is no way for the spectator to know what emotions are at play inside her. Spitzner's wax model had a mechanical movement intended to emulate breath so

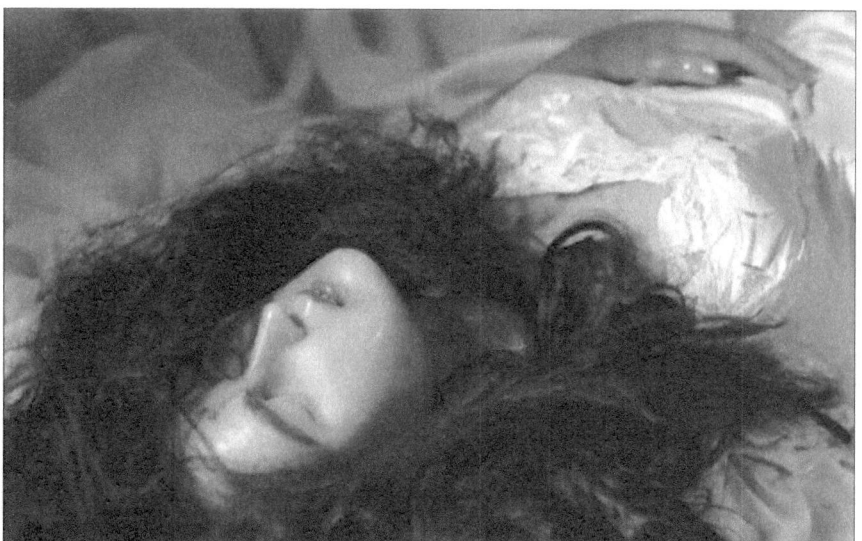

Spitzner's Sleeping Venus, an eerie wax model used in Varda's film

that her chest rose and fell as she lay on a bed in her white nightgown. Like many other anatomical waxworks, her body could be opened to reveal her organs to the scrutinising gaze of doctors-in-training or the audience of a fair. The comparison between the mother and this model (which straddles life and death in sleep) is all the more eerie because the audience knows that what leads to the sale of the property is a tragedy involving the mother which compelled the husband to leave the house with all his children. In the film, the mother remains an unresolved character, repeatedly associated with other wax figures including one of a woman having a Caesarean and delivering twins. Her indecipherability shows that individuals remain a mystery despite a detailed knowledge of their anatomy, reproductive organs or brain functions. They may express some of their emotions through dialogue, but they remain largely unknowable. Some of the most inventive lines in *7p., cuis., s. de b., ... à saisir* confirm this point, for instance, when the doctor tells a younger colleague: 'Je répète à l'envie un texte de systémique zoologicienne en conjugant des activités fabricatrices, déclamatoires, symboliques, fantasmatiques, gesticulatoires, testiculatoires, avec des activités logiques, rationnelles et axiomatiques' ('I'm doing a zoologistical sytemic that conjugates fabricatory, declamatory, symbolic, fantasmatic, testiculatoric acts with logical, axiomatable acts').

Besides the classic love/anger dynamic between the father and his daughter, and within the family more generally, there are a number of other emotions evoked in *7p., cuis., s. de b., ... à saisir* Sadness and resignation are expressed through other participants, such as the former residents of the hospice. Elderly people and former residents haunt the space of the house at regular intervals. Even if they left the premises years ago and belong to a fairly distant past, their presence and their voices remind the audience that this building is a receptacle for layers of different past experiences. In the beginning of the film, by their mere presence a group of old people make us question the imaginary harmony usually maintained between the soundtrack and the images. Sitting on chairs set up against the walls, they are all neatly dressed and silent in what could be the waiting room of a doctor's practice, but at the same time the slow tracking left on an elaborate display of white sculpted heads in the centre of the room, and Barbaud's violin make the scene both mysterious and uncanny. Some of these elderly people also appear unexpectedly in empty rooms, stating their attachment to the house they had to leave ('je ne voulais pas quitter cette maison'). They are either standing in the distance, as two tiny lines at the end of a long room, or their face appears over the walls while we hear their off screen voice. The short testimony of a previous occupant adds to the dizzying quality of the emotions that the audience is exposed to. She remembers the light filtering through the plane trees behind the windows and what it felt like to live in this space. Her careful diction and nervous tics make her effort to describe her memories all the more poignant. As an image and an incarnated voice, she is a striking but also fleeting repository of past memories. This array of mysterious and haunting emotions summoned by the house contributes to the hallucinatory nature of *7p., cuis., s. de b., … à saisir* They also complement the sensory triggers that Varda uses on numerous occasions and which need to be discussed to address the carnality of her *cinécriture*.

While many of the situations at hand in *7p., cuis., s. de b., … à saisir* necessitate an intellectual effort from the spectator, some only require an openness to the immediacy of images and sound. The emphasis on the senses in certain scenes illustrates the incarnate character of Varda's cinematographic vision. Sometimes she creates unexpected juxtapositions and transforms the space of the former hospice into a magical and eerie place. The kitchen empty and, as the estate agent claims, full of potential is turned into a wild garden, with grass on the hob, bright blue jelly and gurgling water in its pots and pans, and live turkeys gobbling and walking free. The collective bathrooms are transformed from austere whiteness to a plush Eden, where Adam is an infant lying in a tub full of feathers and Eve an old naked woman who is enjoying a shower of feathers before looking at us from a chair. In these extreme yet familiar places, Varda gives prominence to the corporeal dimension of cinema. She reinvents the standardised language of cinema, which usually 'appeals more to narrative identification than to bodily identification' (Marks 2000: 171). Sometimes she favours a less bold and more humorous evocation of sensations. In a memorable scene served by Moreau's wonderful acting, Varda jumps from sensation to word play to performance. In the green kitchen, the maid played by Moreau breaks eggs relentlessly and recites adages like 'Y'a pas d'omelette sans casser des oeufs' ('you cannot make an omelette without breaking some eggs') as if in a trance. At the end of the sequence, she spits in the container in front of her, explaining that 'Monsieur les aime bien baveuses!' ('The boss likes him omelettes runny', *baveuse* literally meaning dribbling in French). This conclusion echoes the rebelliousness of Louise, who seems to consider Yolande as an ally and a confidante, but the close up on her hands swishing the eggs around, and the noise of the slippery mixture privileges the material presence of the image, and interpellates the body of the spectator through this attention to sensations. In a quote where she discusses her use of colour, Varda confirms how a sensual apprehension of the real is at the core of her practice:

Two of the film's surreal tableaux: the semi-wild kitchen (left) and a plush Eden and its mature Eve (right)

'J'aime l'irrégularité des sensations colorées ou pas. Le cinéma c'est le mouvement des sensations' (quoted in Smith 1998: 26).

In the film as a whole, Varda refuses to separate body and mind and interpellates her audience through emotions and sensations. In all the scenes where we face the body in its variety of shapes and states, as it is, for instance, hurting, thinking, moving, loving, the director reminds us of cinema's materiality and she demonstrates its potential to jolt us into thinking. When she films silent and contemplative sequences, or edits Barbaud's music over eerie and haunting scenes, Varda also goes against more traditional uses of music and sound. She experiments with various associations, and explores textures and sensations on screen, from the softness of feathers to the pounding hearts of young lovers. Claudia Gorbman, who is an expert on the various uses of music and sound in film, describes utilitarian music as something that 'lulls the spectator into being an untroublesome (less critical, less wary) viewing subject' (2003: 40). In *7p., cuis., s. de b., ... à saisir* Varda, inspired by this space and its surreal *mise en scène*, creates an eerie *rêverie* that provokes the spectator and reasserts cinema's 'capacity to weave together the sensual and the conceptual' (Beugnet 2007: 60). She is not, like Noel Carroll argues of Hollywood movies, trying to achieve a 'flow of action [which] approaches an ideal of uncluttered clarity' (1998: 180). On the contrary, Varda's film is destabilising and provocative. It refuses to satisfy our desire for order and to create a fantasy of intelligibility through its assaults on our senses. Varda's carnal *cinécriture* reminds us that bodies and minds are splendidly complex and messy, as well as elusive and mysterious. In this hallucinatory *rêverie*, the camera probes different spaces, different times and different people, establishing symbolic connections while deconstructing relationships, but it does not achieve any sort of plenitude or transparency. What we face time and again in *7p., cuis., s. de b., ... à saisir* is our thwarted desire to see, to make sense of, and to master the world around us. The only way out of frustration and powerlessness may then be to accept and embrace that our 'consciousness is harnessed to flesh' (Sontag 2012: 86), an avenue that Varda explores many times in her work.

Notes

1   'Varda's filmmaking may best be understood, I would contend, as a performance of feminist phenomenology deriving from her woman-subject's desire, experience,

and vision, a carnal cinécriture she has now developed and refined for more than half a century' (Ince 2012: 14).

2   The website of l'INA (National audiovisual institute) contains several interesting joint interviews, see, for instance, http://www.ina.fr/video/CPF86644616 (accessed December 2012).

3   Aragon was born out of wedlock and was only told once he was an adult that his sister was his biological mother, and his godfather, after whom he had been named, his biological father Louis Andrieux. 'Un collier aux initiales d'autrui' ('a necklace bearing someone else's initials') is the way he refers to his father's legacy. This quote from *Le Roman inachevé* (1956: 400) shows the burden associated with biological links. His determination to do away with this kind of determinism was also obvious when from 1926, with the publication of *Le Paysan de Paris,* he removed his first name Louis from the covers of all his books.

4   Henry Miller and Yanco Varda supposedly met in the 1940s, and Miller later published in *Circle Magazine*, a magazine of art and literature, the article entitled 'Varda the Master-Builder'.

5   Cocteau's real quote, 'Everything one achieves in life even love, occurs in an express train racing towards death. To smoke opium is to get out of the train while it is still moving' (1996: 36), is about the importance of direct sensual experiences and the inevitability of death but it originates from his attempt to do without opium.

6   'Imaginary families, I love you!' ('Famille imaginaire, je vous aime!') exclaims Varda before she first embraces Yanco, no doubt a subvertion of André Gide's famous 'Families, I hate you!' ('Famille je vous hais!') in *Les Nourritures terrestres*.

7   Susan Hayward labels this period as one of 'revival' for the documentary genre (2004: 311).

8   In the director's note published by Zeitgeist Films, Varda describes her adventure as follows: 'I also wanted to roam around. To meet people. To seek them out. Rather than a road movie, I would say a "wandering-road-documentary".'

9   In a long conversation with Shirley Jordan, Varda explains what vision she had for Mona in *Sans Toit ni Loi* thus: 'I wanted to create a character that is escaping me, and I don't feel like a demiurge creating and knowing everything. I like to create characters that I cannot control in a way; they start to have their own lives, and I do what I can to say who they are' (Jordan and Varda 2011: 188).

10 Ydessa closed the well-loved gallery space she had used for twenty five years in Toronto in October 2012 but has declared that she would carry on exhibiting and curating in other places. For more details see this article from the Globe and Mail. http://www.theglobeandmail.com/arts/art-and-architecture/end-of-an-era-ydessa-hendeles-has-closed-her-toronto-gallery-doors/article4775659/ (accessed October 2012).

11 La Grande Carte Postale in her show at la Fondation Cartier and the photographic triptychs in Sète are perfect example of her recent experimentations with the medium of photography. Her most recent exhibition commissioned by the Conseil Régional des Bouches du Rhône is also dominated by photos taken in

Marseilles showing locals posing in their neighbourhood with other members of the community. For details, see the exhibition press-kit http://unpoissonnomme-marcel.files.wordpress.com/2013/01/dp-varda.pdf (accessed January 2013).

12 Information on this project is contradictory at best. For instance, Varda claims that her contribution was edited out by Marker (the final editor) even if she had asked Joris Ivens to film specific footage for her during his trip to Vietnam. Thomas Waugh's article on Ivens's work in Cuba, a country Varda visited too, makes manifest the difficulties scholars face when dealing with the lyrical collective essays of the 1960s. For more details see: http://www.ejumpcut.org/archive/onlinessays/JC22folder/IvensInCuba.html (accessed September 2012).

13 Varda followed the request of the TV channel Antenne 2 but some of the close ups were cut off before it was broadcast to avoid problems with the legal system. An intertitle makes this clear: 'Plan interdit par l'article 283 du code pénal', ('shot forbidden based on the article 283'). This article forbids any indecent shot or scene contrary to accepted standards of behaviour (Sera puni d'un emprisonnement ou d'une amende quiconque aura [...] fabriqué, [...] projeté, [...] distribué [...] tous films ou clichés [...] contraires aux bonnes moeurs.). Varda explains how she had negociate with the channel executors in *Cinéma 75*. (Quoted in this notice: http://www.autourdu1ermai.fr/fiches/film/fiche-film-1075.html (accessed January 2013).

14 Smith describes, for instance, *Réponses de Femmes* in terms of 'aggressive use of nudity' (1998 105).

15 *L'une chante, l'autre pas* an unconventional musical about the struggles of two female friends across time opens with de Beauvoir's famous phrase, confirming Varda's allegiance or at least acknowledging how influential *The Second Sex* is to her.

16 'Je n'aime pas les femmes. L'amour est à réinventer, on le sait.' In *Une saison en enfer* (Délires I. Vierge Folle), was written while Rimbaud was bedridden after Verlaine had shot him twice in the chest during an argument between the two lovers.

CONCLUSION

Agnès Varda's influence on the world of cinema cannot be fully understood from a limited set of canonical examples. One would need several books to do justice to the rich and elaborate production of this 'cinéaste au féminin singulier', but the emphasis placed here on mostly unexamined works and other visual productions highlights significant historical, cultural and political connections not typically associated with Varda. At the end of this journey, my hope is that her love of images, her willingness to embrace chance and unpredictable encounters, and her wit have also come through the various chapters of this book.

Forced from her first venture into filmmaking to justify her unorthodox choices, and being surrounded in the 1950s and 1960s by a group of more famous young Turks was certainly formative. What do you do when you are the only woman in the field, and you are trying to develop an approach in keeping with your vision of meaningful and committed cinema? Varda appears to have surrounded herself with like-minded, generous collaborators like Resnais, Mamou and Aviv. This allowed her to continue to forge her own path, as did the decision to alternate between commissioned and more personal projects. Since her debut, Varda has walked a fine line between trying to shock the viewers through formal experimentation, and making works of art which are democratic, in the sense that they try to appeal to as wide an audience as possible. Some films have been resounding successes like *Les Glaneurs et la glaneuse* and *Sans Toit ni Loi* which was seen by over a million spectators in France in 1985.[1] Others, like *Réponses de Femme,* and *7p., cuis., s. de b., … à saisir* did not find their audience upon release. But these eclectic films are now available on DVD for current appreciation, and Varda's recent foray in visual art provides exciting new ways to discuss her approach in the white cube of the gallery.

A brief survey of her works demonstrates that she enjoys working on a variety of projects and that she never really settled on a single, comfortable, safe format which would have guaranteed a regular audience of followers. Rather than adopting a particular genre, like the 'melodrama of protest' (Lee 2002: 151) favoured by filmmakers like Ken Loach, Varda has alternated between different formats and genres and produced a variety of documentaries, short films and long features, unhindered by previous commercial relative failures. The formal eclecticism of Varda's oeuvre does not mean that her practice cannot be examined and interpreted transversely. In this study, I have put to use a set of overarching concepts to shed light on significant connections between otherwise disparate productions. These final pages draw upon these concepts to highlight their significance to understand Varda's oeuvre and their potential for further investigation in future scholarship.

Praxis, Aesthetics and Reception

– Varda as a Cinéaste Passeur
Many of Varda's projects were the result of her response to a specific encounter, a personal experience, or the work of fellow artists. Her attention to others and her love of new encounters have been a constant throughout her work. In interviews, she makes no secret of this; for example, she mentions how *L'Opéra Mouffe* and *Daguerréotypes* were both influenced by her pregnancies, and how *7p., cuis., s. de b., … à saisir* started with an exhibition in Avignon whose lingering impression remained with her long after. Her long features are no different. *Sans toi ni loi* was inspired by her reaction to a news headline about the death of a young and homeless girl. This is why the idea of a 'cinéaste passeur' is essential to interpreting Varda's films. Because of her status as a creative and opiniated director, Varda becomes a significant mediator not only between the filmed subjects and the spectators, but also between a specific space and time and the moment of the screening. When Varda gives the marginal centre stage and an active role in her film's narrative as she does in *Sans Toi ni Loi, Les Glaneurs et la glaneuse, Deux Ans Après*, or even *Documenteur*, when she captures images of those whom cinema often rejects, she makes a significant ethical and aesthetic choice. The subversive and irreverent edge to her work should not distract from the analysis of her specific praxis. When, for example, she juxtaposes Claude M., Gislaine and Bébert, three homeless alcoholics in *Les Glaneurs et la glaneuse*, with established artist and psychiatrist Louis Pons and Jean Laplanche, she makes it clear that they are all worthy of attention.

– Poetics of Space
Although Varda's films are often seen as quintessentially Parisian, the location she chooses to situate her creations varies from film to film, which is why a close examination of her works' poetics of space is essential. In this book, I use an eclectic corpus of films including *Cléo de 5 à 7, Du Côté de la Côte, Plaisirs d'amour en Iran*, as well as three recent installations: *Ping Pong Tong et Camping, La Cabane de l'Échec*, and *Dépôt de la cabane de pêcheur* in order to analyse Varda's understanding and creative use of space. In Varda's work, space is neither objective nor topographic, and often it is invested by someone's presence and by his or her embodied subjectivity. In *Cléo de 5 à 7*, Varda creates a specific emotional geography associated with the epony-

mous heroine who will, by the end of the film, accept change and truly become open to others. Another essential characteristic of Varda's poetics of space is its relational quality. Looking at documentaries like Varda's exuberant picture of the Riviera, *Du Côté de la Côte*, illustrates how space is used to establish various connections between different images, *clichés*, individuals and the director. When Varda edits her documentary employing garish images of the Riviera and *clichés* about la Côte, archival footage and reproductions, and her own often Tati-esque footage, she transforms the everyday and mundane (like hats and parasols) into something marvellous (flowers and crowns), and proves that she is a relentless '*enchanteuse du quotidien*', a true enchantress. Similarly, in the installations I analyse, landscapes, and beachscapes in particular, become creative opportunities to summon up a multiplicity of connections, memories and experiences.

– Technique and Collaborations
Some of these connections between the filmmaker, her collaborators and the participants are an integral part of the making of the film. Unfortunately, these are often either considered anecdotal, or relegated to the margins of scholarly analyses. But the work of scholars interested in performance, star studies, sound design as well as music (like Geoff Dyer, Claudia Gorbman and Ginette Vincendeau) encourages scholars to look beyond the narrow prism of auteurism to reconsider actors, composers and collaborators as equally important contributors. This study tries to follow these specialists' cue in considering the contribution of participants whose collaboration may generally not be acknowledged.[2] *La Pointe Courte,* Varda's first attempt to mix documentary and fiction in Sète, and *Agnès de ci de là Varda*, her recent kaleidoscopic TV series offer two examples which demonstrate that Varda's projects, as different as they may be, should be looked at as the result of a complex amalgam of efforts, encounters, and influences. In *La Pointe Courte*, the film that established her as an *auteur* in France, I go back to the making of the film and to its various participants in order to underline the collective nature of this cinematographic enterprise. Resnais, the editor, and Barbaud, the composer, are among the figures I examine to see what role they played at the time. In *Agnès de ci de là Varda*, a peripatetic journey that takes the audience from Paris to Brazil, Spain, Mexico and Sweden, Varda presents the work of various artists and ponders their artistic *persona*. In these two works, by pointing to a performative and self-reflexive idea of authorship, Varda challenges two fantasies: the transparency of the cinematographic medium and the overarching importance of the almighty director.

– The Question of Reception
If recognition of Varda's influence by young directors is a sign by which one can judge the importance of her work, then we can only conclude that she has succeeded in her attempts to entertain, provoke, question and move her audience at home and abroad.[3] Whatever the format or topic that she chooses, what Varda strives for is to reach the spectator, and to make them aware of the conflicting dynamics at work in art beyond the limiting categories of art house, blockbuster, auteur or 'europudding'[4] productions. Her particular way of assembling images, voices and sound provokes the spectator with

its blank acting style (in *La Pointe Courte*), its blend of surreal décors and authentic characters (in *7p., cuis., s. de b., … à saisir* and *Les Créatures*), and its use of sensory signs and tactile impressions (in *Du Côté de la Côte* and , *les ours et etc.*). Whether it is screened in cinemas or experienced in the space of galleries and museums, Varda's body of work refuses 'to fit the category of the déjà vu' (Cooper 2006: 86). Her portfolio may contain incredible variety, but a common thread connecting her films is that they rarely offer the spectator an illusion of plenitude or transparency. Rather, they make us aware time and again of our thwarted desire to see, to make sense of, and to master the world around us. They ask questions but do not provide clear-cut answers. Varda refuses to use her characters as a mouthpiece. She is happy to incorporate discordant and even oppositional voices in her films, and in doing so she adopts a truly polyphonic type of enunciation and narrative whose trajectories are open-ended rather than pre-determined or clichéd.

In the opening of *Salut les Cubains!* the crowd of photographers and filmmakers points to this desire to understand and capture events before they fade away.[5] Varda's film does not present post-revolutionary Cuba as a univocal, pastoral paradise. Varda and Piccoli comment on different aspects, and do not necessarily speak in perfect unison. What the film does do, however, is to invite the audience on a musical, sensual and intellectual journey that presents itself as self-reflexive and subjective. In short, through her singular *cinécriture*, Varda experiments with the cinematographic medium and reasserts cinema's 'capacity to weave together the sensual and the conceptual' (Beugnet 2007: 60).

Feminism and Politics

Varda's vision of the world has often been described as original both for her time and for her generation, which may explain why she has not always fit in well-defined categories and groups. Even if some critics have had doubts about the politics of her work, I would argue that the attention that she has paid to different women's experiences and to the corporeal more generally testifies to her feminist commitment. *L'Opéra Mouffe*, *Daguerréotypes*, and *Les Veuves de Noirmoutier*, three essayistic examples discussed at length earlier in this text, show that Varda's work not only captures a variety of images of women across time, but also rejects limiting versions of female subjectivity. By focusing on many different women and their experiences, Varda invites the spectator to reconsider their views, and to question specific images associated with women in the 1950s, in the 1970s and at the end of the twentieth century. Making all her films accessible to viewers who may not have experienced the conservatism of the 1950s or the heyday of feminism in the 1970s first-hand is a clever way to allow present day spectators to place feminist issues within a historical continuum, while also reflecting on past concerns through the prism shaped by contemporary society.

Regardless of the project she works on, Varda is, like some of her subjects (including the Black Panthers), loud and proud: 'Les femmes soit disant on est toutes les mêmes! Emmerdeuses, futiles, bavardes, connasses, salopes, etc!' ('Because we women are supposedly all the same! Nuisances, frivolous, gossips, bitches, sluts, etc!'). This quote from *Réponses de Femmes,* one of Varda's boldest polemical shorts, is representative of her desire to seize the spectator's attention, and to take them out of their comfort zone. Some, like Claire Johnston in the 1970s, have not been convinced by the feminist contribution in her films, and argue that Varda's production is too essentialist to be feminist (see Johnston 2000). But it must be remembered that the audiences she addresses are quite different from those for the early *cinétracts*, made in 1968, which were preaching to the converted and not really trying to reach people beyond a limited circle of already politically active citizens. Varda's 'in your face' manifesto was made to be broadcast on prime time television, and testifies to her desire to bring feminist questions to the fore, so that they can be debated in the public arena. When questioned about her strategy for *L'une chante, l'autre pas*, a musical about abortion, marriage and motherhood, Varda is clear: 'Make it clear, simple, not too complicated. If I put myself on the screen – very natural and feminist – maybe I'd get ten people in the audience. Instead, I put two nice young females on the screen, and not too much of [sic] own leftist conscience. By not being too radical but truly feminist, my film has been seen by 350 000 people in France. It's better if they all got half the message than to have 5000 people seeing a courageous 16mm film' (Varda and Peary 1977).

This study shows how Varda's work is committed to feminism in many different ways as it compels the viewer to question established definitions of gender, and to review the patriarchal structures of French society. In the past, Varda has put her money where her mouth is by signing the famous 'manifeste des 343' and by providing practical assistance to women who needed help to have an abortion (this mention in *Les Plages d'Agnès* is more than an anecdotal detail but a revelation that Varda was involved both personally and politically). The example set by these 342 women has not been forgotten and their courage is still inspirational today.[6] For example, politician and activist Clémentine Autain convinced women in late 2012 to sign a manifesto called 'le manifeste des 313' which aims to break the silence around rape (via an online campaign http://www.contreleviol.fr/, the publication of testimonies in *Viol, elles se manifestent* and the screening on France 2 of a documentary on that subject).[7]

Because her career spans almost sixty years, Varda's films are also enlightening documents which illustrate legal changes and evolving attitudes in France, which bear witness to activism, and confirm the provocative potential of feminist issues both in France and abroad. The reason why her work may not be recognised as feminist to all is, I suspect, her reluctance to be over-didactic. As Neupert remarks in relation to *Le Bonheur*: 'Varda avoided making large moralizing social statements about the movie or its characters' (2007: 348). The absence of a distinct political message is coherent with her conception of cinema as a medium able to use the polemical potential of the corporeal on screen, an idea that she takes even further when creating installations. She will be asking a set of questions, or provoking interrogations, and we, as spectators or viewers, need to find our own answers. In *Les Veuves de Noirmoutier*, for example, by focusing on bereavement, she makes the intangible palpable and appeals to our grieving selves, thus reminding us how implicated we all are in shaping the community we live in. Overall, both her commitment to making documentaries and her relentless solicitation of the viewer's emotions and sensations show that Varda wants the audience to become 'subjects of (potential) agency and actors in history' (Rabinowitz 1994: 8). Her cinema and her art, both past and future, will continue to challenge and stimulate spectators in France and around the world.

Notes

1. Tim Palmer recently published an interesting article on female directors and their position within the so called 'club des millionaires', that is to say films that attracted over a million paying admissions (for more detail, see Palmer 2012).
2. Catherine Portuges adopts a similar approach when she underlines the contribution of Hélène Louvart, a talented director of photography whose attention on the corporeal is undeniable in Wim Wenders's *Pina* (2011), Dominique Cabrera's *L'autre côté de la mer* (1997) and *Les Plages d'Agnès* (see Portuges 2009: 58).
3. Joshua Moore, the director of *I Think it's Raining*, is one of the many filmmakers who acknowledges Varda's influence. For details see this interview http://atlantafilmfestival.com/atlff-news/2013/8/14/atlff12-i-think-its-raining-now-on-vod-we-interview-director-joshua-moore (accessed September 2013).
4. Leach describes 'europudding films' as large budget co-productions which are encouraged by the European Union meant to compete with Hollywood (2004: 4).
5. The whole paraphernalia of the film's shooting and the reflexivity it creates because of its disruptive character is also something 'that 'art film' of the 1960s seized upon with relish' (Aumont 1989: 179).
6. The manifesto was signed twice by Liliane Siegel (one of Sartre's lovers) who used her maiden's name.
7. To see how the magazine *Le nouvel observateur* was involved in diffusing both manifestos in 1975 and 2012, see the following thread: http://tempsreel.nouvelobs.com/viol-le-manifeste (accessed January 2013).

FILMOGRAPHY

1954
La Pointe Courte
Length: 89 mins
Director: Agnès Varda
Screenplay: Agnès Varda
Editing: Alain Resnais
Music: Pierre Barbaux
Leading Cast: Philippe Noiret, Silvia Monfort
Production Company: Tamaris Films, France

1957
O Saisons, O Châteaux
Length: 22 mins
Director: Agnès Varda
Screenplay: Agnès Varda
Editing: Janine Verneau
Music: André Hodeir
Cinematography: Quinto Albicocco
Producer: Pierre Brauberger
Production company: Films de la Pléiade

1958
L'Opéra Mouffe
Length: 17 mins
Director: Agnès Varda
Screenplay: Agnès Varda
Editing: Janine Verneau
Music: George Delerue, Agnès Varda
Leading cast: Dorothée Blank, André Bourseiller, José Valera, André Rousselet
Production Company: Ciné-Tamaris

1958
Du Côté de la côte
Length: 24 mins
Director: Agnès Varda
Screenplay: Agnès Varda
Editing: Henri Colpi, Jasmine Chasney
Music: George Delerue
Producers: Anatole Dauman, Philippe Lifchitz
Production Company: Argos Films

1961
Cléo de 5 à 7
Length: 90 mins
Director: Agnès Varda
Screenplay: Agnès Varda
Editing: Janine Verneau, Pascale Laverrière
Music: Michel Legrand

Leading cast: Corinne Marchand, Antoine Bourseiller, José Luis de Vilallonga, Sami Frey, Michel Legrand
Producer: George de Beuarrgard, Carlo Ponti
Production Company: Ciné-Tamaris

1963
Salut les Cubains!
Length: 30 mins
Director: Agnès Varda
Screenplay: Agnès Varda
Editing: Janine Verneau
Production Company: Pathé Cinéma

1964
Le Bonheur
Length: 82 mins
Director: Agnès Varda
Screenplay: Agnès Varda
Editing: Janine Verneau
Leading Cast: Jean-Claude Drouot, Claire Drouot, Marie-France Boyer
Producer: Mag Bodard
Production company: Ciné-Tamaris, Parc-Film

1965
Elsa la Rose
Length: 20 mins
Director: Agnès Varda
Screenplay: Agnès Varda
Leading cast: Elsa Triolet, Louis Aragon
Editing: Jean Hamon
Production company: Ciné-Tamaris, Pathé Cinéma

1965
Les Créatures
Length: 105 mins
Director: Agnès Varda
Screenplay: Agnès Varda
Editing: Janine Verneau
Music: Pierre Barbaud

Leading cast: Michel Piccoli, Catherine Deneuve, Lucien Bodard
Producers: Mag Bodard
Production company: Parc Film, Madeleine Films

1967
Loin du Vietnam
Length: 115 mins
Director: Joris Ivens, William Klein, Claude Lelouch, Agnès Varda, Jean-Luc Godard, Chris Marker, Alain Resnais
Editing: Chris Marker
Music: Michel Fano, Michel Chapdenat, Georges Aperghis
Production Company: SLON Films

1967
Oncle Yanco
Length: 22 mins
Director: Agnès Varda
Screenplay: Agnès Varda
Editing: Jean Hamon
Leading cast: Jean Varda, Agnès Varda, Rosalie Varda, Tom Luddy
Production company: Ciné-Tamaris

1968
Black Panthers
Length: 28 mins
Director: Agnès Varda
Screenplay: Agnès Varda
Editing: Paddy Monk
Production company: Ciné-Tamaris

1969
Lions Love (and Lies
Length: 110 mins
Director: Agnès Varda
Screenplay: Agnès Varda
Editing: Robert Dalva
Music: Joseph Byrd
Production company: Ciné-Tamaris

1974
Daguerréotypes
Length: 80 mins
Director: Agnès Varda
Screenplay: Agnès Varda
Editing: Gordon Swire
Cinematography: Nurith Aviv
Production company: Ciné-Tamaris, INA, ZDF

1975
Réponses de femmes
Length: 8 mins
Director: Agnès Varda
Screenplay: Agnès Varda
Editing: Marie Castro
Production company: Ciné-Tamaris, Antenne 2

1976
Plaisirs d'Amour en Iran
Length: 6 mins
Director: Agnès Varda
Screenplay: Agnès Varda
Editing: Sabine Mamou
Cinematography: Nurith Aviv, Charlie Vandamme
Leading cast: Valérie Mairesse, Ali Raffi
Production company: Ciné-Tamaris

1976
L'une chante, l'autre pas
Length: 120 mins
Director: Agnès Varda
Screenplay: Agnès Varda
Editing: Joëlle Van Effenterre
Leading cast: Thérèse Liotard, Valérie Mairesse, Ali Raffi, Mathieu Demy, Robert Dadiès
Production company: Ciné-Tamaris, SFP, INA, Contrechamp, Paradise Film, Population Film

1980
Mur Murs
Length: 81 mins
Director: Agnès Varda
Screenplay: Agnès Varda
Editing: Sabine Mamou, Bob Gould
Leading cast: Juliet Berto, Mathieu Demy
Production company: Ciné-Tamaris

1980-81
Documenteur
Length: 63 mins
Director: Agnès Varda
Screenplay: Agnès Varda
Editing: Sabine Mamou
Music: George Delerue
Cinematography: Nurith Aviv
Leading cast: Sabine Mamou, Mathieu Demy, Lisa Blok, Tom Taplin
Production company: Ciné-Tamaris

1982
Ulysse
Length: 22 mins
Director: Agnès Varda
Screenplay: Agnès Varda
Editing: Marie-Jo Audiard
Music: Pierre Barbaud
Production company: Garance

1984
Les Dites Caryatides
Length: 13 mins
Director: Agnès Varda
Screenplay: Agnès Varda
Editing: Hélène Wolf
Production company: Ciné-Tamaris

1984
7 P., cuis., s.de b. (à saisir)
Length: 27 mins
Director: Agnès Varda
Screenplay: Agnès Varda

Editing: Sabine Mamou
Director of photography: Nurith Aviv
Music: Pierre Barbaud
Leading Cast: Louis Bec, Yoland Moreau, Hervé Mangani
Production company: Ciné-Tamaris

1985
Sans toit ni loi
Length: 105 mins
Director: Agnès Varda
Screenplay: Agnès Varda
Editing: Agnès Varda, Patricia Mazuy
Music: Joanna Bruzdowicz, Frédéric Chichin
Leading cast: Sandrine Bonnaire, Macha Meryl, Stéphane Freiss, Yolande Moreau
Production company: Ciné-Tamaris, Films A2

1987
Jane B. par Agnès V.
Length: 97 mins
Director: Agnès Varda
Screenplay: Agnès Varda
Editing: Agnès Varda, Marie-Joe Audiard
Music: Joanna Brudowicz
Leading cast: Jane Birking, Jean-Pierre Léaud, Philippe Léotard, Farid Chopel
Production company: Ciné-Tamaris, La Sept

1987
Kung Fu Master
Length: 78 mins
Director: Agnès Varda
Screenplay: Agnès Varda
Editing: Marie-Joe Audiard
Music: Joanna Brudowick
Leading cast: Jane Birking, Mathieu Demy, Charlotte Gainsbourg, Lou Doillon
Production company: Ciné-Tamaris

1990
Jacquot de Nantes
Length: 118 mins
Director: Agnès Varda
Screenplay: Agnès Varda, Jacque Demy
Editing: Marie-Joe Audiard
Leading cast: Philippe Maron, Édouard Joubeaud, Laurent Monnier
Production company: Ciné-Tamaris

1992
Les Demoiselles ont eu 25 ans
Length: 63 mins
Director: Agnès Varda
Screenplay: Agnès Varda
Editing: Anne-Marie Cotteret, Agnès Varda
Music: Michel Legrand, Jacques Loussier
Leading cast: Catherine Deneuve, Michel Legrand, Mag Bodard, George Chakiri
Production company: Ciné-Tamaris

1993
L'univers de Jacques Demy
Length: 90 mins
Director: Agnès Varda
Screenplay: Agnès Varda
Editing: Marie-Jo Audiard
Music: Michel Legrand, Michel Colombier
Leading cast: Anouk Aimée, Richard Berry, Nino Castelnuovo, Danielle Darrieux, Catherine Deneuve
Production company: Ciné-Tamaris

1994
Les Cents et une nuits
Lenghth: 120 min
Director: Agnès Varda
Screenplay: Agnès Varda
Editing: Hugues Darmois
Leading cast: Michel Picolli, Marcello Mastroianni, Julie Gayer, Mathieu Demy
Production company: Ciné-Tamaris

2000
Les Glaneurs et la glaneuse
Length: 82 mins
Director: Agnès Varda
Screenplay: Agnès Varda
Editing: Agnès Varda, Laurent Pineau
Music: Joanna Bruzdowicz
Leading cast: Agnès Varda, François Wertheimer
Production company: Ciné-Tamaris

2002
Deux Ans Après
Length: 64 mins
Director: Agnès Varda
Screenplay: Agnès Varda
Editing: Agnès Varda
Music: Joanna Bruzdowicz, Isabelle Olivier, George Delerue
Leading cast: Agnès Varda, Macha Mackeieff
Production company: Ciné-Tamaris

2003
Le Lion volatil
Length: 12 mins
Director: Agnès Varda
Screenplay: Agnès Varda
Editing: Agnès Varda, Sophie Mandonnet
Leading cast: Julie Depardieu, Valérie Donzeli, David Deciron
Production company: Ciné-Tamaris

2004
Ydessa, les Ours, et etc…
Length: 42 mins
Director: Agnès Varda
Screenplay: Agnès Varda
Editing: Agnès Varda, Jean-Baptiste Morin
Music: Isabelle Olivier
Leading cast: Agnès Varda, Ydessa Hendeles
Production company: Ciné-Tamaris

2006
Quelques Veuves de Noirmoutier
Length: 69 mins
Director: Agnès Varda
Screenplay: Agnès Varda
Editing: Jean Baptiste Morin, Agnès Varda, Baptiste Filloux
Music: Ami Flammer
Production company: Ciné-Tamaris, Arte France Cinéma

2008
Les Plages d'Agnès
Length: 110 mins
Director: Agnès Varda
Screenplay: Agnès Varda
Editing: Jean Baptiste Morin, Agnès Varda, Baptiste Filloux
Music: Isabelle Olivier
Leading cast: Agnès Varda, Rosalie Varda, Mathieu Demy, Stéphane Vilar
Production company: Ciné-Tamaris, Arte France Cinéma

2011
Agnès de ci de là Varda
Television documentary
Length: 5 episodes of 45 mins
French TX date: 19-23/12/2011
Director: Agnès Varda
Screenplay: Agnès Varda
Editing: Jean-Baptiste Morin, Johan Boulanger
Production company: Ciné-Tamaris, Arte France Cinéma

BIBLIOGRAPHY

Agacinsky, Sylviane (2003) *Time Passing: Modernity and Nostalgia*. New York: Columbia University Press.
Allison, Maggie (2000) 'Women and the Media', in Abigail Gregory and Ursula Tidd (eds) *Women in Contemporary France*. Oxford: Berg, 65–87.
Aragon, Louis (1956) *Le Roman inachevé*. Paris: Gallimard.
Aumont, Jacques (1989) 'The Fall of the Gods: Jean-Luc Godard's *Le Mépris* (1963)', in Susan Hayward and Ginette Vincendeau (eds) *French Film: Texts and Contexts*. London and New York: Routledge, 174–89.
Bachelard, Gaston (1969) *Poetics of Space*. Boston: Beacon Press.
Bal, Mieke (2007) 'Exhibition as Film', in Paul Basu and Sharon McDonald (eds) *Exhibition Experiments*. London: Blackwell, 16–43.
Baqué, Dominique (2004) *Pour Un Nouvel Art Politique: De L'art Contemporain Au Documentaire*. Paris: Éditions Flammarion.
Bardaud, Pierre (1964) *Cinéma 64*, 89. Fédération Française des Ciné Clubs (FFCC): Paris.
Barnet, Claire (2011) '"*Elles-Ils Islands*": Cartographies of Life and Death by Agnès Varda', *L'Esprit Créateur*, 51, 1, 97–111.
Bastide, Bernard (1991) 'Agnès Varda Photographe, ou, l'apprentissage du regard', in Michel Estève (ed.) *Agnès Varda*. Paris: Minard, 4–12.
____ (2009) 'Agnès Varda, une auteure au féminin singulier' in Antony Fiant, Roxane Hamery and Éric Thouvenel (eds) *Agnès Varda: le cinéma et au-delà*. Rennes: Presses universitaires de Rennes, 15–24.
Bénézet, Delphine (2009) 'Spatial Dialectic and Political Poetics in Varda's Expatriate Cinema', *Journal of Romance Studies*, 9, 2, 85–100.
Beugnet, Martine (2004) 'French Cinema of the Margins', in Elizabeth Ezra (ed.) *European Cinema*. Oxford: Oxford University Press, 283–98.
____ (2006) 'Screening the Old: Femininity as Old Age in Contemporary French Cinema', *Studies in the Literary Imagination*, 39, 2, 1–20.

____ (2007) *Cinema and Sensation: French Film and the Art of Transgression*. Edinburgh: Edinburgh University Press.
Bogue, Ronald (2003) *Deleuze on Cinema*. London and New York: Routledge.
Bouchard, Vincent (2005) 'Transmettre l'expérience d'une rencontre; le cas du cinéma léger synchrone', *Intermédialités*, 5, 81–97.
Bounoure, Gaston (1974) *Alain Resnais*. Paris: Seghers.
Boyle, Claire (2012) 'Self-Fictions and Films: Varda's Transformative Technology of the Self in *Les Plages d'Agnès*', *XXXXI Critical Review of Contemporary French Fixxion*; http://www.revue-critique-de-fixxion-francaise-contemporaine.org/rcffc/issue/view/11/showToc.
Briggs, Jonathyne (2012) 'Sex and the Girl's Single: French Popular Music and the Long Sexual Revolution of the 1960s', *Journal of the History of Sexuality*, 21, 3, 523–47.
Bruzzi, Stella (2006) *New Documentary*. London and New York: Routledge.
Burch, Noël (1979) *To the Distant Observer: Form and Meaning in Japanese Cinema*. Berkeley, CA: University of California Press.
Butler, Judith (2003) 'Violence, Mourning, Politics', *Studies in Gender and Sexuality*, 4, 1, 9–37.
Carroll, Noel (1998) *Mystifying Movies: Fads and Fallacies of Contemporary Film Theory*. New York: Columbia University Press.
Chamarette, Jenny (2011) 'Spectral Bodies, Temporalised Spaces: Agnès Varda's Motile Gestures of Mourning and Memorial', *Image and Narrative*, 12, 2; http://www.imageandnarrative.be/index.php/imagenarrative/article/view/144.
____ (2012) *Phenomenology and the Future of Film: Rethinking Subjectivity Beyond French Cinema*. London: Palgrave Macmillan.
Charpentier, Laure (1981) *Toute honte bue: l'alcoolisme au féminin*. Paris: Denöel.
Cheu, Hoi F. (2007) *Cinematic Howling: Women's Films, Women's Film Theories*. Vancouver: University of British Columbia Press.
Chevrier, Henri-Paul (2012) *Le Cinéma de répertoire et ses mises en scène*. Québec: Les Éditions de l'instant même.
Chion, Michel (1994) *Audio-Vision: Sound on Screen*. New York: Columbia University Press.
Chrostowska, Dorotha (2007) 'Vis à vis the Glaneuse', *Angelaki: Journal of the Theoretical Humanities*, 12, 2, 124–33.
Cocteau, Jean (2001) *Opium – The Diary of His Cure*. London: Peter Owen.
Comolli, Jean Louis (2004) *Voir et pouvoir, l'innocence perdue: Cinéma, Télévision, Fction, Documentaire*. Paris: Verdier.
Comolli, Jean-Louis and Jacques Rancière (1997) *Arrêt Sur Histoire, Supplémentaires*. Paris: Centre Georges Pompidou.
Conway, Kelley (2009) '*L'Île et Elle*: lieu, temps, écran, récit', in Antony Fiant, Roxane Hamery and Éric Thouvenel (eds) *Agnès Varda: le cinéma et au-delà*. Rennes: Presses universitaires de Rennes, 209–18.
____ (2010) 'Varda at Work: *Les Plages d'Agnès*', *Studies in French Cinema*, 10, 2, 125–39.

Cook, Hera (2004) *The Long Sexual Revolution: English Women, Sex, and Contraception, 1800–1975*. Oxford: Oxford University Press.
Cooper, Sarah (2006) *Selfless Cinema?: Ethics and French Documentary*. London: Legenda.
____ (2007) 'Introduction: the Occluded Relation – Levinas and Cinema', *Film-Philosophy*, 11, 2; http://www.film-philosophy.com/2007v11n2/introduction.pdf.
Corrigan, Timothy (1990) 'The Commerce of Auteurism: A Voice without Authority', *New German Critique*, 49, 43–57.
____ (2011) *The Essay Film: From Montaigne, After Marker*, Oxford: Oxford University Press.
Cruickshank, Ruth (2007) 'The Work of Art in the Age of Global Consumption; Agnès Varda's *Les Glaneurs et la glaneuse*', *L'Esprit Créateur*, 44, 2, 119–32.
Crofts, Stephen (1998) 'Authorship and Hollywood', in John Hill and Pamela Church Gibson (eds) *The Oxford Guide to Film Studies*. Oxford: Oxford Universty Press, 310–24.
Dardenne, Luc (2005) *Au Dos de nos Images, 1991–2005*. Paris: Seuil.
Davilà, Arlene M. (2004) *Barrio Dreams: Puerto Ricans, Latinos and the Neoliberal City*. Berkeley, CA: University of California Press.
De Baecque, Antoine (2006) 'Écrans, le corps au cinéma', in Jean-Jacques Courtine (ed.) *Histoire du corps 3: Les Mutations du regard. Le XXème siècle*. Paris: Seuil, 385–406.
De Beauvoir, Simone (2009) *The Second Sex*. Trans. Contance Borde and Sheila Malovany-Chevallier. London: Jonathan Cape.
De Certeau, Michel (1984) *The Practice of Everyday Life*. Berkeley, CA: University of California Press.
Déchery, Laurent (2005) 'Autour de Mona dans *Sans toit ni loi* d'Agnès Varda', *French Review*, 79, 1, 138–47.
Deleuze, Gilles (1985) *Cinéma 2: L'image-temps*. Paris: Éditions de Minuit.
De Navacelle, Marie-Christine and Claire Devarrieux (1988) *Cinéma Du Réel: Avec Imamura, Ivens, Malle, Rouch, Storck, Varda. Et Le Ciné-Journal De Depardon*. Paris: Autrement.
DeRoo, Rebecca J. (2008) 'Unhappily ever after: visual irony and feminist strategy in Agnès Varda's *Le Bonheur*', *Studies in French Cinema*, 8, 3, 189–209.
____ (2009) 'Confronting Contradictions, Genre Subversion and Feminist Politics in Agnès Varda's *L'une chante, l'autre pas*', *Modern and Contemporary France*, 17, 3, 249–65.
Dyer, Richard (1979) *Stars*. London: British Film Institute.
Éluard, Paul (1959) *Médieuses: Oeuvres complètes*. Paris: Gallimard.
Everett, Wendy (2007) 'Colour as Space and Time', in Wendy Everett and Axel Goodbody (eds) *New Studies in European Cinema. Vol. 6: Questions of Colour in Cinema*. Oxford: Peter Lang. 105–26.
Faulkner, William (2000) *The Wild Palms*. London: Vintage Books.
Flitterman-Lewis, Sandy (1996) *To Desire Differently: Feminism and the French Cinema*. New York: Columbia University Press.

____ (1998) 'Documenting the Ineffable: Terror and Memory in Alain Resnais's *Night and Fog*', in Barry Keith Grant and Jeannette Sloniowski (eds) *Documenting the Documentary: Close Readings of Documentary Film and Video*. Detroit: Wayne State University Press, 204–22.

____ (2008) 'Varda: The Gleaner and the Just', in Marcelline Block (ed.) *Situating the Feminist Gaze and Spectatorship in Post-war Cinema*. Newcastle: Cambridge Scholars Publishing, 214–25.

Forbes, Jill (2002) 'Gender and Space in *Cléo de 5 à 7*', *Studies in French Cinema*, 2, 2, 83–9.

Froger, Marion (2004) 'Don Et Image Du Don: Esthétique Documentaire Et Communauté', *Intermédialités*, 4, 115–40.

Gaut, Berys (1997) 'Film Authorship and Collaboration', in Richard Allen and Murray Smith (eds) *Film Theory and Philosophy*. Oxford: Clarendon Press, 149–72.

Gorbman, Claudia (2003) 'Why Music? The Sound Film and its Spectator', in Kay Dickinson (ed.) *Movie Music: The Film Reader*. London and New York: Routledge, 37–49.

____ (2012) 'Finding a Voice: Varda's Early Travelogues', *Substance*, 41, 2, 40–57.

Günther, Renate (2004) '"Une Femme qui boit, c'est scandaleux": Marguerite Duras and Female Alcoholism in France' in Allison Aggie and Yvette Rocheron (eds) *The Resilient Female Body: Health and Malaise in Twentieth Century France*. Oxford: Peter Lang, 87–100.

Handyside, Fiona (2011) 'The Feminist Beachscape: Catherine Breillat, Diane Kurys and Agnès Varda', *L'Esprit Créateur*, 51, 1, 83–96.

Hayward Susan (1990) 'Beyond the Gaze and Into Femme-Filmecriture', in Susan Hayward and Ginette Vincendeau (eds) *French Film Texts and Contexts*. London and New York: Routledge, 269–80.

____ (1992) 'A History of French Cinema 1895–1991: Pioneering Filmmakers (Guy, Dulac, Varda) and Their Heritage', *Paragraph: A Journal of Modern Critical Theory*, 15, 1, 19–37.

____ (2000) *Cinema Studies: The Key Concepts*. London and New York: Routledge.

____ (2004) *French National Cinema*. London and New York: Routledge.

Hendeles, Ydessa (2012) 'Interview with Alexander Ferrando', *FlashArt Online*; http://www.flashartonline.com/interno.php?pagina=articolo_det&id_art=902&det=ok&title=Ydessa-Hendeles.

Herzog, Dagmar (2005) *Sex After Fascism: Memory and Morality in Twentieth-Century Germany*. Princeton, NJ: Princeton University Press.

____ (2006) 'Between Coitus and Commodification', in Axel Schildt and Detlef Seigfried (eds) *Between Marx and Coca Cola: Youth Subcultures in Western Europe, 1960–1980*. New York: Berghahn Books, 261–86.

Hottell, Ruth (1999) 'Including Ourselves: The Role of Female Spectators in Agnès Varda's *Le Bonheur* and *L'Une chante, l'autre pas*', *Cinema Journal*, 38, 2, 52–71.

Ince, Kate (2012) 'Feminist Phenomenology and the Film World of Agnès Varda', *Hypatia*; http://onlinelibrary.wiley.com/doi/10.1111/j.1527–2001.2012.01303.x/references.

Johnston, Claire (2000) 'Women's Cinema as Counter-Cinema', in E. Ann Kaplan (ed.) *Feminism and Film*. New York: Oxford University Press, 22–34.

Jordan, Shirley (2009) 'Spatial and Emotional Limits in Installation Art: Agnès Varda's *L'Île et Elle*', *Contemporary French and Francophone Studies,* 13, 5, 581–8.

____ (2011) 'Writing Age: Annie Ernaux's Les Années', *Forum for Modern Language Studies*, 47, 2, 138–49.

Kausch, Frank (2008) '*Les Plages d'Agnès*: la mer éternellement recommence', *Positif,* 574, 15–16.

Lagny, Michele (1994) 'Film History: or History Expropriated', *Film History*, 6, 1, 26–44.

Leach, Jim (2004) *British Film*. Cambridge: Cambridge University Press.

Leigh, Jacob (2002) *The Cinema of Ken Loach: Art in the Service of the People*. London: Wallflower Press.

Livingstone, Paisley (2009) *Cinema, Philosophy, Bergman: On Film as Philosophy*. Oxford: Oxford University Press.

Mai, Joseph (2007) '*Corps-Caméra*: The Evocation of Touch in the Dardennes' *La Promesse* (1996)' *L'Esprit Créateur*, 47, 3, 133–44.

Marks, Laura U. (2000) *The Skin of the Film: Intercultural Cinema, Embodiment, and the Senses*, Durham, NC: Duke University Press.

Mary, Philippe (2006) *La Nouvelle Vague et le Cinéma d'auteur: Socio-Analyse d'une révolution artistique*. Paris: Seuil.

Maule, Rosanna (2008) *Beyond Auteurism: New Directions in Authorial Film Practices in France, Italy and Spain since the 1980s*. Bristol: Intellect.

McClung, Alexander William (2002) *Landscapes of Desire: Anglo Mythologies of Los Angeles*. Berkeley, CA: University of California Press.

McMahon, Laura (2012) *Cinema and Contact: The Withdrawal of Touch in Nancy, Bresson, Duras and Denis*. London: Legenda.

McNeill, Isabelle (2009) 'Agnès Varda's Moving Museums' in Peter Collier, Anna Magdalena Elsner and Olga Smith (eds) *Anamnesia: Public and Private Memory in Modern French Culture*. Oxford: Peter Lang, 283–94.

____ (2010) *Memory and the Moving Image: French Film in the Digital Era*. Edinburgh: Edinburgh University Press.

Mesnil, Michel (1991) 'Agnès Varda la voyeuse, ou l'art de la pointe courte', in Bernard Bastide (ed.) *Agnès Varda: Études Cinématographiques*. Paris: Minard, 179–86.

Morissey, Jim (2008) 'Paris and Voyages of Self-Discovery in *Cléo de 5 à 7* and *Le fabuleux destin d'Amélie Poulain*', *Studies in French Cinema*, 8, 2, 99–110.

Moore, Joshua (2013) 'Interview with Charles Judson'; http://atlantafilmfestival.com/atlff-news/2013/8/14/atlff12-i-think-its-raining-now-on-vod-we-interview-director-joshua-moore.

Mouton, Janice (2001) 'From Feminine Masquerade to Flaneuse: Agnès Varda's *Cléo in the City*', *Cinema Journal*, 40, 2, 3–16.

Murcia, Claude (2009) 'Soi et l'Autre, *Les Glaneurs et la glaneuse*', in Antony Fiant, Roxane Hamery and Éric Thouvenel (eds) *Agnès Varda: le cinéma et au-delà*. Rennes: Presses universitaires de Rennes, 43–8.

Murphet, Julian (2001) *Literature and Race in Los Angeles*. Cambridge: Cambridge University Press.

Neupert, Richard John (2007) *The History of the French New Wave*. Madison: University of Wisconsin Press.

O'Doherty, Brian (2000) *Inside the White Cube: The Ideology of the Gallery Space*. Berkeley, CA: University of California Press.

Orpen, Valerie (2007) *Cléo de 5 à 7*. London: IB Tauris.

O'Shaughnessy, Martin (2007) *The New Face of Political Cinema: Commitment in French Film Since 1995*. Oxford: Berghahn Books.

Ostrowska, Dorota (2008) *Reading the French New Wave: Critics, Writers and Art Cinema in France*. London: Wallflower Press.

Özgen Tuncer, Asli (2012) 'Women on the Move: the Politics of Walking in Agnès Varda', *Deleuze Studies*, 6, 1, 103–16.

Palmer, Tim (2011) *Brutal Intimacy: Analysing Contemporary French Cinema*. Middletown, CT: Wesleyan University Press.

____ (2012) 'Crashing the Millionaires' Club: Popular Women's Cinema in Twenty-First Century France', *Studies in French Cinema*, 12, 3, 201–14.

Portuges Catherine (2009) 'French Women Directors Negotiating Transnational Identities', *Yale French Studies*, 115, 47–63.

Powrie, Phil (1999) 'Heritage, History and "New Realism": French Cinema in the 1990s', in Phil Powrie (ed.) *French Cinema in the 1990s: Continuity and Difference*. Oxford: Oxford University Press, 1–21.

____ (2011) 'Heterotopic Spaces and Nomadic Gazes in Varda: From *Cléo de 5 à 7* to *Les Glaneurs et la glaneuse*', *L'Esprit Créateur*, 51, 1, 68–82.

Prévert, Jacques (1946) *Paroles*. Paris: Gallimard.

____ (2011) 'Heterotopic Spaces and Nomadic Gazes in Varda: From *Cléo de 5 à 7* to *Les Glaneurs et la glaneuse*', *l'Esprit créateur*, 51, 1, 68–82.

Rabinowitz, Paula (1993) 'Wreckage upon Wreckage: History, Documentary and the Ruins of Memory', *History and Theory*, 32, 2, 119–37.

____ (1994) *They Must be Represented: The Politics of Documentary*. London: Verso.

Rachlin, Nathalie (2006) 'L'exclusion au cinéma: le cas d'Agnès Varda', *Women in French Studies*, 59, 88–111.

Rascaroli, Laura (2009) *The Personal Camera: Subjective Cinema and the Essay Film*. London: Wallflower Press.

Reineke, Sandra (2011) *Beauvoir and Her Sisters: The Politics of Women's Bodies in France*. Urbana, IL: University of Illinois Press.

Renov, Michael (2004) *The Subject of Documentary*. Minneapolis: Minnesota University Press.

Rosello, Mireille (2001) 'Agnès Varda's *Les Glaneurs et la glaneuse*: Portrait of the Artist as an Old Lady', *Studies in French Cinema*, 1, 1, 29–36.

Russel, Catherine (1999) *Experimental Ethnography: The Work of Film in the Age of Video*. Durham, NC: Duke University Press.

Russel, Deirdre (2007) 'Contemporary Trends in Personal and Popular French Cinema', in Isabelle Vanderschelden and Darren Waldron (eds) *France at the*

Flicks: Trends in Contemporary French Popular Cinema. Newcastle: Cambridge Scholars Publishings, 75–88.

Sartre, Jean-Paul (2003) *Being and Nothingness: An Essay on Phenomenological Ontology.* London: Routledge.

Schwartz, Vanessa (2010) 'Who Killed Brigitte Bardot? Perspectives on the New Wave at Fifty', *Cinema Journal*, 49, 4, 145–52.

Sellier, Geneviève (2008) *Masculine Singular: French New Wave Cinema.* Durham, NC: Duke University Press.

Sinclair (2003) 'Audition: Making Sense of/in the Cinema', *Velvet Light Trap*, 51, 17–28.

Smith, Alison (1998) *Agnès Varda.* Manchester: Manchester University Press/New York: St. Martin's Press.

____ (2007) 'The Other Auteurs: Producers, Cinematographers and Scriptwriters', in Michael Temple and Michael Witt (eds) *The French Cinema Book.* London: British Film Institute, 194–208.

Sobschack, Vivian (2004) *Carnal Thoughts: Embodiment and Moving Image Culture.* Berkeley, CA: University of California Press.

Sontag, Susan (2013) *Diaries 1964–1980: As Consciousness is Harnessed to Flesh.* London: Penguin.

Staiger, Janet (2003) 'Authorship Approaches', in David A. Gerstner and Janet Staiger (eds) *Authorship and Film.* London and New York: Routledge, 27–57.

Starr, Jerold M. (1985) 'Cultural Politics in the 1960s', in Jerold M. Starr (ed.) *Cultural Politics: Radical Movements in Modern History.* New York: Praeger, 235–94.

Tarr, Carrie and Brigitte Rollet (2001) *Cinema and the Second Sex: Women Filmmaking in France in the 1980s and the 1990s.* New York: Continuum.

Thornham, Sue (2007) *Women, Feminism and Media.* Edinburgh: Edinburgh University Press.

Tyrer, Ben (2009) 'Disgression and return: aesthetics and politics in Agnès Varda's *Les Glaneurs et la glaneuse* (2000)', *Studies in French Cinema*, 9, 2, 161–76.

Tyler, Parker (1959) 'New Images', *Film Quaterly*, 12, 3, 50–3.

Varda, Agnès (1975) 'Autour et alentour de *Daguerréotypes*', *Cinéma*, 204, 39–53.

____ (1994) *Varda par Agnès.* Paris: Cahiers du cinéma.

Varda, Agnès and Laura Adler (2010) 'Semaine Agnès Varda avec Laure Adler et invités variés', *France Culture*; http://www.youtube.com/watch?v=YqD-5SMV6xo.

Varda, Agnès and Melissa Anderson (2001) 'The Modest Gesture of the Filmmaker', *Cineaste*, 26, 4, 24–7.

Varda, Agnès and Yvonne Baby (1999 [1962]), 'The Struggle between Coquettishness and Anguish', in Jean Douchet (ed.) *The French New Wave.* Paris: Éditions Hazan-Cinémathèque Française, 219.

Varda, Agnès, Shirley Jordan and Marie Claire Barnet (2011) 'Interviews with Agnès Varda and Valérie Mréjen', *l'Esprit créateur*, 51, 1, 184–200.

Varda, Agnès and Jacqueline Levitin (1974) 'Mother of the New Wave: An Interview with Agnès Varda', *Women and Film*, 1, 5–6.

Varda, Agnès and Andrea Meyer (2001) 'Gleaning, the Passion of Agnès Varda'; http://andreameyerwriter.com/articles.asp.

Varda, Agnès and Gerald Peary (1977) 'Interview with Gerald Peary', *The Real Paper*; http://www.geraldpeary.com/interviews/stuv/varda.html.
Varda, Agnès and Philippe Piguet (2007) 'Entretien', *L'artabsolument*; http://media.artabsolument.com/pdf/article/20407.pdf.
Varda, Agnès and Barbara Quart (1987) 'Interview with Agnès Varda', *Film Quarterly*, 40, 2, 3–10.
Varda, Agnès and Julie Rigg (2001) 'Gleaning Agnès Varda', *ABC Arts Online*; http://www.abc.net.au/arts/film/stories/s424327.htm.
Varda, Agnès and Felix Von Boehm (2010) 'Interview: Varda on Poetry', *Cine-fils magazine*; http://www.cine-fils.com/interviews/agnes-varda.html.
Vogel, Amos (1997) 'Interview with Scott MacDonald', *Wide Angle*, 19, 1, 49–83.
Vincendeau, Ginette (1987) 'Women's Cinema, Film Theory and Feminism in France', *Screen*, 28, 4, 4–18.
____ (2013) *Brigitte Bardot*. London: British Film Institute.
Wagstaff, Peter (2005) 'Traces of Places: Agnès Varda's Mobile Space in *The Gleaners and I*', in Wendy Everett and Axel Goodbody (eds) *Revisiting Space: Space and Place in European Cinema*. Oxford: Peter Lang, 273–91.
Waugh, Thomas (2011) '*Loin du Vietnam* (1967), Joris Ivens and the Left Bank Documentary', *Jump Cut*; http://www.ejumpcut.org/archive/jc53.2011/Waugh Vietnam/text.html.
Wild, Florianne (1990) 'Ecriture and Cinematic Practice in Agnès Varda's *Sans Toit ni Loi*', *L'Esprit Créateur*, 30, 2, 92–104.
Wilson, Emma (2005) 'Material Relics: Resnais, Memory and the Senses', *French Studies*, 59, 1, 25–30.
____ (2009) *Alain Resnais*. Manchester: Manchester University Press.
Wood, P. Mary (2007) *Contemporary European Cinema*. London: Bloomsbury Academic.

INDEX

Agnès de ci de là Varda 3, 7, 58, 60, 62, 64, 68, 71, 141
authorship 4, 6, 42, 60, 62, 64, 68, 141
autobiography 20, 37

Bachelard, Gaston 89–90, 108
Barbaud, Pierre 48–49, 134–5, 141
bereavement 32, 34, 143
bonimenteur 11, 37, 82, 115, 126,
body, bodies 5–7, 10, 12–13, 16, 19, 23–6, 28–31, 33, 38, 45–7, 50, 55, 65, 67, 77, 84–5, 90–1, 93–4, 99–101, 104, 107, 123, 126–32, 134–5, 140, 142

chance 9, 31, 55, 59–60, 66, 73, 75, 86, 91, 94, 106, 114, 119, 122, 130, 139
cinéaste passeur 5, 7, 71, 75–6, 79, 82, 86, 140
cinécriture 2, 4, 7, 111, 119, 122–3, 127, 132, 134–5, 142
cinétract 128–30, 143
Cléo de 5 à 7 3–4, 7, 9, 78, 90, 108, 112, 140
corporeal 3, 6, 10–11, 13, 16, 19, 22, 24, 29–32, 120, 123, 127, 134, 142–4

Daguerréotypes 6, 22–31, 58, 62–3, 65, 76, 140, 142
De Beauvoir, Simone 1, 19, 28, 70, 112, 129–30, 137

Dépôt de la cabane de pêcheur 7, 102, 106, 140
Deux Ans Après 7–8, 58, 60, 112, 120–2, 140
documentary 1, 5, 7, 10–11, 19–21, 24, 29–32, 38, 42, 46, 67–8, 73–6, 79, 84–7, 90, 94–5, 100, 106–7, 113, 115, 118, 122–3, 127, 136, 141, 143
Du Côté de la Côte 7, 94–5, 98–100, 102, 104–5, 107–9, 140–2, 143

eclecticism 4–5, 7, 71, 98, 140
emotion, emotional 21–2, 32, 43, 46–7, 49, 54–7, 68, 82–4, 89–91, 94, 102, 104, 107, 111, 116, 122, 125, 127, 131–4, 140, 143
encounter(s) 6–7, 25, 31, 33, 60, 64, 66, 71–9, 91, 96, 104, 106, 116, 118–19, 139–41
ethics, ethical 3–4, 7, 32, 53, 71, 75, 78, 812, 86, 71, 140
experimentation, experimental 2, 4, 6–7, 10–11, 13, 23, 29, 51–3, 56, 58, 69, 94, 103–4, 111, 113, 125, 130–2, 135–6, 139, 142

femininity 4, 17, 21, 70
feminism 4–5, 10, 128–9, 142–3
fiction 5, 20, 43, 58–9, 74, 76, 82, 84–7, 90–1, 93–4, 99, 102, 107, 113, 125, 141

Jacquot de Nantes   31, 34, 58, 109

La Cabane de l'Échec   7, 102, 104, 140
La Pointe Courte   3, 6, 9–10, 37, 42–4, 46–58, 60–1, 71, 111, 116, 141–2
L'Île et Elle   31, 34, 58, 103–4
Les Créatures   48, 69, 103, 142
Les Glaneurs et la glaneuse   3, 7–10, 32, 60, 69, 76, 78, 84–6, 94, 112, 116, 118, 120–3, 139–40
Les Plages d'Agnès   31, 37, 39, 58–9, 61–3, 94, 102, 106, 143–4
Les Veuves de Noirmoutier   6, 10, 31–6, 39, 76, 81, 142
Lions Love (...and Lies)   123
L'Opéra Mouffe   3, 6, 9–13, 15–16, 18–22, 24, 36–7, 82, 90, 97, 107–8, 115, 120, 125, 140, 142
loss   33–6, 57
L'une chante, l'autre pas   10, 91, 137, 143

margins, marginal   36–7, 75, 81–2, 84–6, 123, 140–1
mourning   32, 63, 104
Mur, Murs   7–8, 10, 72–82, 84, 86, 108
music   2, 7, 11, 14, 20, 22–3, 27, 33, 37, 48, 50–1, 60, 65, 73–4, 77, 82, 95, 97, 99, 108, 116–18, 121, 126–7, 135, 137, 141–3
new wave   3–4, 8, 10, 37, 41, 43, 68–9, 82, 130

Paris, Parisian   1–2, 7, 10–11, 13, 19–23, 25, 31, 34, 36–8, 42–3, 46–8, 51, 55–9, 65–6, 82, 89–90, 94, 102, 105, 108–9, 112, 114, 116, 118, 122, 125, 136, 140–1
photographs, photography   1–3, 5, 9, 26–7, 29, 34, 45–6, 49, 52–3, 58, 60–1, 64–8, 74, 78, 80, 104–5, 111, 114, 123–7, 136, 142, 144
Ping Pong Tong et Camping   7, 102, 104–6, 140
Plaisir d'Amour en Iran   3, 7, 92
politics, political   1–6, 8, 10, 16, 18, 20, 23, 26–8, 31, 36, 51, 59, 63, 66–8, 73–5, 81–2, 112, 114–15, 117–19, 122, 131, 139, 142–3

poetics   76, 86, 94, 102–3, 140–1
portrait, portrayal   2–4, 13, 23, 25, 28–35, 46, 57, 59, 64–6, 68, 72–5, 82, 84–5, 90, 93–4, 96, 108, 116, 118
praxis   65, 81–2, 111–12, 140
pregnant, pregnancy   11–16, 18–20, 22, 82, 90, 125, 130, 140

Resnais, Alain   2–3, 9, 42–3, 48, 51–7, 61, 94, 128, 139, 141
rêverie   4, 7, 11, 15, 17, 93, 98, 132, 134

Salut les Cubains!   1–3, 5, 8, 52, 74, 78, 142
Sans Toit ni Loi   3–4, 7, 9, 58, 82, 84–6, 123, 136, 139
sensation   57, 91–2, 100, 102, 111, 126, 131–2, 134–5, 143
senses, sensory   5–8, 12, 14, 37–8, 50, 52, 56–7, 94, 100–2, 104, 106, 127, 134–5, 142
7p., cuis., s. de b., ... à saisir   7, 9, 58, 70, 123, 131–5, 139–142
sound, soundscape, soundtrack   2, 7, 11–15, 17, 20, 22, 25–6, 29–30, 33, 36–8, 43, 46–51, 55, 58, 73, 77, 82, 95, 104–5, 111, 121, 125, 127, 130, 134–5, 139, 141
space   5, 7, 10, 14, 19, 24, 31–3, 35, 54, 64–6, 71, 76, 79, 82, 85–6, 89–95, 97–9, 101–7, 109, 120, 123–4, 126–9, 131–6, 140–2
surreal, surrealism, surrealist   10, 12, 16, 19, 70, 75, 93–4, 102, 113, 121, 127, 135, 142

Vallaux, Christophe   58, 63, 102

widow(s), widowhood   31–5, 38–9
women   1–6, 13, 16–28, 30–7, 45–6, 50, 53, 57–8, 61, 63, 66, 74, 92, 94, 97–9, 113, 128–31, 142–3

Ydessa, les ours et etc.   7–8, 58, 123–7, 131, 142

GPSR Authorized Representative: Easy Access System Europe, Mustamäe tee
50, 10621 Tallinn, Estonia, gpsr.requests@easproject.com

www.ingramcontent.com/pod-product-compliance
Lightning Source LLC
Chambersburg PA
CBHW021952290426
44108CB00012B/1037